The Story of English Literature

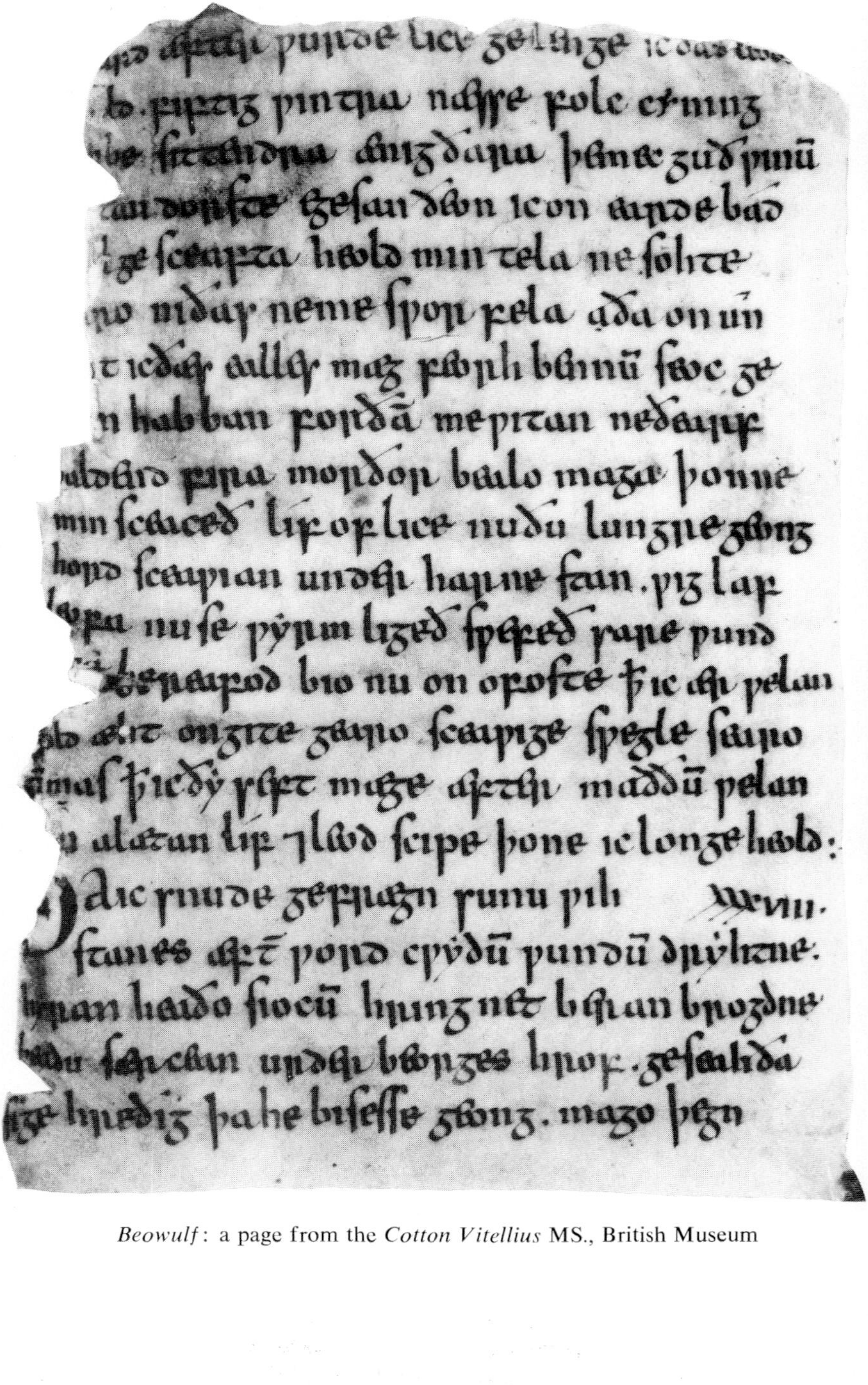

Beowulf: a page from the *Cotton Vitellius* MS., British Museum

ANNE TIBBLE

The Story of English Literature

A Critical Survey

PETER OWEN · LONDON

ISBN 0 7206 7604 5

PETER OWEN LIMITED
12 Kendrick Mews Kendrick Place London SW7

First British Commonwealth edition 1970
© Anne Tibble 1970

Printed in Great Britain by
Falmouth Packet Ponsharden Cornwall

*For Hilary and Robin, Audrey and Patrick,
and their like*

CONTENTS

ACKNOWLEDGEMENTS

My thanks are due to Michael Levien for his great care and patience in editing this book; to Patrick G. Scott, of the Department of English in the University of Leicester, Joan Simon and Phoebe Lathom, for their reading and checking of the manuscript and for many suggestions; to Maud Denham for unfailing help in typing many drafts; to the librarians of the Northampton County Library and of the Northampton Reference Library for their hunting of books not easily obtainable; and to the Trustees of the British Museum for permission to reproduce the page from *Beowulf*.

' The English are a dumb people. They can do great acts, but not describe them. . . . It is complained that they have no artists: one Shakespeare indeed: but for a Raphael only a Reynolds; for Mozart nothing but Mr. Bishop; not a picture, not a song. And yet they did produce one Shakespeare: consider how the element of Shakespearean melody does lie imprisoned in their nature.'

Thomas Carlyle, *Past and Present*

INTRODUCTION

This book is meant for readers, young and older, both overseas and in Britain, who want to know in outline the long story of English literature.

I have tried to offer a non-formal, compact account which is not without elements of cultural unfolding. Some scholars say that English literature starts only with Chaucer in the fourteenth century. This story begins well before Bede, the first known prose writer, and Caedmon, the first named poet in the seventh century, with a very brief sketch of the peoples of Britain and their languages before their prose and poetry began to be written down and so became literature.

Clearly I am much in debt to literary historians such as Professors Stopford Brooke, Emile Legouis, Louis Cazamian, Cook, Nevill Coghill, Dorothy Whitelock, for facts and dates; to the authors of *The Cambridge History of English Literature* and *The Oxford Companion to English Literature*; and to scholars and critics such as Professor F. R. Leavis, G. S. Fraser, Dr A. Kettle, Professor Dame Helen Gardner, Professor Frank Kermode and James Reeves, among many others.

I do not think I shall alienate readers by confessing at once that occasionally I had to halt for weeks to become better acquainted with an individual poet's or novelist's or dramatist's work—even after a quarter of a century's reading. Trying to avoid labels such as ' great ', ' lesser ', ' average ', ' minor '—the fascinating thing is to read, and re-read, individual novels, poems and plays, which for overt or hidden reasons attract; then, and then only, to read commentaries on them. Of course, with Anglo-Saxon poetry one relies on translations and renderings such as Michael Alexander's in *The Earliest English Poems*, or Kevin Crossley-Holland's modernization of *Beowulf* alongside the Anglo-Saxon text.

By reading independently one finds out what one thinks. What one thinks will alter, slowly, as one advances. There is no need to believe, at least not too sedulously, all that the experts say. To rely too much or too long on ' value-judgments ', or to ask students of whatever age to do so, is to linger, and to advise coming generations to linger, victims of an enforcement that is an enemy not only of joy in reading, but of spontaneity and independence, and so of any true education. It is actually to demand that the majority remain neophytes, in subjection to what does not exist, the ' disinterested intellect ' of gurus. We learn to distinguish what is worth while partly because we listen, wanting to know what those whom we respect appreciate and what they think worth while. Reading for sheer interest, as J. R. R. Tolkein once said, cannot begin until student days are over. But this book is for those who want to read with the pleasure that is part of the need for independence of thought in all of us. It is for that minority which, as Richard Hoggart has said, is ' potentially very much more numerous than we've been used to thinking '.

In spite of a present temporary focus of attention on ' concrete ' poetry and a return to oral communication, there is little fear that a millennium of written literature (some five thousand years, if we remind ourselves of the Middle East *Gilgamesh,* the first known poem in script) will be superseded.

Learning begins in interest, but must pass beyond the pleasure principle. Something of English literature I should like to help pass on, chiefly to the young, in our own and in other countries. If this aim is too wide, it is simple and non-specialized. For, despite the splendid drive for World Literacy set on foot in 1964, there is a long, long, uphill road to climb before those works in English literature which form part of world literature can even begin to become the ' strands in the lives of all men ' that, as Lascelles Abercrombie used to point out, they were once and ' literacy ' again can make them. In a so-called literate Britain good books are still far from being strands in the lives of most of us. On the contrary, they are often unreasonably and mysteriously ' out of print ' or ' unobtainable '.

Literature is a deeper part of our lives than is sometimes agreed on, or than perhaps we yet know: not as ' uplift ', or therapeutically, but as a basic part of our ' Immense Journey ' from shore-going fish, tarsiers and first cousins of primates. Devoted scholars maintain and expand poetic beauty. They further knowledge of language's complexity. Writers themselves constantly explore this knowledge and those traditions to transcend rule and law and create new literature. Nearly always writers' voices are relevant in that they reflect the life and times they live in; they point new directions; often they plead a necessary balance or foresight.

There is not the least evidence, to date, that if all books which have stood time's test were easy to find, if radio and television were more inclusive of plays from novels and of straight reading of novels and poems, young and old would not read more and enjoy more of what is too stuffily and 'squarely' cut off as literature. Perhaps the 'great divide' between literary and popular poetry and prose, as that 'divide' has developed in Britain since the days of Caedmon, was inevitable. But that there must be always a 'select few' and a long-miscalled 'vulgar' many, makes a distinction that is not valid. Whether or not such hiatus remains, the overall aim of this book is no more than to try to extend the pleasure and interest lying hid in much poetry and prose to a few more of the many.

ANNE TIBBLE

I

From Early Times to the Norman Conquest

B.C. - 1066

The beginnings of English literature lie among unrecorded songs and stories of our earliest ancestors. Before a people's verbal art is written down it goes through a long prehistoric stage. Warrior-minstrels praise mythical or semi-historical or actual heroes. Heroic doings become confused with myths of gods. Poetry, song and dance are not then separate. Stories are told by thousands of unknown grandmothers and grandfathers to children. Songs are sung, accompanied by music and dance, often by groups of girls or women, at births, bridals, feastings, deaths.

A little later, individual poets, almost always men, chant praise-songs or dirges about the brave deeds or valiant deaths of particular kings and known leaders. Gods, kings, heroes, and the songs and poems about them, become more and more confused with each other as time goes on. These individual poets or singers hand their memoried stories down by word of mouth to younger poets or singers apt enough to carry on the art. Memories before the invention of printing were astoundingly long. Earliest known Celtic poets were the *bardd*. This name, still used, is mentioned, Gwyn Williams writes in his foreword to *The Burning Tree*, at the beginning of the first century B.C. Anglo-Saxon poets were called *scôps*, shapers of deeds and words; the British or Celtic *scôp*, *bard* or *filé* was a poet who sang or chanted to a musical instrument.

The first written poetry and prose of the British Isles, as is the first written art of words of any culture, were—by the time poetry was distinct from prose and both had separated from music and dance—products of a long age of verbal experiment and enjoyment.

There is no trace of prose and poetry among the first peoples who lived in Britain after the last ice melted. At some time during the occupation of these earliest of our forefathers, the wind-swept

15

Atlantic rose with the melting snows and ice and cut off the mainland of Europe, to make Britain a storm-held group of rocky islands. Wrapped in skins our Old Stone Age ancestors lived for unknown centuries in caves above swamp, treacherous bog, impenetrable forest. The often rainy summers were short; the long winters were hard. Cheek by jowl, Stone Age hunters dwelt with sabre-toothed tiger, woolly rhino, lion, hyena, grizzly bear, bison and beaver. They killed the beasts with flint-tipped arrows, ate them and used their skins and bones for clothes, tools, ornaments. Almost certainly these people strove to shorten and make less fearful the long northern nights by the telling of stories or the reciting of poems. Some of their members, those with the best memories and the most vivid imaginations, became noted for their entertainment round the fire. They were valued by young and old.

The next peoples, Neolithic (New Stone Age and Bronze Age men and women), undoubtedly also told stories and invented poems. If these were rhymed, the rhyme was to help the entertainers remember, as well as to emphasize events and feelings. Megalith builders who made Stonehenge and other ancient Circles (' giants ' to later peoples) were perhaps sun-worshippers and may have had verbal poets. Battle-Axe people, Beaker people, Windmill-Hill people—some of these Bronze Age and Neolithic tribes are said to have been related to peoples as far apart on the earth as Hittites, Etruscans, Abyssinians, Berbers and the people of south India. Blood, as well as myth and verbal arts, relates our earliest ancestors to diverse peoples of Europe, Asia, Africa; and some of our early literature certainly has links with theirs.

In the last millennium B.C. three ' nation-groups ' of Celts came from Europe or from farther afield. These slave-keeping warrior Celts were Goidels or Gaels, related to Gauls; Brythons related to Bretons and Welsh; Belgae related to Belgians. The Celts brought the first iron swords into Britain. Thus, four or more Neolithic peoples, and the Celts, and more to come, form the richly mongrel British make-up. Their verse and prose, prehistoric and historic, must form the base of what we now call English literature. All must have offered some contribution, however small, to the variety of fourteen hundred years of written prose and poetry. The Brython Celts, importing amber from Europe with which to deck themselves, and ivory from the Land of Cush for tools, and exporting corn, gold, silver and slaves, were those who gave the land the name Britain.

Still no verse or prose was written. There was but the raw material for both poetry and prose—the live and ever-changing word. Its users thought this held magic for charm, spell or curse. They accumulated lore or history, in lament, praise and war-boast. Celtic and Gaelic, the languages the two tribe-groups of Celts and Gaels spoke, are two of many forms of a mother tongue that again probably unites peoples as far apart as India and Britain. This supposed earliest ancestor of our language, as well as of French, Latin, Greek, Slavic, Hindi and Russian, is called Indo-European.

But the Celtic and Gaelic languages were doomed. Under continued ravages of successive invaders of Britain's shores, Celtic and Gaelic could not survive over the greater part of the land. The two languages remain to this day in part of North Wales, in northern Scotland and in the remoter parts of western Ireland. From Gaelic and Celtic the succeeding tongues inherited a persistent lilt, half a dozen words and a few place-names. The name of a Celtic god is said to have suggested the name of Britain's capital city.

Celtic and Roman Britain

Julius Caesar, from empire-making Rome, forced an entry into Britain in 55 B.C. and again in 54 B.C. In A.D. 43 Claudius conquered the south east of the land and made it a Roman province. The Romans found the Brythonic Celts in possession of most of the east coast and south centre of the land, with the Goedels and the Neolithic peoples pushed into north-west Scotland, Ireland and Wales. As the Celts had at first enslaved what they could of the Neolithic peoples, so Romans enslaved Brythons, particularly women and children. Roman historians, Pliny the Elder, Diodorus, Tacitus and Caesar himself have left confused pictures describing the inhabitants they found in Britain: barbarians hunting deer, wolf, boar; fishing and fowling with primitive weapons; dressed in skins; painted in dye from the bright yellow-green woad plant that still grows in a few places up and down the land in summer; some keeping cattle, pigs and goats in settled farming, others brilliantly skilful in manoeuvring knife-axled, horse-drawn war-chariots;

practising human sacrifice: not one word about the poetry or prose the Celts, later, were proved to have had.

Cassivellaunus at Verulam, Caractacus with pre-Celt Silures under his banner, Boadicea and the Iceni tribe fought desperately against Roman cruelty and foreign domination. All were defeated, and almost all died. Our literature—any literature—would not be what it is had hero after hero not resisted tyranny, to be remembered in story and legend.

The government of Agricola under Vespasian, the rule of Hadrian and that of Antoninus—after Suetonius' cruelty under Nero—quietened British chiefs from the Forth and Clyde southward in a *pax Romana*. Elements of that mutual acceptance after strife which goes to make a nation were not yet discernible. The earliest owners of the land, those from Scotland and North Ireland, raided the north and west of Britain in the third century A.D. On the east and south east more and more pirates from Europe were by A.D. 290 on Britain's shores. The Romans stayed some 350 years. But beset at home by Vandal and Visigoth, soon after the close of the fourth century, Rome had left Britons to look to their own defence.

There is an early connection between literature and nationalism; but British tribes did not yet understand unity. They could only fight desperately and separately, hopeless of success against an ever-increasing number of invaders. One chief actually sought the foreign invader's help against the pre-Celts, Picts and Goidels. That was a turning-point. The conquest of Britain by Jutes, Angles and Saxons went apace. But there is still no trace of any prose or verse they may then have had.

The Romans built strongly fortified towns—Aquae Sulis (Bath), Verulam (St Albans), Camulodunon (Colchester), where before had been hilltop forts or scattered villages. They made roads where before had been ancient tracks or ridgeways. They drained fens and marshes. They built, with British slave labour, public baths and country houses (chiefly for Romans and collaborators) with heating and drainage. All these were marvels to be admired, envied, emulated, remembered.

Romans brought Christianity. Most of us remember the legend, told and retold, of how Gregory saw fair-haired slave-children in the Roman market-place and thought them ' angels not Angles '. That old story is among the first to stay in the memory even of today's schoolchildren. When Gregory became Pope he sent a mission to Britain. By A.D. 590 Canterbury had a Christian minster. The Roman Christian faith did not penetrate far among the heathen of the interior and the north. But soon afterwards Glastonbury was Christianized by Irish monks, and its abbey built. Literature might be said—hiddenly—to be about to begin.

Three and a half centuries of Roman influence left on ordinary British people a deep desire to be ' free ', to advance by themselves. It left them, too, the Latin language. Latin had come from Sumerian pictographs, through Phoenician and Greek lettering. But, as in the continent of Africa a century ago, so in Roman Britain seventeen centuries since, Christianity meant writing. Writing meant learning. Writing makes possible poetry and prose art forms. In Britain we still use Roman lettering, though Gothic lettering gave us our non-capital letters. But Latin was to be the language of British scholars for twelve centuries. It both retarded and deformed vernacular prose. There were men like Gildas, the first British historian, so proud to be a Roman citizen that he bewailed the passing of Roman civilization from Britain—in Latin.

Northern Invaders

The next invaders, by this time already on British shores, were Teutonic or Germanic tribes. These had emerged from the land mass of south-east Russia, though there is no positive proof that this was their original homeland, and they were being driven westward by tribes of Huns and Goths. Teutonic and Germanic slave-owning savages thus passed along the rivers Oder, Elbe and Rhine, and the north European coast, moving in bands as people did in those migratory days. In the fifth century, by destruction, enslavement and intermarriage, Angles were masters of British land north of the Humber almost to the Forth, Jutes ruled Kent, and Saxons held the coast south of the Thames.

Celts were driven west and north into what is now Cumberland, Devon, Cornwall, south Somerset and the Welsh borders. Throughout the next two or three hundred years, slowly the new conquerors imposed their own language. This grew, in the imperceptible way languages do grow, into a mixture of Saxon and related Anglian.

It is remembered as Anglo-Saxon and was to be the English language for six or seven centuries. The Angles of Northumbria, that part of Britain between Humber and Forth, bestowed on the land the new name of *Englalond*, now England.

Both Teuton and Celtic tribes were developing their hierarchic society. Chiefs were tribal heads. Land in both peoples belonged nominally to these petty rulers. It was farmed and used communally. Neither Celtic nor Teuton women were subject or inferior. They could hold land, be consulted. Both Celt and Anglo-Saxon still lived in thatched beehive or in round, stone huts. Celts believed in an Earth-mother goddess, Teutons in an All-father, an Earth-mother, their son Woden, and Woden's fate-maidens, victory women, the Valkyrie. Thor, the Teutonic All-father, has bequeathed his name to one of our days of the week, Woden to another.

Both peoples had a pantheon. Gods and goddesses, spirits of wisdom, good, light and fertility warred against demons and monsters of dark, hate, barrenness, night and evil. Pre-Celts, *and* Celts and early Teutons, sought, by sacrificing daughters, to wrest food in good harvests from the powers they deemed supernatural. That kind of fearful bargaining is found among many primitive peoples. Driven by famine they may, at some time, have been cannibals. By the sixth century A.D. both Celtic and Teutonic culture had reached that stage when they attempted to limit vengeance to ' an eye for an eye '. One death—but not, as before, often more than one—revenged a life taken or lost.

Rapine, and conquest by the Anglo-Saxons, went on. Rebellion by the previous holders of the land did not cease. But by the seventh century, in quiet areas, fines were taking the place of the most savage physical torture. Law, slowly enough and inspired by both Christian law and Roman civil law, was growing. Something approaching what we now think of as ' justice ' might occasionally have been seen to be meted out in folk-moot and court-leet among hard-drinking warriors and their farming brothers.

Slowly the land accepted Roman Christianity. Probably there was little persecution in the earlier centuries of British conversion. Stories already current in those pristine days, nature myths of the year's death and rebirth, of Yule and Eostra, of summer joys, corn-gathering and winter endurance all joined with rejoicing at the stories of Christ's birth, and with sorrow and hope at the story of his forgiveness of his murderers and his crucifixion. Gladness in earth's mysterious renewal responded to the Christian story of Jesus's conquest of death. But all this, in Britain, was still verbal.

The Celtic communities prized imagination; the English were powerfully practical. Both were singing people, poetic that is. They had bard or *scôp* or *filé*, who chanted of joy, grief, freedom or brave deeds. Most of the earth's peoples then on the move between Africa and Asia, and Asia and Europe, had singers, minstrels or oral poets among them, as very rural communities have today.

Brythons who had retreated to Cambria and Cumbria—now Wales and north-west England—seeing the need for unity, joined with each other and with the pre-Celts in the west. All these began to call themselves Cymry—fellow-countrymen. And Brythons and Gaels had what must now be called the beginnings of a literature. Four great Cymru, Celtic or Welsh, bards lived in the sixth and seventh centuries. Their stories and poems exist in the Four Ancient Books of Wales. The manuscripts in existence date only from the twelfth century; but scholars say that they concern sixth-century and seventh-century Cymry struggles against the Angles. To Celts of that date we owe the story of King Arthur and his Knights of the Round Table. Earlier than the Welsh books are the Ancient Books of Ireland. These contain the second earliest written literature of all Europe. Certain stories or motifs in them run through our poetic thought to this day: the desire for a land of eternal happiness and peace; the admiration of our own peculiar idea of beauty; the yearning for continued youth; the idea of search or quest linked to an unremitting, trial-beset striving for ' better ', finer, far-off things. These motifs run through most known literatures. They hint, if they do not prove, how basic, how elemental, poetic thought, equally with trade and commerce, is.

Bede and Caedmon in the Eighth Century

In the seventh century England was still disunited. Each of five sections was ruled by a petty king. Northumbria, first Christianized by Celtic-Irish monks and then ordered to conform to Roman Christianity by the Synod of Whitby, produced the first English school of learning and of poetry and prose. At the monastery of Jarrow the Venerable Bede drew scholars and writers together and

himself collected the first British library. Overwhelmingly industrious, Bede—so the legend reaches us—finished the last sentence
in his last book only a few minutes before he died tranquilly in 735.
Bede brought to a close his *Historia Ecclesiastica Gentis Anglorum*
(History of the English Church and People) in 731. Forty other
books are sometimes spoken of as being the work of Bede's School
of Jarrow. At Bede's death the centre of learning moved to York.
York became the greatest seat of culture outside Rome, with a good
collection of books.

Bede wrote both prose and poetry at Jarrow. Although he was
educated by Irish monks, he wrote in the Roman conquerors'
Latin. But these Celtic or Gaelic monks believed that learned men,
poets and ordinary people all needed their native tongue. Bede
began English prose—Anglo-Saxon prose, that is—with a translation of St John's Gospel. To Bede we owe a hint of how the first
English poetry was made and written down in runes learned from
the Irish.

Caedmon, Bede records, was a herdsman at the monastery of
Streaneshalch (Whitby), on the sea-cliffs of what is now Yorkshire.
Whitby was ruled by the Abbess Hild (or Hilda); Caedmon, born
a heathen, was there between A.D. 660 and 680. His Celtic-sounding
name has caused some doubt about Caedmon's real or individual
existence. Perhaps he *was* Celtic. We know no more about him than
what Bede wrote down for us. Caedmon, Bede says, was old as well
as poor. Whenever a feast was held, the custom was that each in
turn, rich or poor, was required to sing. Knowing no song Caedmon
slunk away ashamed before the harp was passed to him. One night
after such a feast he fell asleep among the animals. Then, Bede
goes on:

> One stood by him, and saluting him, said, 'Caedmon, sing me
> something.' And he answered, 'I know not how to sing, and for
> this reason I left the feast.' Then the other said, 'Nevertheless,
> you will have to sing to me.' 'What shall I sing?' Caedmon
> replied. 'Sing,' said the other, 'the beginning of things created.'

And Caedmon found himself able to sing, to chant a poem that
is. In the morning he hastened to tell the town-reeve of his dream.
The reeve or bailiff brought Caedmon to the Abbess Hild. Caedmon

sang again. After that he was honoured by Northumbrian scholars but continued to live devoutly and humbly.

Whether or not it was Bede who wrote down the first, or the only one, of Caedmon's lyrics at the back of the manuscript of Bede's *Historia Ecclesiastica* is not known. Whether Caedmon lived or not, the most ancient of English lyrics was written down not later than A.D. 736. It is in the dialect of the Anglo-Saxon speech spoken by the Angles:

> Nu scylun hergan hefaenricaes uard,
> Metudes maecti end his modgidanc,
> Uerc uuldurfadur; sue he uundra gihuas
> Eci Dryctin or astelidae.
> He aerist scop aelda barnum
> Heben til hrofe; haleg scepen !
> Tha middungeard; moncynnaes uard !
> Eci Dryctin ! AEfter tiadae
> Firum foldu; frea allmectig !

> Now must we greet with praise the guard of Heaven's realm,
> The Maker's might, and of his mind the thought,
> The glorious Father's works, and how to wonders all
> He gave beginning, He, the Eternal Lord !
> He at the very first formed for the bairns of men,
> He, Holy Shaper ! Heaven for their roof ;
> Then Middle-garth He made: He, of mankind the Ward !
> Lord everlasting He ! And then He let arise
> The earth for man; He is Almighty God ![1]

The School of Northumbria produced other, longer, Christian poems: poems in which Christ replaces the heathen hero and the whole battle of human life between Good and Evil from the myth of Adam's and Eve's ' Fall ' to the Son's Redemption is recounted. These are in the Junius manuscript which contains *Genesis A*. Caedmon is said to have died as Bede died, greeting death after a lifetime of happy work.

Among the Anglo-Saxon heathen the *scôp* was sometimes a noble. Attached to the chief, he held land from him, went into battle with him. Each was a trusted comrade, necessary to the other. But the

[1] The Rev. Stopford Brooke's translation. A. Stopford Brooke, *English Literature from the Beginning to the Norman Conquest* (Macmillan, 1919), p. 129.

scôp, it seems, might also have been a wanderer. Then, from poor or rich, the poet-singer claimed hospitality. An important thing to remember is that most men, Teuton or Celt, and most women in their own precincts, could chant in those days either in chorus or singly, a lay, a gnomic verse, a glee, a dirge, a riddle. Poetry in that early, less time-pressed, culture was honoured. Teutons thought the gift of it came from the gods. Christian abbots and monks and scholars believed Caedmon's gift came from God.

Old English Heathen Charms

The oldest heathen poems, from the four Old English manuscripts in which the bulk of surviving Old English poetry is preserved, are *Charms*. Charms, or prayers, had a magic, or mantic, even a sacred quality, whilst being part of everyday life. They were pleas to the spirits of the fruitful earth for harvest and other blessings. Images, sounds and phrases from the Charms linger, unrecognizably now divorced from their pristine sense, in nursery rhymes and in children's games. Being heathen, many of them were overtaken and quietly overlaid by Christianity. A Charm such as the following may have been sung by some of the earliest of our ploughmen ancestors:

> Erce, Erce, Erce ! O Earth our mother !
> May the All-Wielder, Ever-Lord, grant thee
> Acres a-waxing, upwards a-growing,
> Pregnant with corn and plenteous in strength;
> Hosts of grain-shafts and of glittering plants !
> Of barley the blossoms,
> And of white wheat ears waxing,
> Of the whole land the harvest. . .
> Hale be thou Earth, Mother of men !
> Fruitful be thou in the arms of the god.
> Be filled with thy fruit for the fare-need of man ![2]

[2] MSS. in the British Museum and also in the Library of Corpus Christi College, Cambridge. Translation in Brooke, op. cit., p. 43. *Sweet's Anglo-Saxon Reader* [see General References] contains two Charms; but *Sweet's Oldest English Texts* has none.

Beowulf

The longest early saga of folk-legend and nature-myth in Old English is a long tale of Anglo-Saxon continental origins: *Beowulf*. With some likeness to ancient Euro-Asian-African modes of poetry, it has long lines with four main stresses. These lines are without end-line rhyme and have a pause in the middle of each line. The sonorous music of the verse of *Beowulf* comes from its repeating the initial letter of the key-stress (which is the first stressed word after the mid-line pause) in one or two of the main stresses in the first half-line. The fourth stress of the line must not have the same initial letter. This Old English, strictly formed verse is said to follow speech rhythms, which in turn follow heart rhythms and breath rhythm. Alliterative poetry contains, twentieth-century imagist poets have said, English literature's only indigenous metre.

Its richness lies in its synonyms and images: these *kennings*, as they are called, are the germs of metaphor and simile and are found in most early people's poetry. In the ' heroic ' verse to which *Beowulf* belongs the Anglo-Saxons likened and linked one thing to another to enhance it: the sea was ' the swan's way ' or ' the whale's bath '; a man was ' a sword-wielder '; the sun ' the world's candle ', poetry a ' word-hoard '. We do not know who wrote the poem *Beowulf* down or who composed it, or anything of its history whilst it was being told over and over as spoken poetry before it was transcribed.

There is not one word about England or the English in *Beowulf*. The poem's 3,183 lines tell of a sea-daring prince-hero, Beowulf, son of Ecgtheow and nephew of Hygelac, King of the Geats of south Sweden. The young Beowulf hears that a ferocious man-beast, Grendel, is troubling the people of Hrothgar, the King of the Danes. He offers himself in combat against the monster. Beowulf slays Grendel, then Grendel's horrifying, man-eating mother. He is rewarded by money and an alliance with the Danish king. For fifty years Beowulf rules, after Hygelac's son, as the mildest King of the Geats. At eighty he rids his own people of another dragon; he wins for them glittering gold and an all-golden banner of strange, light-shedding handiwork, inwoven with magic songs. But the dragon's fiery breath and poisonous claws give Beowulf his death-blow. He has no son sprung from his loins. His last words to Wiglaf his loyal kinsman disclose to us how poetry kept alive in those early minds not only the virtues of kingly dedication to service and valour but also virtues of peace and fidelity in heathen but not ignoble days.

> . . . Ic on earde bād
> māel-zescaefta, hēold mīn tela,
> ne sōhte searo-niðas, ne mē swōr fela
> āða on unriht.

[Beowulf says, dying:] In my own land I awaited the fate allotted for me. I guarded well what was mine, I did not pursue crafty spites, I did not swear any oaths unjustly.[3]

Parts of the *Beowulf* epic would have been chanted among the English conquering Britain in the seventh century. Parts belong to earlier days still. The poem was not set down in the form we know until about the year 1000, though some think the saga reached its present form by about the eighth century. Not until the eighteenth century was it transliterated, then translated into a form we can understand. There is but one manuscript of *Beowulf*, the *Cotton Vitellius A.15*. The poem is in the West Saxon dialect, and the manuscript is in the British Museum.

The myth of a man-eating monster and a ferocious dam belongs to the heritage of oral legends of ogres, giants, dragons, beast-men and trolls that we share with many other peoples of the world. When our forefathers seized land from earlier owners, those previous inhabitants, retreating to bare mountain and marsh, driven by famine and a desperate will to survive, no doubt made wild descents by night, carrying off what and whom they could. Grendel and his dam are of this cohort of cannibal beings made fearful to others in the grim, early struggle for life.

The last part of the epic, where the aged king overcomes the new dragon, is a nature myth: Beowulf (Beowa), the cloud-sweeper, a fertility god, a sun-hero, conquers the dragon of winter's ice and snow. Like a good king, a saviour, he gives his life to bring to his

[3] *Beowulf*, ed. A. J. Wyatt and R. W. Chambers (Cambridge Univ. Press, 1914; repr. 1920), p. 136, lines 2736-9. Kevin Crossley-Holland has recently made a verse translation (Macmillan, 1968). The translation given here is from G. N. Garmonsway, Jacqueline Simpson and Hilda Ellis Davidson, *Beowulf and Its Analogues* (Dent, 1968), p. 72.

suffering people the longed-for treasures of spring, summer, food.

There is no possibility that the poem can be read without its language being learned. But Kevin Crossley-Holland's verse modernization (1968) is an admirable way back into the heroic days of Britain's tribal past.

Cynewulf

In the late eighth or early ninth century a Christian poet, whom we know as Cynewulf, followed Caedmon and what is called Caedmon's 'school of poetry'. Most likely Cynewulf belonged, as Caedmon belonged, to Northumbria; both in that case would be Angles. Cynewulf may, however, have been Mercian. Cynewulf's four signed poems show he knew and shared the island love of the sea, the rocky cliffs, the perils of seafaring. But the poems of his school, ' The Harrowing of Hell ' and ' The Dream of the Rood ', interpret the sorrows of Christianity rather than the Christian joy in life's creation which Caedmon voiced.

This is not to be wondered at. Soon after Caedmon's and Bede's deaths disaster swooped again on Britain. More pirate-invaders reached Northumbria's shores. Northmen, or Norsemen, related in their European homes to Dane and Jute, landed in the creeks and gullies among the storm-beaten cliffs on the Yorkshire coast. Foraging up the rivers inland, these laid waste as they went. The library and centre of learning at York fell. Monasteries and abbeys, Jarrow, Wearmouth, Whitby and elsewhere were burnt or shattered. The invaders killed or scattered monks and scholars. Ruin and death spread again down the east coast of Britain.

But the Norsemen-Danes could not impose a new language. Their own, cognate with Anglo-Saxon, left some influence in place-names such as Whitby, Rugby, Cleethorpes, Lowestoft and other -*bys*, -*thorpes*, -*thwaites* and -*tofts*. Danes settled. Steadily they pressed inland. They married English women—when they had conquered the land. Yet the Anglo-Saxon tongue remained. In time the beaten English Christianized the triumphant, heathen Danes.

Personal, elegiac, and half-contemplative poems, gnomic verses and riddles, are in an eighth-century outpouring. Heathen image and Christian idea are often fused in them. ' Widsith ' (the wide-ranger or traveller) and ' Deor's Lament ' bewail past glories and present ills, the loss of *cynn* or family group, the loss of *cyn-ing*, the comrade, protector, the king. ' The Seafarer ', ' The Wanderer ' and the fragmentary ' Waldere ' describe Britain's storm-wracked, enemy-haunted frontiers, the enchantment of cuckoo-song after gloomy winter. Soon after these, poetry in the north of the land was silent. *The Song of Brunanburh* (937) and *The Battle of Maldon* (991) in the *Anglo-Saxon Chronicle* are war chants.

The eighty-ninth Riddle, scholars think by eighth-century Cynewulf himself, tells us a little of what one of the first of the individually known poets was like: in his youth Cynewulf began as a wandering singer; probably he carried a harp, a tabor or a pipe; a lover of tempest, sea, animal, bird and nature both terrifying and peaceful, he sang for any man who asked a song. He was as ready, he asserts, with an earthy stave for a peasant as he was to praise a hero. Poetry in the Britain of the eighth century was not divided into learned and popular. Most of it could be enjoyed by the many. It did not wait on learning.

But division was at hand. The poems actually signed by Christian Cynewulf and belonging perhaps to his later life show a shorter line (than the *Beowulf* line). Rhyme has entered. Apart from blank verse, rhyme was to lure poetry onward until the twentieth century. Cynewulf was adopting new rules for his poetry. For good or ill the long divergence that overtakes all arts had set in. Inevitable hiatus, between poetry as the strand it had been in the lives of men in the days of Beowulf, Bede and Caedmon, and poetry for a learned few, begins to be discernible in the poetry of the first eighth- or ninth-century individual poet of England.

Alfred

The lead in learning passed from Northumbria to Wessex, from York to Glastonbury, then to Winchester. By 870 or 880 Danish ravagers, with their poets called *scalds*, were at the frontiers of the land of Ethelred, the King of Wessex, who ruled the West Saxons. He himself died in battle. Of Ethelred's many sons, the youngest Alfred was his father's favourite. As a small boy Alfred had been to Rome and the Frankish court. Unlike his brothers Alfred loved books. He prized the volumes which monks of his day spent so much of their solitary lives copying. Up to 1476, when Caxton brought Gutenberg's and Schoeffer's invention of Printing to England, such copying was the only means by which books could be made. The monks' illuminated volumes, rare and precious then and now, are the forerunners of our multitudinous libraries.

On the death of his father, Alfred, at twenty-two, became, in 871, King of Wessex. The outlook for his kingdom was wellnigh hopeless. The neighbouring kingdom of Mercia was in the hands of the conquering Danes. For months outlawed by the foreigner Alfred was secretly collecting forces. Sallying out, he defeated the Danish array and extracted from their leader the Peace of Wedmore (Chippenham) in 879. This confined the Danes within the Danelaw, that part of the land east and north of the Roman road of Watling Street, a line from north west to south east, from Ribble to Thames. England was ripped in two. But in Alfred the Truthteller, new love of learning and traditional heroism met. No sooner had he the Danes at bay than he turned to educating his people. This was a harder task than rescuing them from the Norsemen. Yet for his profound common sense, humility and Christianity, ' the Angelcyn turned to Alfred, except those in bondage to Danish men '.[4]

Alfred believed in the English mother tongue. He had a translation made by his group of scholars, the ' palace school ', from Gregory's *Cura Pastoralis* (Pastoral Care), Bede's *Historia Ecclesiastica* and Boëthius's *De Consolatione Philosophiae* (The Consolation of Philosophy). But Alfred's own jottings contain a fine common sense:

> For me, I dread no ill weirds, They can neither help nor harm a man. Ill luck is even happiness, though we do not think it is. One can trust it; what it promises is true.[5]

Alfred's palace school was almost alone. The monks were not enthusiastic for learning. Grown worldly under duress and superior, conquering strangers, they were indifferent to prose and even to piety. Alfred died lonely and disappointed.

[4] The *Anglo-Saxon Chronicle*, quoted from Brooke, op. cit., p. 216.
[5] Ibid., p. 233.

More Conquerors—Danes and Normans

The Danes pressed on. There were the good kings of Wessex such as Athelstan, Alfred's grandson whose queen is said to have been a peasant girl. Then came Ethelred the Unready. By the eleventh century the Danes held England.

Religious vitality had returned to the monasteries, following the Cluniac revival. In the first quarter of the eleventh century Alfric, the monk of Winchester and Cerne and then Abbot of Eynsham, wrote his *Homilies* (990-2) in the English tongue. Wulfstan, Archbishop of York, also wrote in the vernacular his *Sermo Lupi ad Anglos*, straight-speaking homilies against the low morale of the English under Danish oppression. The second Wulfstan, Bishop of Worcester, preached against the English selling of their own people as slaves, and he procured some cessation. But after Alfric and the two Wulfstans, except for the *English Chronicle*, kept up until 1154, Anglo-Saxon prose was mostly silent for over a century.

Canute, the first Danish King of England, was himself more English than Dane. Alfred had united the half of England not under the Danish heel. Canute was the first King of all England from what are now the Welsh and Scottish borders to the Channel. If at first Canute the Dane used measures that seem oppressive, soon he was sending preachers to civilize the Scots and appointing Englishmen to positions of authority in England. By the time he died Canute had grown, in spite of opposition from Godwin, Earl of Wessex, and his family, almost as wise and as trusted a ruler as Alfred. But he wrote no books, and the writing of books languished.

For even then Britain was not nationally united enough to hold herself free of invader and conquerer. Edward the Confessor, educated in France, brought Norman-French friends and supporters to England. By 1066 William Duke of Normandy was claiming, on the strength of this connection, the very throne of England. Relatives of the Norsemen, he and his Normans landed on the beach at Hastings. In one sweep, almost, England lay a fifth time under the foreigner's heel.

The Anglo-Saxon language went underground. Norman-French became the language of King and court, of the educated, of Law. Latin was strengthened as the only dignified medium of prose.

Yet an unsuspected thing was happening. Earlier Normans
(northmen) had been kin of Danes and Saxons. In France Norsemen
had taken the French language, French culture, French ways.
After the Normans' arrival in England, King, court, Norman baron
and Norman household spoke Norman French. The aspiring and
wealthy among the English sedulously copied them.

But ordinary people in village and small market-town, at fair
and feast, went on with their own means of communication. The
very threat of the foreign Norman-French may have strengthened
determination to hold on to native Anglo-Saxon. It changed, as
the living speech of living people must change. English enriched
itself with new words and ideas, from Norman chivalry, luxury,
religious fervour, from French law, music and literature of the
University of Paris. It dropped—slowly, of course—the cumber-
some case-endings which had made it a language of synthesis,
powerful, descriptive, practical, but wordy, involuted and clumsy.
It was in process of becoming an analytic language, lighter, quicker,
clearer, as rich but altogether subtler. And—perhaps through the
very hardship of dominating change—it grew far more adaptable.

The Normans actually helped this evolution. In Edward I's
onslaughts against Scotland and Wales, Normans felt themselves
English. Norman and Dane cherished their own sagas and myths,
some of which were similar to Celtic and Anglo-Saxon myths.
When, in the wars against France, King John lost Normandy in
1204, Normans felt cut off from their former land. Patriotism for
Britain grew. Religion in Britain found British and Normans wor-
shipping together.

Normans joined in the speech and songs of the people more and
more. If they could not pronounce a word, slowly that word
changed to fit speaker and hearer. Thirteenth-century and fourteenth-century English is bespattered with these new words, new
sounds, new phrases. In 1362 English became the language of
law. By 1399, when England began to feel herself a nation at last,
the strong usurper Henry IV used English for the first time in
Parliament.

The Rise of Middle English

But it was no longer the Anglo-Saxon language, such a process had it undergone of what we must call organic evolution. In manners, melody, reason, knowledge of poetic forms, and ideas, so different did it emerge from Anglo-Saxon, that we call it Middle English. It is for this reason that some argue that English literature begins only after the twelfth-century development into Middle English.

Not less than five, perhaps more, racial strands make up the basis of the tongue which has produced English literature. The Neolithic peoples, the Celtic, the Anglo-Saxon, the Danish-Norse and the Norman—each has a share in it, however small. Perhaps the Stone Age peoples passed on some power of symbols, the ' magic ' of making inanimate things live by words ? The Brythonic Celts brought to English their idealistic imagination, their passionate melancholy, their as passionate self-mockery; the Irish, directly or through Breton and Norman, supplied many of the richly various rhythms for its lyric poetry. The Anglo-Saxons gave the tongue supple, subtle restraint, reasonableness, philosophic capacity, but also an enduring sense of the sea, of storm, of grave, even sinister, peril and adventure always to be undertaken.

As the vehicle for both poetry and prose, English was slowly to acquire both depth of feeling for human character and for nature, as well as power of thought. All these are vital for prose and poetry. From Norman-French, English derived what Emile Legouis has called ' movement, gaiety, and light '.[6] Gaiety and light wove themselves into the Anglo-Saxon, northern awareness of the end of all earthly things.

This was the confused mixture out of which Middle English rose from the ashes of its former self. It is perhaps through its prolonged struggle from this time onward that English literature has developed its particular strength. And through the centuries up to today Celtic and Anglo-Saxon language and literature, tradition and change, in Scots, Irish, Welsh and English writers, have enriched each other and prevented each other from stagnating, until the sophisticated or mature complexity of today's English literature is reached.

[6] Emile Legouis and Louis Cazamian, *A History of English Literature* (Dent, 1926), p. 61.

II

From the Norman Conquest to Chaucer

1066 - 1400

For almost a century and a half after the Norman conquest English as a written art held silence. The existence of manuscripts and of illuminated books depended entirely on the devoted labours of monkish scribes and clerks. What schools there were the Church kept. Few, either children or grown-ups in secular Britain, could read or write. The fervour of what had been the Christian conversion lost its sense of rapture.

In such a situation much pre-Christian poetry disappeared. A few monks kept historical records, such as the *Anglo-Saxon Chronicle*.

Richard Coeur de Lion holds a very modest place among twelfth-century poets. During his reign, 1189-99 (only six months of which were spent in England), this 'ideal knight' was the friend of Provençal poets such as Piere Vidal and Bertran de Born. He is said to have written many poems, but in French. G. H. Needler has translated Richard's 'Prison Song', one of the two poems which can with any authenticity be attributed to him, and said to have been written in an Austrian prison before his minstrel found him by singing outside the prison walls:

1.   A prisoner boots it nought to tell his wrong,
   As mute endurance doth to grief belong:
   Yet may a man for comfort make a song:
   Poor are their gifts, tho' rich my friends and strong,
         Shame be to them that I two winters long
             For ransom lie in bonds.

2.   Now well must all my knights and barons know
   In Gascony, England, Normandy, Poitou,
   That I count not the poorest serf so low

To leave him ransomeless imprisoned so;
This say I not contempt on them to throw,
    But still I lie in bonds.

3. This truth doth now itself to me commend:
A prisoner, like a dead man, hath no friend.
If they their gold and silver will not spend,
Hard fate for me; yet will a worse attend
Themselves in the reproach after my end,
    They left me thus in bonds.

4. No wonder is it that my heart is sore:
My lord to turmoil now my land gives o'er,
And thinks upon the solemn oath no more
That we together to the Almighty swore:
Yet know I well 'twill not be long before
    I shall be free of bonds.

5. Companions whom I loved, and cherish still,
Of Cahors and of Perche, I live until
'Tis sung that they no longer oaths fulfil,
Tho' knew they ne'er in me a recreant will.
The deed of caitiffs, should they treat me ill
    While I remain in bonds!

Not until about the time of *Magna Carta* did recorders think openly
of rejecting Latin for English. The chronicler William of Malmes-
bury, of Norman and English parentage, boldly helped to unify
Normans and English by writing in English; Henry of Huntingdon
helped too. Matthew Paris, a Norman chronicler, was almost
purely English in sympathy.

Geoffrey of Monmouth

Geoffrey of Monmouth, a Welsh priest at Henry I's court in the
twelfth century, collected—from Old Welsh scripts and from the
compilations of the historian known as Nennius—stories of remembered history when Arthur was said to have been King of Britain

or part of Britain. Geoffrey stirred that feeling for their past which grows in a people just beginning to feel nationhood. But Geoffrey wrote in Latin.

Layamon

About 1205 Layamon, a monk who lived on the Severn banks, near the Welsh-English border, turned current legends from Wace's *Brut* into alliterative verse. Layamon told of Lear, the old king who, with trusting folly, divided his kingdom between his three daughters, two elder ones and the younger, filial one. Layamon brought his story down to Athelstan. Probably an Anglo-Saxon, Layamon imbibed, on the Celtic border, enough of the Celtic imagination to make him the first post-Conquest poet to attempt to reconcile Welsh, English and Norman by heroic tales of their common land. He was influenced by French *trouvères* such as Geoffrey Gaimar; but Layamon's *Brut*, one-third the length of Wace's, told of how Brut(us), great-grandson of Aeneas of Troy, fathered all Britons and founded New Troy on London long before the Romans came; this was homely enough to nourish British need for the heroic boasting which conquest had denied. *The Brut* became popular among the people for whom it was meant; and Layamon knew what he was about: his thirty thousand lines contain scarcely fifty French words.

Thirteenth- and Fourteenth-Century Poems

After Layamon the influence of French story-telling impinged again. *Havelok the Dane* and *King Horn*, though Teutonic legends, are in French eight-syllabled, rhymed lines, not in English stressed, alliterative non-rhyme. *Havelok* (early fourteenth century) shows how time confuses myth with history, attaches incidents to wrong names, identifies hero with quite distinct hero. The origin of *Havelok the Dane* was perhaps Olaf Sitricson who reigned a few years in the tenth century in Northumbria. The story, an attempt to reconcile English listeners to Danish usurpers, is of Grim, a brave fisherman of the ancient sea-town of Grimsby, who brought up in humble simplicity a boy of unusual bravery and beauty, the result of a supernatural birth, Havelok. Havelok married a princess and became a monarch. The manuscript of *Havelok* shows how the minstrel of such a ' praise-story ' of a hero began his lay by begging, of the ' goodmen, wives, and maids ' assembled in hall to hear him, ' a cup of good ale '.

The English language rallied slowly. Stories such as *Bevis of Hampton* and *Guy of Warwick* (*c.* 1300), *Sir Gawayne and the Grene Knight* of the fourteenth century, all have English heroes and English settings. *Sir Gawayne* revived alliterative metre. *Bevis* and *Guy* were made, a sixteenth-century writer tells us, ' for the recreation of the common people '; they were printed and reprinted until at least the nineteenth century. In *The Owl and the Nightingale* (*c.* 1280) the birds quarrelled wordily, as birds and creatures do in almost all early peoples' folk stories. The birds' merits, of music and character, were judged by the English author, Nicholas of Guildford. Richard Rolle was a Yorkshire hermit who wrote an enormous amount of ecstatic prose and fervent, saintly poetry. *The Ancrene Riwle* was one of many books, then and to come, devoted to giving rules of conduct for both the devout and the worldly. This Rule for Anchoresses was written by a priest for three women recluses. They were to live as shyly as birds of the air. They were not to attempt what some women tried to do—to teach the young; they were themselves too ignorant. *Pearl* (*c.* 1350-80), probably by the author of the heroic, courtly *Sir Gawayne and the Grene Knight*, is about the death of the poet's daughter. He loses the child of two in a garden. He goes seeking her. Falling asleep, he sees her in a dream—happy; but he cannot cross to her visionary paradise. The child bids him not mourn: how can he be sad to see her happy ? They talk. Finally the father accepts—but sadly—the loss of one ' so small, so sweetly fragile '. The *Pearl* is skilfully yet simply written in twelve-lined, octosyllabic stanzas with the French ornament of intricate rhyme. From this time onward rhyme does much to lighten English verse. The poet of *Sir Gawayne* and *Pearl* and of two more story-poems illustrating the virtues of purity and humility, *Cleanness* and *Patience*, may have lived in Lancashire, on the Celtic border.

All these poems were written down somewhere near the time of their composition. Before this, poems might have been passed down by word of mouth for generations. Christian manuscripts such as those of the Lancashire poet were carefully preserved. It was the pre-Christian poetry which perished, in what quantities we do not know. Before the enterprising Caxton in the fifteenth century spent a busy life printing and publishing, copies of manuscripts multiplied. Yet some waited until the eighteenth or nineteenth century to be printed, edited, modernized. *Havelok the Dane* has but one manuscript, now in the Bodleian Library; Richard Rolle's 150 are scattered in European libraries. The single manuscript of *Pearl* was not printed until 1891. There were forty manuscripts of John Gower's only English poem, the *Confessio Amantis* (Confession of a Lover). Caxton printed part of this inordinately long poem, and its Middle English was translated into modern by Morley in the late eighteenth century and by Macaulay in 1901. Though there is an excellent modernization of about one-third of the whole,[1] there is no edition in print today of the original *Confessio*.

The heathen *scôp* disappeared after Christianity came. Before printing, before the building of schools, when news could travel and the arts of prose and poetry spread, not otherwise than by word of mouth, when serfdom and slavery which bound people to one place were still in slow process of ending in this country—as soon as freedom to move could be seized, people moved. They wandered about the country. Palmers, minstrels with harp and base- or treble-viol, gleemen, pedlars, players and entertainers of many kinds increased in number. As money began to take the place of service and payment in kind, old values were lost. Work grew scarcer. Worldly wise singers and reciters asked for money instead of a pot of ale. These had, still, by memory, their word-hoard, their stock of poems. But versions of poems and ballads multiplied. Corruptions added themselves to older forms; often amalgamation of new incidents changed old stories out of all recognition.

Population in Britain was growing. Minstrels still entertained at court, lord's or baron's hall, country manor house, at marriage, feast, funeral, and the country fairs still kept up in plenty. There were all manner of minstrels, church players and mimers, and folk and ballad singers. In days when there were fewer pastimes, darkness was lit by taper or rushlight, and toil was longer, quieter, heavier, varied, and hence not tedious. Then, work and play were closer, not so separate. Often whole families, including children, grandparents and relatives, worked together in field or house.

[1] Terence Tiller, *The Lover's Shrift* (Penguin Classics, 1963).

Men, women and children often sang to lighten labour. They gathered to listen to story and poem or to sing or recite ballads themselves round the Yule log at Christmas and New Year and Hallowe'en, or under the oak on May eve, midsummer eve or Martinmas.

In retrospect, divergence between popular and learned was not yet wide or deep enough to be consistently discernible. Just as there were very few stories, especially for the young, so there was no such thing as literature as we know it.

Not until the thirteenth century did the English lyric emerge to sight again for the first time since Caedmon. The lyric, a song sung to the lyre, often at times of deep feeling such as births, bridals and burials, was frequently the work of women. Between the seventh century and the thirteenth, lyrics must have continued to be sung. Many were lost. Survivors were those which took French forms such as the *rondel* and the *balade*. This last is not to be confused with the Old English ballad, though both words stem from the French *ballet*, a song with music and dance.

The Middle English lyric which has been preserved and is earliest in date is ' The Cuckoo Song ' of between 1240 and 1250. This has survived because the beauty and grace of its music and setting mark an epoch, rather than for its merits as verse. Its music, for six voices, is said to have been composed in 1226 by John of Fornsete, a monk of Reading Abbey, and begins the first English School of Music. Its form, chorus and coarse, gay realism suggest that it was sung by many country voices before being written down.

The cuckoo's long-awaited call after winter and Britain's dismally delaying spring must always have been hailed with relief; indeed, with a certain rapture. Undoubtedly lyrics, ballads and ancient poems in the versions in which we have them today were once the work of individuals. Present-day poetry groups show how convivial communal verse can be. Until Britain's open-field agriculture and common-land grazing broke up in the late eighteenth century there was little break in the singing of festive, country-oriented song and ballad such as:

> Sumer is icumen in,
> Lhude sing cuccu !
> Groweth sed, and bloweth med,
> And springth the wude nu—
> Sing cuccu !

Awe bleteth after lomb,
  Lhouth after calve cu;
Bulluc sterteth, bucke verteth,
  Murie sing cuccu !

Cuccu, cuccu, well singes thu, cuccu:
  Ne swike thu náver nu;
Sing cuccu, nu, sing cuccu,
  Sing cuccu, sing cuccu, nu ![2]

Another lyric of northern spring, written down about 1310, is
' Lenten ys come with love to toune ' (' Spring has come, with love,
to the village '). A third of about the same date is ' When the
nytegale singes '. The second has a twelve-line stanza, the third an
eight-line stanza; both have three- and four-stressed lines with
French-influenced rhyme. All these lyrics have the same gaiety as
' The Cuckoo Song '.

Still other lyrics from the Böddeker manuscript, both of 1310,
are love-songs: ' Alisoun ' and ' Blow, northern wind '. Both of
these have eight-line, three-stressed, rhymed stanzas. Both hint a
growing refusal of rigid beat and metre which will make English
lyric poetry supple, musical, essentially varied. Both songs betray,
too, emotional values which owe less to French medieval chivalric
art than to a primary idealism that is deeply Celtic-Anglo-Saxon.

An handy hap Ichabbe y-hent;
Ichot from hevene it is me sent;
From alle wymmen me love is lent,
  And lyht on Alysoun.

A happy fate has come to me;
I think it sent from heaven;
From other girls my love is turned,
  And lights on Alisoun.

The chorus of ' Blow, northern wind ' shows how it was meant
to be sung, as a round, or roundelay:

[2] Lhude=loud; sed=seed; med=meadow; awe=ewe; lhouth=loweth;
sterteth=leaps; verteth=farts; murie=merry; swike=cease.

> Blou, northerne wynd,
> Send thou me my suetyng !
> Blou, northerne wynd !
> Blou, blou, blou !

The fourteenth-century monk, Robert Mannyng of Brunne (Bourne, Lincolnshire), translated the *Manuel des Pechiez*, on the ten commandments and the seven deadly sins, as *Handlyng Synne*. This is said to throw light on the oppression of barons and lords. The Scottish John Barbour's *The Bruce*, and Barbour's lyric ' Freedom ', of about 1375, were popular in North Britain:

> A ! Fredome is a noble thing !
> Fredome mays man to haiff liking;
> Fredome all solace to man giffis,
> He levys at ese that frely levys !

In 1339, the century after these lyrics and poems were first recorded, Edward III began the first campaign of the Hundred Years' War with France. The French wars showed Normans on which side their final loyalty lay; but however much English bowmen triumphed in 1346 at Crécy, war increased miseries at home. Kings had no means of raising funds other than by fine, loan or levies on subjects great and small. Bitter rivalries among the powerful barons made it imperative that the King should be one who by warrior prowess as well as by a knightly or traditional sense of justice could hold his throne amid plot, counter-plot, murder, or secret, incessant, virulent enmity. Loyalties were in the melting-pot. National loyalty was in the making.

As the feudal hierarchy accepted since the Norman conquest grew less rigid, poetry could begin to reflect the sense of liberty instinctive in a developing people.

Hand-to-mouth poverty had been so common in the feudal age it was accepted among the many as God's plan. Crafts, and strip-farming, with animal-keeping under Manor or Monastery gave subsistence level to most lives. Rich baronial lords were few, but they were very rich indeed, chiefly in land. Yet a subterranean sense was growing—as money, land and independence became more and more to be desired—that poverty resulted from mismanagement either among the poverty-haunted or among leaders.

Injustice and thriftlessness must therefore both be sung and spoken against wherever they were caught sight of.

With scant medical knowledge, with a rising population and primitive sanitation, people accepted disease and ill-health as well as poverty as a fact of life. Death overtook most people before they were forty years old; the average lifespan was about nine years. General attitudes reflect themselves in the literature of the time.

The Plague, the Black Death, which fell on the country in 1349, 1362 and 1369, carried off one-third of the people. Amid misery and terror they turned again to the religion that had languished.

Wyclif

John Wyclif (or Wycliffe), chaplain to Edward III, banned by the Pope, and sometimes called the first Protestant, was responsible for translating the Gospels, the New Testament, and, about 1388, part of the Old Testament, from Latin into English. Wyclif wished people to be able to read in their own tongue the Bibles still chained in churches. As Wyclif's ' poor priests ' carried his vigorous prose pamphlets among the populace, so the times helped call into being a poet who voiced prevalent feelings and fears. This poet wrote against corruption in high and low places, in the royal court, among ecclesiastics, in the common man. Social life and the habits of high and low alike were held up for the most uncompromising scrutiny by this poet who declared when King Richard, a boy of eleven, ascended the throne: ' Wo to thee thou land whose king is a child.'

Langland

The new poet's cry was against tyranny, corrupt power and wealth which exploited the weaker, against hypocrisy in priests, against idleness in the growing number of the unenergetic, the ' lollers ' (a corruption of Lollards), as well as against dishonesty in workmen. It is clear that Wyclif, Wyclif's Lollards and the new poet were not so foolish as to propound at such a time that all men were equal, when men all too patently languished, as they had languished for centuries, in inequality. When Wyclif and the new poet called for a search of conscience in all, they restated the Word of Christ: men are equal in their claims on mercy, God's and their fellows'.

The new poet who demanded greater social justice was William (or Robert) Langland (or Langley). He is thought to have been born in Shropshire or Warwickshire—again a resurgence from, or near, the Celtic border—about 1330. His long poem, *The Vision of William Concerning Piers Plowman*, is attributed to William Langland of Cleoburg Mortimer. The first version was written probably in 1362, when Langland had left the Malvern hills to settle in London. One part of the poem, the sixth, is the source of most of what knowledge we have of the poet. He describes himself as ' long-cloaked ' and tonsured; he was one of the scores of chantry priests; himself a ' spill-time ', a ' loller ', ' little to be praised '. Others called him ' Long Will '; he lived in Cornhill with his wife and his daughter Calote. He was too ' long ' to work at farming. Ill-health, wit and understanding had made of him an idle poet.

We do not know whether Langland himself chanted or sang his poem at the funeral masses for souls he was paid as a common chantry-priest to say for a few pence. Relatives of most people in the fourteenth century had to afford a mass for departed souls' well-being. Langland would certainly be able to gather people by his chantry labours. *The Vision* was popular enough to make Langland (or somebody else?) write, in 1377, a second version, another vision about pestilence and evil as the direct results of general sin. A third, still longer, vision, belongs to 1398. Langland is thought to have died about 1400. The three versions of *Piers Plowman* were all printed in the sixteenth century; but not until 1886 were they edited from the preserved manuscripts and investigations made to discover their authorship.[3] It remains uncertain whether the three versions are the work of two or more men.

Piers Plowman is the last poem in traditional English, alliterative, non-rhymed verse. Its frank preaching is passionately sincere. Its music, though but occasional, is based on natural English speech rhythm. Though it is said to owe something of its form and tone to the second author of the French *Roman de la Rose*, Jean de Meung, *Piers Plowman* is in content, strongly indigenous. Picture after

[3] For a modernization of *Piers Plowman*, by Arthur Burrell, see Everyman Library edn (1915; repr. 1938).

picture, rough-hewn with merciless vigour, outline English people of the fourteenth century. The author declares he saw in a vision this ' Field full of folk ' when he fell asleep one May morning on the Malvern hills:

Of alle maner of men   —the mene and the riche—
Worchyng and wandryng,   as the worlde asketh . . .

Ac japers and jangelers,   Judas chylderen,
Feynem hem fantasies,   and foles hem maketh . . .

Bidders and beggeres   fast about gede,
With her belies and her bagges   of bred ful ycrammed;
Fayteden for here fode,   fougten atte ale;
In glotonye, God it wote   gon hii to bedde,
And risen with ribaudye,   tho Roberdes knaves; . . .

Heremites on an heep   with hoked staves,
Wenten to Walsyngham,   and here wenches after; . . .

I fond there freris—   all the foure ordres
Preched the peple   for profit of hemselven;

All manner of men,   rich and poor,
Working and wandering   as in the world we must . . .

Jesters and janglers,   Judas' children,
Feigning their fancies,   and fooling the crowds . . .

There were tramps and beggars   fast about flitting,
Crammed with bread,   in wallet and belly,
Lying for their food,   and fighting in the taverns,
Going to bed in gluttony,   rising from bed in ribaldry,
Gangs of mean thieves . . .

Hermits, a heap of them,   with hooked staves,
Were walking to Walsingham   —each had his wench with
                                                                                him—

Friars ? All the four orders,   I found them there,
Preaching to the people   and glosing the gospel
For their own profit.[4]

[4] *A Literary Middle English Reader*, ed. A. S. Cook (New York: Ginn & Co., 1915), pp. 335-7; modernization in Everyman Library edn. pp. 4-5.

Yet I dreamed more   of mean men and rich,
Barons and burgesses,   bondmen of villages;
I saw in this assembly,   as ye shall hear after,
Many a butcher, baker, brewer,   tailors and tinkers,
Woolweavers, linenweavers,   toll-takers in the markets
Masons and miners   and many another craft,
Ditchers and delvers,   that do their work ill,
And spend the livelong day in song . . .[5]

After the vision of the ' Field full of folk ' which for Langland
was the English scene, Piers dreamed of Holy Church and of Lady
Meed; Meed stands for bribery, then an evil very prevalent in
Britain; Meed is said to stand, too, for the woman who had been
Edward III's mistress. Visions of Conscience and of Reason follow;
visions of the search for Truth. The two sisters, Mercy and Peace,
offer Piers Plowman counsel to give to pilgrims. Peace tells how:

Love, my dear one   such letters sent me,
That my sister Mercy and I   mankind should save,
And that God hath forgiven   and granted to all mankind.
That Mercy and I   shall go bail for all.
Christ hath changed   the nature of righteousness
To fear and pity . . .[6]

Visions follow of God's Bull of Pardon which Piers got for men.
There are three further dreams in the second and third versions of
the poem, the visions of Do-well, Do-better, and Do-best. In the
third, with Piers half-identified with Christ, the allegory almost
overreaches itself:

. . . then I called Conscience   to tell me the truth;
' Is this Jesus the Jouster   that the Jews did to death ? '
' Or is it PIERS PLOWMAN;   who painted him so red ? '
And Conscience kneeled,   ' These be Piers arms,
His colours, his coat-armour,   but He that cometh so bloody
It is Christ with his Cross   Conqueror of Christendom.'[7]

Langland has used his allegory to remind readers, as Wyclif
reminded his, that the Jesus of record was a poor man's son who

[5] Everyman Library edn, p. 11.
[6] Ibid., pp. 156-7.
[7] Ibid., p. 167.

had little use for riches. It is not the search for wealth or the quest for happiness which brings men closest to some deeply desired integrity of thought and of action. This far-off ideal the author of *Piers Plowman* nursed in his severe, indignant mind. Christ, he was long before his time in saying, wished not to be known as ' perfect God ', but as the friend of the poor and of the underdog.

For all Langland's vigorously crude criticism of friars, of Sleuthe the parson, of pardoners, ' Rome-runners ', the ' robber Pope of France ' and cardinals with ' furs and palfreys ', he was no rebel. He had no reform to offer other than the searching of consciences for the English Church founded by the ' good Gregory ' and of which he himself was so insignificant a member. He recommended a system for the country in which a wise king, with a parliament and a loyal, hard-working people, joined to promote a common weal. He could even accept the still current slavery:

> no clerk should be tonsured   save he be the son
> Of frankleyns and free men   and of wedded folk;
> Bondmen and bastards   and beggars children,
> *These* are the sons of labour,   *these* are to serve lords.[8]

But he could also set down:

> feed on thine own loaf   and be free.

In Langland's by no means consistent allegory we watch thirteenth-century Britain struggling to rid herself of the centuries-old feudal evil of serfdom; to rise above common theft and corruption; make better laws, as well as pronounce absolutes of human conduct. Langland was well aware of ' Covetise ': envy was ' so keen a fighter ', it prompted the lazy poor to rail against the more fortunate and the better off. He allows Covetise, one of the deadly sins, ' knowing no French ', to declare humorously, ' rifling *was* restitution ', since Christ himself refused wealth. If any man knew ordinary medieval people in all their poverty, ignorance, riotous good will and patient endurance, William Langland knew them.

Yet the long struggle went on. The poet wakes from his final vision only to set out afresh; a pilgrim must:

[8] Ibid., p. 65.

walk as wide   as the world lasteth.

He seeks, must go on hoping for, must trust to find goodness and wisdom in each ordinary man.

This compassionately ruthless insight makes Langland one of the two fourteenth-century poets who brought English poetry and the English language to life again after almost two centuries' French imitation and English search for identity. *Piers Plowman* is a foil and a complete contrast to Geoffrey Chaucer's *Canterbury Tales*.

Gower

John Gower, the third considerable name in fourteenth-century English literature, was, it is said, blind in his later years, and came of a landed Kentish family. A clerk or scholar, he had a lifetime in which to read and write. He preferred city life in the aura of the court to life on his country estates. He was, he himself tells us, a friend of Geoffrey Chaucer. Chaucer described him as the ' moral Gower '.

In his youth Gower produced some fifty love *balades* in the bizarre French-English soon to die from sheer lack of vitality. Later he wrote three very long poems. The first, in French, was *Speculum Meditantis* or *Mirour de l'Omme*; the second, some say his best, was *Vox Clamantis* (*c.* 1381) in Latin; the third, *Confessio Amantis* (1390), which, in spite of its Latin title, was in English. Shocked and startled into guilt as an absentee landlord, he wrote in *Vox Clamantis* of the Peasants' Revolt of 1381 in the county where his estates were. Dismayed fear is apparent in his pictures of the populace as wild beasts without reason. He transfers blame by making a moral attack on the disorder in the Ship of State. Gower was medieval enough to think still in terms of three orders of British society—clerks, warriors (knights and nobles), and serfs or slaves. All are chidden, as all Langland's people were chidden. Gower ends with a plea to Richard II to heed the voice of the people. This voice, Gower thinks, with a premonition of British liberalism, is often the voice of God.

Admonished, King Richard yet remained Gower's patron. It was he who commanded Gower to write again. This time Gower produced *Confessio Amantis*. In the octosyllabic couplets of French romance, this long string of more than a hundred stories are translations from Ovid and other Latin or Greek authors. These Gower retailed at inordinate length to illustrate his own failings in love, confessing them to Genius the Priest of Venus. Gower used this form of the *Gesta Romanorum*—stories strung together— before Chaucer did.

The *Confessio*'s fluent verse has been said to be tedious. But no medieval poem was meant to be read alone and for long stretches. Terence Tiller's modernization of about one-third is the best way to enjoy the *Confessio Amantis*, but not without comparing it with the original.

Growing old, admitting to lechery, pride, avarice and all the Deadly Sins of medieval thought, Gower confessed that the mystery of human love was ' beyond all medicining ':

> For Love's true nature is perverse,
> Ever some barrier or some curse
> That gives too little or too much:
> How may a man delight in such
> Pursuits unless he be no man ?
> There is another Love, which can
> Dwell in his heart unchangingly,
> Being sealed in him by Charity.
> Such Love is very good to have. . . .[9]

Fourteenth-Century Background

Up to the late fourteenth century the literature of Britain had consisted, as early literatures usually consist, chiefly of poetry and prose celebrating gods, princes, kings and warriors. Incidents of British and English heroes, historical and legendary, had become inextricably entwined with myths of supernatural beings, other-world supposed happenings and anthropomorphic creatures. The epic of King Arthur and his democratic Round Table, from its original Celtic sources, under Breton, Norman and English pens, had grown into an enormous cycle. Its romance of adventure was at this time in process of being transformed into an intricate

[9] Tiller, op. cit., pp. 286-7.

Christian allegory. Relationship with the Normans and with France, as well as the travel-lure of the Crusades between 1090 and 1290, widened horizons and saved Britain temporarily from her incessant liability to ingrowth. Stories and myth now poured in from classical Greece and Rome, such as the *Orpheo* and the *Recuyell of the Historyes of Troy*. Legends of Charlemagne, one of the early Christian kings of the Franks, grew into cycles, at first heroic in tone, later elaborately courtly. From Byzantium and still farther east came stories such as *King Alexander* and the Persian-Egyptian *Arabian Nights' Entertainments*; from Africa came Aesop's animal fables. All these mingled with Norse, Danish, Celtic and English tales. The term ' Dark Ages ' is, in terms of literature, a rather narrow Western one ; it does not take into account the classical age of Arabic scholarship or Byzantium's one thousand years up to 1453, or Africa's moral fables.

In Britain the fourteenth century was still part of that most poetic of eras, the Middle Ages. A great accumulation of lore, history and legend, both indigenous and foreign, grew. Of the stories, songs, ballads, lays and romances, many fell into oblivion. Oblivion did not swallow only the work of local or less than average minstrels. It overtook vigorous enough lays such as the late thirteenth-century *Richard Coer de Lyon* [*sic*.]. In this lay Richard was endowed with a fabulous fay for a mother to explain his dauntlessness in war. He was also depicted as serving, to his gallant enemy Saladin's messengers, a meal of their slain relatives' heads.

Lays, romances and stories all used supernatural additions of god, monster, witch, giant, talking animal or bird, spell, charm, vision and dream—the cornucopia of most early peoples' beliefs. Usually, heroes were exempted from earthly parentage and from common death. Most stories exalted ancient personal principles of loyalty, courage, generosity, chastity, gentleness. Courtesy was not new—to the aged, the poor and the weak. Respect for women was an early Teutonic characteristic. The medieval worship of the Virgin strengthened respect for women in one way. But Christian distrust of the fierce forthrightness of primordial love aided a growing legal protection and hence subordination of women. Whilst softening, civilizing and repressing, a worldly, wealth-seeking Church helped to bring about double, conflicting attitudes. Energetic ambition collided with generosity. Fidelity and private understanding between a young man and a girl (often a very young girl in those days) were sometimes lost in the newer custom of social and economic alliances and property marriages. But the fascinating thing is how earlier standards of character and conduct emerge again in poetry and prose about this time, highlighted as new. After fourteen centuries, four foreign conquests, amid grinding general workaday life, foreign war, famine, plague, revolt and growing wealth and magnificence for the few, the fourteenth-century English were still seeking their identity, in ideal and in language; they tried to outline these in their arts of poetry and prose.

They had no machines besides plough and loom, but they had leisure and quiet. They still listened by moonlight, firelight or rushlight, to long, didactic, allegories as well as to romances and lays. There were still animal fables pointing morals. Personified virtues and vices illustrated Peace, Beauty, Love, the Seven Sins of Pride, Envy, Greed, Anger, Avarice, Gluttony and Lechery. Such stories and fables do not belong specifically to Christian literature. They are fairly common in the lore of pre-literate cultures.

Geoffrey Chaucer was born about 1340. His father and grandfather were London wine-merchants. The boy was given the kind of education then fashionable: he attended St Paul's Almonry; by sixteen he was a page in the household of the Duke of Clarence, being taught in Courtesy or Chivalry. His work would be to run errands, carry messages, wait at table, help the great of the land to dress, learn to ride, to use a sword, to joust. In 1359 he went to France as a soldier. After being imprisoned and ransomed, he is heard of in various missions to the Continent, twice to Italy. He married Philippa, sister of John of Gaunt's third wife. When John of Gaunt, Chaucer's lifelong patron, went out of favour, Chaucer lost his place at court. But the engaging audacity of his lyric ' The Compleynt to His Purse ', addressed to the new king, Henry Bolingbroke, murderer of Richard II and ' conquerour of Brutès Albioun ', gained Chaucer a pension which filled his empty purse and so lightened the poet's last days. He died in 1400 and is buried in Poet's Corner in Westminster Abbey.

Like Gower Chaucer, an avid reader with a capacious memory, began his poetic life by writing love-lyrics. None of these has survived. 'The Compleynte unto Pite', which tried out his now famous, then original stanza, the seven-line rhyme-royal, is his earliest lyric to be preserved. It reveals a beauty of form struggling with a poet's gravest thought about his art and his world. ' Pity,' Chaucer says, ' is dead ' and : ' no wight woot that she is dead but I '. Assurance, Wisdom, Wealth, Contempt and Authority stand, ' withouten any wo ', at Pity's graveside. But of what use are these so-called new manners of ' gentlemen ' ? Of what use ' gentilesse ' itself, or ' Youthe and Honestee ', without true feeling ? This was one of the deeply hid, great questions of Edward III's and Richard II's days. Actual physical bravery might be no longer as necessary for all men as once it had been. The question was what took its place for manhood. If chivalry and manners had become romantic and legendary, non-useful, what made a real enough, commercial ' gentleman ' ? This question of maturity or manhood underlies developing literature because it underlies civilization and life itself.

To between 1382 and 1390 belongs Chaucer's lyric, ' Truth ', or ' The Balade de bon Conseyl '. No doubt this owes its theme to Boëthius's well-known *De Consolatione Philosophiae*. But again the ring of conflict is audible in Chaucer, a struggle between the genial, social side of a court poet and the graver reflection which did not fail to visit the Chaucer who, to achieve his poetic output, must have spent much of a busy life in solitude :

> Flee fro the prees, and dwelle with sothfastnesse
> Suffice unto thy thyng though hit be smal;
> For hord hath hate and clymbyng tikelnesse,
> Prees hath envye, and welé blent overal;
> Savour no more than thee bihové shal;
> Werk wel thy-self, that other folk canst rede,
> And trouthe shal delivere, it is no drede.

> Tempest thee noght al crokèd to redresse
> In trust of hir that turneth as a bal;
> Greet restè stant in litel besynesse;
> An eek be war to sporne ageyn an al;
> Stryve noght, as doth the crokkè with the wal.
> Daunte thy-self, that dauntest otherès dede,
> And trouthè shall delivere, it is no drede.

That thee is sent, receyve in buxumnesse,
The wrastling for this worlde axeth a fal.
Her nis non hoom, her nis but wildernesse.
Forth, pilgrim, forth ! Forth, beste, out of thy stal,
Know thy contree, look up, thank God of al;
Hold the hye wey, and lat thy gost thee lede,
And trouthe shall delivere, it is no drede.

Flee from the crowd and so keep steadfastness;
Content with what you have though it is small;
Plenty breeds hate, ambition fickleness,
The crowd will envy well-being over all.
Have no more appetite than what's behove;
Work well yourself that others may see clear;
And truth shall set you free, there is no fear.

Don't fret to put all right that you think wrong.
Or trust in (fortune) turning like a ball:
Great rest is in restraint from meddling;
Beware you be not stubbed on a sharp awl;
Don't strive. Be still as water in its wall.
Subdue yourself who would be others' peer,
And truth shall set you free, there is no fear.

What (fate) is sent to you, receive obediently,
Wrestling for worldly goods asks for a fall.
Here is no home, here's but a wilderness.
Forth, pilgrim, forth ! Forth, beast, out of your stall,
Know (heaven) your country, look up, thank God for all.
Hold the highway, step close in your spirit's rear,
And truth shall set you free, there is no fear.

Spelling in the fourteenth century was almost individual, certainly far from formalized; grammar was not made into any system until the eighteenth century. Final ' e ' was sounded in poetry, as it was in speech before consonants, but not before ' y ' or before vowels. Double negatives were not only permitted. They strengthened the negative case, as in the line: ' Her nis non hoom, her nis but wildernesse.'

After those early lyrics Chaucer put himself to a long and severe apprenticeship in poetry. Under French influence he wrote the long *Boke of the Duchesse*, a lament for the death, in 1369, of Blanche, the well-loved wife of John of Gaunt. Courtly, as befitted the work of a court poet, artificial, the poem follows French poetic conventions. Yet underneath, a poet who lamented for posterity the death of ' pity ' in that hard age shows himself. He wrote, for the one son we know him to have had, the learned but dull prose *Treatise on the Astrolabe*, but did not finish it. He went on to translate many of the stories Dante, Petrarch and Boccaccio wrote or used. In prose he translated Boëthius's *De Consolatione Philosophiae*, which had been one of the most read and valued books since its publication in Latin in the early sixth century. It is nearly as dull as the *Treatise on the Astrolabe*: we do not think in the terms it used.

Between 1372 and 1385 Chaucer produced *The Parlement of Foules*, *The Hous of Fame* and *The Legende of Goode Women*. All these are medieval works using classical figures, well-known stories, with talking birds of early cultures, abstractions and gods and goddesses of vice and virtue. Also before 1380 he translated (probably with the help of a northern poet) the French verse romance, by Guillaume de Lorris and Jean de Meung, *Roman de la Rose*. This almost interminable poem is an exposition of Love. By Love, Chaucer says, he meant: ' pitee/Frendshipe, love and all bounte '. The medieval Christian cult of the Virgin had brought about this expansion of interest in the side of our nature opposite to aggressiveness and need for ascendancy. Far from having no interest for us today Chaucer's partial translation, titled *Romaunt of the Rose*, is a necessary signpost of the developing cultural consciousness.

Between 1382 and 1385 Chaucer produced his first masterpiece, *Troylus and Cryseyde*. Though it is based on his contemporary Boccaccio's *Il Filostrato*, which in turn was based on the *Roman de Troie* written in the twelfth century, and though the story of Cressida's perfidy would be well known, Chaucer, having no need to heed what we now value as originality of theme, yet produced one of the most moving, tragic yet laughable stories. His Cressida is not the unpractised, giddy jilt which, as Hazlitt says, Shakespeare made of her. Chaucer does not ramble among the warlike heroes of Greece and Troy, Hector, Agamemnon, Achilles and Paris. His story is a precise, psychological presentment of the daughter of a traitor. Lonely and insecure, Cressida, through feminine softness and through her father's example, perhaps, failed in the ideal of faithfulness set up by the age succeeding the warlike-heroic.

Chaucer did not finish the *Romaunt of the Rose*, or *The Hous of*

Fame, or *The Legende of Goode Women*. He was trying to break through to a reality of his own. He was seeking his true voice, of mild irony and wide sympathies. It has been said that Chaucer did not presume to ascend to Paradise, or to venture down to Hell in the manner of his admired Dante, who died in 1321. He sought, as his Welsh or English contemporary William Langland sought, to portray real men and women. Yet he was not concerned, as Langland had been, to denounce, much less condemn. He did not, even in his less mature work, evoke long-term Justice, or call, as John Gower called, for State or Clergy to put things right. He simply delighted in men and women as vivid, various, fallacious, cunning, lustful, laughable, loving, loyal or disloyal human beings.

This translator and adaptor of Italian, French, and European writing, turned finally, about 1386, to create something entirely English. This was his second masterpiece, *The Canterbury Tales*. He imagined thirty pilgrims from as many walks of life setting out on the not unusual pilgrimage from London to the shrine of Thomas à Becket at Canterbury. Making a social occasion of the journey as the custom was, the pilgrims were each to tell two tales to help pass the time. This enormous (and not particularly original) scheme was not completed before Chaucer's death. But its *Prologue* is sometimes said to be the first English novel.

Part of the stories' fascination lies in what they reveal about those who relate them. Some were written by Chaucer much earlier than 1386; some may have been written when his genius was failing. Most are translations from French, Italian, classical or other European sources. One or two are in Chaucer's dullish prose. ' The Canon's Yeoman's Tale ' is said to be Chaucer's own invention, perhaps his only one. The chief fascination of *The Canterbury Tales* lies in what Dryden called the ' God's plenty ' of Chaucer's loving descriptions of the Pilgrims: their dress, talk and attitudes.

A Doctor of Physic, a Man of Law, a Clerk of Oxford, and the poet himself, represented the learned class. A Knight, his son a Squire, and a Yeoman, represented the fighting class. A Miller, a Ploughman, a Reeve and a Franklin represented the land. A Merchant, a Shipman, a Wife of Bath, a Haberdasher, a Carpenter, a Webbe (weaver), a Dyer, a Tapycer (tapestry maker), a Maunciple (purveyor of food), a Cook and the keeper of the Tabard Inn (the Host of the Pilgrimage) were craftsmen and traders. Of the clergy there was a poor village parson, a Sompnour (summoner to the ecclesiastical courts then still in use as well as civil courts), a Canon (who disappeared leaving his yeoman to tell the tale of a fraudulent alchemist), a Benedictine Monk, a Prioress and her Chaplain, a Nun, a mendicant Friar, and a Pardoner (one who sold pardons for money).

Though the Cook and the Friar and the Parson might be poor enough, most of the Pilgrims were not the indigent whom Langland knew: ' bidders and beggars ', ' tailors and tinkers ', ' ditchers and delvers ' could not have set out on what was clearly a not inexpensive pilgrimage. Chaucer's company were a cross-section of all but the poorest of English society of his day. His keen eye for how colour, dress and speech betray and set off character was unknown to Langland or Gower and unprecedented in English writing. His humorous, easy tolerance gives us for the first time, in the *Prologue* and in the outspoken, revealing, ' murye wordes ' amongst the Pilgrims between the tales, highly individual men and women.

Here is his portrait of the Squire, the Knight's son. This young squire has been brought up in a courtly household. That was the kind of ' education ' boys of wealthy parents then received:

> A lovyere and a lusty bacheler,
> With lokkės crulle as they were leyd in presse.
> Of twenty yeer of age he was, I gesse.
> Of his stature he was of evene lengthe,
> And wonderly delyvere and greet of strengthe;
> For he hadde been somtyme in chyvachie,
> In Flandrės, in Artoys and Pycardie,
> And born hym weel, as of so litel space,
> In hope to stonden in his lady grace
> Embrouded was he, as it were a meede
> Al ful of fresshė flourės whyte and reede;
> Syngynge he was, or floytynge al the day;
> He was as fressh as is the monthe of May.
> Short was his gowne, with slevės longe and wyde;
> Wel koude he sitte on hors and fairė ryde;
> He koudė songės make and wel endite,
> Juste and eek daunce and weel purtreye and write.
> So hoote he lovedė that by nyghtertale
> He sleep nomoore than dooth a nyghtyngale.
> Curteis he was, lowely and servysable,
> And carf beforn his fader at the table.[10]

[10] Chaucer, *Works*, Globe edn (Macmillan, 1919), p. 2.

This squire of twenty was the son of the ' verray parfit, gentil knyght '; and in both these characters it might be thought that the court poet shows through, had Chaucer not given us just as generous a picture of the ' Poure Persoun of a Toun ', the village parson. To contrast the Parson with Langland's ' Parson Sloth ' is to be aware of Chaucer's genial, ' ful brode ' kindliness beside Langland's severity.

Chaucer's garrulous, much-travelled Wife of Bath is perhaps his best-known character. Her every word betrays what is still thought of as feminine deceits, as well as her unabashed earthiness. Roundly she declared what was coming to be thought: that manners and courtesy—the new civilizing influences—were not to be seen as virtue or as the results solely of noble birth. They could be attained by the so-called ' base-born '; some of the ' simple ' had them naturally. She thought a woman should be the match in argument and strength of mind of a man. The Clerk's Lombard tale of Griselda's reward for her unbelievable patience, the Merchant, ' heart-scalded ' with a bad wife, and his tale of senile January and faithless May, the Second Nun's story of the early Christian Church's valuing of purity before life itself, the Franklin's tale of affection and trust—all these may be added to the Wife of Bath's outlook on the subject of human feeling. Contrary to what was held in the French Courts of Love Chaucer indicates that love and marriage might not be incompatible; but he was too good an artist to assert any one viewpoint.

The form of *The Canterbury Tales* is as clumsy as are Langland's sometimes incoherent visions. Not all the tales accord with their tellers; a few, like the Parson's dull sermon, make some of the hearers grumble. The Host serves strong wine for supper and ' vitaille of the best ', to stave off the quarrels that come near arising in those hastier days when blows or fisticuffs were readily resorted to, if ' honour ' demanded, among even civilized or educated Britons.

The *Prologue* to the *Canterbury Tales* is in five-beat, iambic lines, rhyming in pairs. Later to be called the heroic couplet, neither this verse-form nor ' rhyme-royal ' was Chaucer's invention. But his use of both was a gift to English poetry.

His literary legacy to posterity is also in his control of English as a language capable of many rhythms; he encloses his depth and width of human sympathy within poetry full of vivid simile: the

Ploughman's mouth was wide as ' a greet forneys ', the Prioress's
' eyen greye as glas '; the Doctor of Physic's ' study ', ' but litel
on the Bible ', the Monk's bridle ' Gynglen . . . as cleere . . . as
dooth the chapel belle '. The sympathy of this metrically new, and
graphic, poetry triumphed over metrical uncertainty and medieval
abstraction. It opened a window for Britain's literature and a gate
towards human tolerance and understanding. We may call his
poetry realist and his quality humanism. The *Prologue, Troylus
and Cryseyde* and *The Canterbury Tales* mean more than both these
words mean.[11]

Whilst poetry was freed by Chaucer prose remained fettered.
Scholars and churchmen insisted on Latin. Fourteenth-century
English prose was chiefly theological and scientific. The problematic Sir John Mandeville in his ' Voiage ', or *Travels*, was prolix,
naïve and medieval in recounting ' wonders ' on the way to the
Holy Land. Yet his *Travels* were enjoyed on their appearance in
the last years of the fourteenth century when growing numbers of
people were learning to read.

The Paston Letters

These literates show themselves in the volumes of the *Paston Letters*.
The *Letters* reveal the rise of an energetic, legal and trading family
interested in landholding, titles and family aggrandisement. Often
betraying mercenary and material outlooks, their *Letters* are yet
fascinating to others besides historians. Three generations of this
Norfolk family pass before our eyes. The family rose about 1422
from the yeoman peasantry to a baronetcy and an earldom, to
drop back towards peasantry in the sixteenth century. The *Letters*,
sometimes from managing Paston women to sons, daughters,
husbands, cousins and servants, trusted and distrusted, deal with
money, land, leases, lawsuits, domestic improvements and in-
volvements. These writers lend books, precious because still scarce.
Oddly modern yet completely medieval, the *Letters* reveal a con-

---

[11] If we cannot guess our way through them as Chaucer wrote them, Nevill Coghill's modernization of the *Tales* and Margaret Stanley-Wrench's of *Troilus and
Criseyde* are keys to this room in our past [see General References].

tinuity of human ways that sometimes we overlook. There are few flights of imagination. But instance after instance evinces the courage of women and men in days when to speak your mind in England might be to endanger your head. Quaintly formal address to parents and husbands conceals loyalty and enduring respect, though often based on hard economics. The sternness of fifteenth-century English towards their young glares from the *Letters*. But youthful independence is also vocal. Some of those Pastons rise against the hitherto unquestioned assumption of parents that offspring could be used to further family ambitions. Finally the *Paston Letters* show English prose, roundabout and clumsy, in slow process of becoming a better means of mutual comprehension.

Malory

By 1470 Sir Thomas Malory, a knight who lived at Winwick near Rugby, had completed a prose version of the King Arthur stories. Malory wrote *Morte Darthur* in the Midland dialect which had been Chaucer's, and which was to be Shakespeare's, and so was to become Standard English. The legends of Arthur, his Round Table, and his knights, Tristram, Gawayne, Lancelot, and his Queen Guinevere, had grown into a bewildering cycle of romance, to which the still more immense cycle of the pagan-Christian Quest of the Holy Grail had been added. Malory is said to have written *Morte Darthur* in prison whilst serving a sentence for murder and other crimes.

The originals of many of these stories lie far back among heathen, Celtic myths. These had become blent with saintly themes of devotion, perseverance and seclusion. Both Christian and pre-Christian myths were mixed with Breton (Celtic) and French lays and romances. Malory portrayed all the courtesy and some of the Chaucerian ' gentilesse ' of a Britain emerging out of the Middle Ages wherein all still ' hovered betwixt war and wantonness '. He wrote an English prose story which, for all its Middle English dialect, is fascinating and readable.

Back in superstitious days, of giants, talking beasts, ogres, magicians, magic happenings, spells and counter-spells, we are beguiled by beauty and haunted by perilous adventures of Christian heroes and humble men. We are made conscious of the infinitely slow change in human sensitivity towards tolerance, let alone generosity. Roger Ascham, educationist and Royal schoolmaster of Elizabeth I's day, condemned the Arthur stories as immoral. In them, love outside marriage was tolerated, its tragic fidelity tacitly applauded. Though anthropological and humanist insights are currently in some disrepute, it does no harm to remind ourselves that the original object of the search which became the Holy Grail quest, is known to have been a Celtic food talisman, a magic means of making food appear among people never far above starvation. The heroes, often simple and untutored, belong essentially to unlettered days of brutal but heroic life. Three centuries after Ascham, the statesman Edmund Burke, seeing heroic and chivalrous as one age, lamented the passing of those days. If Malory's prison-written *Morte Darthur* shows us anything, it is that ideas such as bravery, loyalty and honesty belong within a continuity of human time.

Caxton and Printing

Caxton printed Malory's story in 1485, soon after that busy, practical publisher established his first printing-press in London under the patronage of a royal woman. Caxton wrote that the Book of Arthur was:

> . . . right necessary to be read. For in it ye shall find the gracious, knightly, and virtuous wars of the most noble knights of the world, whereby they got praising continual. Also it seemeth by the oft reading thereof ye shall greatly desire to accustom yourself in following those gracious knightly deeds—that is to say, to dread God, and love righteousness. . . .[12]

Ballads

Another form of verse which quickened into poetry in the fourteenth century was the ballad. Ballads are found all over early Europe. They are a primary form of popular poetry. They have been dis-

[12] Quoted from W. H. Schofield, *English Literature from the Norman Conquest to Chaucer* (Macmillan, 1906), pp. 257-8.

covered in the greatest numbers in outlying border districts where fear and enmity between groups and tribes linger longest. Many ballads have choruses; and these refrains suggest more than other early poetry that listeners joined in with the bard or minstrel. Some scholars have thought that ballads may have been communally composed. But the more likely fact is that minstrels— in tawny coat and leather buskins, like Anthony Now-Now[13]— used words, phrases, lines, certainly incidents, picked up from audiences in bower, hall and ale-house. The actual form of a ballad, however much this changed as the ballad continued to be sung, was usually the work of an individual poet. By incessant oral repetition change often rendered them beyond recognition, by the time they began to be written down in the sixteenth century. Though the fourteenth century is known to be the date when the historical events celebrated in some British ballads took place, the earlier history of the form is now lost. We do not know for sure where the four-line ballad-stanza came from. Rhyming at the close of the second and fourth lines, the ballad quatrain is surely much older than the eleventh century, the age of the Provençal troubadours and *trouvères*. More likely it goes back, as the Chadwicks say in *The Growth of Literature*, to verbal forms among Steppe horsemen; it may be akin to the four-line, rhymed and rhythmic verse of many early peoples.

In England nobody bothered to collect ballads until Bishop Percy in 1765. Courtly ballads such as ' The Battle of Otterburn', and ' Chevy Chase', can be dated as dealing with episodes belonging to the fourteenth and fifteenth centuries, the Scots and English rivalries on the border, strife between Earls Douglas and Percy, and between England's and Scotland's kings. ' Sir Patrick Spens ' is a confusion of at least three historical tragedies. All these ballads are concerned with the valour of individual fighters and the drama of combat. Philip Sidney confessed in 1581:

. . . I never heard the old song of Percy and Douglas, that I found not my heart more moved than with a trumpet; and yet it is sung but by some blind crowder with no rougher voice than rude stile.[14]

The ballad-cycle of Robin Hood belongs to the fifteenth century.

[13] Minstrel mentioned in Henry Chettle, *Kinde Harte's Dreame* (1593). Chettle complained that crowds gathered to hear children sing immoral songs.
[14] Quoted from Legouis and Cazamian, *A History of English Literature*, p. 177.

We cannot now be certain that an individual called Robin Hood existed. Professor Child, an American collector of ballads in the late nineteenth century, held there was no historical Robin. (King Alfred had been an outlaw before he dared claim his kingdom.) The outlaw was frequently a local champion against oppression. There must have been, up to days when English longbowmen proved themselves at Crécy, more than one archer (besides Randolph of Chester) whose fame spread from mouth to mouth in the ' rude stile ' of an uncivil age. There must have been women, the Nut-Brown Maid and Robin's Maid Marian, faithful to outlaw lovers. There must have been men like Locksley in *Ivanhoe*.

In his introduction to a collection of ballads Robert Graves writes:

> The original character who inspired the legends of Robin Hood is shown by J. W. Walker (*The Archeological Review*, 1944) to have been a yeoman of Wakefield in Yorkshire, born about 1285, and outlawed for joining the rebellion of the Earl of Lancaster, whom King Edward II defeated at Boroughbridge in 1322. Robin was the son of a forester named Adam Hood.[15]

One Robin Hood was said to have been pardoned by Edward II and invited to form a band of archers, as *A Lytell Geste of Robin Hoode* tells. The name, Robert Graves adds, figures in the *Register of Court Expenses* for 1323 and 1324. Whether there was any one Robin who actually lived is of interest chiefly to the specialist-scholar. But the memory of that defier of a growing legal system which often worked against, rather than for, the poor and the obscure, is important for all who are interested in what we obstinately think of as liberty.

There are ballads older than those of the Robin Hood cycle and the Border cycle. The original form of these cannot now be known. They portray days when bloodthirsty tribal revenge often involved the innocent. In remotest districts in north and south-west England, in Scotland, Wales and Ireland, revenge could be, for all time, the most obvious settlement between tribe and tribe, family and family, man and man. Customs continued to include reverence for ancestors; and the dead were thought to hold power, often dread power, to force obedience to their behests, over the

[15] *English and Scottish Ballads* (Heinemann, 1957), p. xviii.

living. Even in the late Middle Ages marriage could be by capture of a girl, willing or unwilling. Battle conquest meant bondage for the conquered. The ballads which tell of these things, such ballads as ' The Twa Sisters of Binnorie', ' Lord Randal', ' The Demon Lover ' and ' The Unquiet Grave', are superstitious and full of crude dramatic action. They deal with primordial feelings that in our early society prompted acts of murder, rapine, hate, but also begot loyalty and bravery; in them love, cruelty and revenge could pass beyond death to haunt the living to their destruction. Some ballads have undergone Christian influence. Such are ' Hugh of Lincoln ' and ' The Cleveland Lyke Wake Dirge '. Many have been lost. Those which have escaped destruction form an important part of Britain's poetic heritage.

III

On to the Great Age of Britain's Literature

1400 - 1616

After Chaucer's death in 1400 more than a century and a half passed by before another poet of stature appeared. But what looks like literary barrenness does not mean that little was happening. On the contrary, much that was vital to letters was taking place beneath the surface among the many unknowns whose lives and work have contributed to the story of literature.

The fifteenth century saw terrible civil conflict in England. The Wars of the Roses, between 1454 to 1485, after a hundred years of war with France, were between two rival lines of claimants, the House of York and of Lancaster. The prize was the kingship. Brother's hand might well be then against brother's; son's against father's: that was no time for studious poetry. National consciousness, hewn out of suffering, as well as compounded of failure, hope, vigour, daring and success, was not yet in being. Language, the very stuff of prose and verse, was still struggling for forms and rhythms of communication.

Parents began to feel it imperative that the younger generations should be able to read and write. Very slowly more and more schools went up. Town and village boy crept, ' like snail, unwillingly ' to them. Girls were taught by mothers and then sent to other homes to learn disciplined home management, herbal medicine, broderie Anglaise, needlework; a very few to read and write. Primary schools were most often set up by local benefactors. Grammar schools were often founded and endowed by wealthy burghers. But the grammar in question, all the grammar taught, was not English grammar, which did not exist, but Latin grammar. Education meant knowing how to read and write, but also, however clumsily and uselessly, conning a little of the admired language of Britain's conquerors of fifteen hundred years before; as also a little classical Greek, the language of that people to whom all Europe owes the bases of its thought.

The English language continued its own development: mute ' e ' slowly dropped out; noun-plurals and verb-forms were changing; spelling and punctuation were so unorganized as to be left to individual choice.

In Europe and the Middle East Arab scholars had been for centuries among the foremost of the time. But before and after the end of the Byzantine Empire, with the fall of Constantinople to the Turks in 1453, European learning received a great quickening from Baghdad and from Christian Byzantium. Western scholars and poets of the Renaissance New Learning such as Dante, Boccaccio and Petrarch revived the interest in Greek and Roman poetry, prose, philosophy and science. The Renaissance reached France; soon it would electrify Britain.

Fifteenth-Century Poets

There were a few fifteenth-century English poets who remembered Chaucer and to a lesser degree Langland. Thomas Hoccleve (or Occleve) and John Lydgate were among these. Imitation and translation from French and Latin were still the fashion or indeed the sole motif in literature. Hoccleve and Lydgate agreed no poet was left ' that worthy was his [Chaucer's] ynkehorne for to holde '. That they did not follow Chaucer's poetic usages was because they did not comprehend his method of versification; and that they did not comprehend was perhaps because the language was too much in flux. Hoccleve translated French romances. He confessed that:

> Chaucer fayne wold have me taught,
> But I was dulle, and lerned lyte or naught.

Yet Hoccleve's *Letter of Cupid* was for a long time said to be by Chaucer.

Lydgate was a learned East Anglian monk who had travelled in France and Italy. He probably wrote more than any other Middle English poet. He is interesting despite his medieval long-windedness; his poetry is occasionally fresh and revealing and gives evi-

dence of the rapid transition of the language towards a modern
form. Lydgate describes in his *Testament* his ' yearys greene '; he
did what most boys do—lied, stole, made game of grown-ups behind backs, forgot to say his prayers, got up on cold winter
mornings as late as he possibly could and:

> Ran in to garydns applys ther I stal
> To gadre frutys sparyd hegg nor wall . . .
> Was moor reedy than for to seyn matynes.[1]

One unknown fifteenth-century poet wrote *The Crede of Piers
Plowman*, and it was taken for Langland's work. Later Dryden
modernized the allegorical poem *The Flower and the Leaf*, thinking
that Chaucer's; but the poem is the work of another of the century's
unknowns. There are many more of these poets lost to us.

Scottish poetry in the late fourteenth and in the fifteenth century
was more vigorous than English poetry of that period. The earliest
Scottish poem is *The Gododdin*, thought to have been written by
Celtic Aneirin of the late sixth century. This is a story—movingly
translated by Professor Hurlestone Jackson—of an onslaught by
three hundred Scottish, Celtic and Pictish cavalry against the
' heathen ' invaders from over the sea, Anglo-Saxons of the newly
formed border kingdom of Deira-Bernicia, soon to be Northumbria.
The three hundred were annihilated—except for the poet, who
escaped to praise those heroes. Perhaps what deeply stirs in *The
Gododdin* is the sense of our northern ancestors' courage in battle,
death and border rivalry centuries before they and we, both sides
of the border, settled into being civilized neighbours. After Robert
Bruce's final manifestation of Scottish independence was celebrated
by John Barbour in *The Bruce*, in the early fifteenth century King
James I of Scotland—captured whilst still a boy on his way to
France and borne to prison in England—fell in love with the
English Lady Jane Beaufort. James wrote, in the seven-line stanza
Chaucer had used, ' The Kingis Quair ' (The King's Book); this
is why the stanza is called ' rhyme-royal '. The poem describes his
love and its happy ending.

Other Scots poets were Robert Henryson, who joined pastoral
poetry to the implicit Celtic love of nature; William Dunbar, who
wrote ' The Thistle and the Rose '; David Lindsay, Alexander

---

[1] Harleian MS. 2255, printed by the Percy Society in 1840.

Scott and Gavin Douglas. All these poets' work, deeply interesting of itself, also reveals how the Scottish language evolved so differently from the English, remaining vocally beautiful and intrinsically itself whilst it passed under the pens of William Drummond, James Beattie, Allan Ramsay, James Thomson, Robert Burns and Walter Scott to Hugh MacDiarmid, Iain Crichton Smith and others of the twentieth century.

Books of Courtesy

Whilst poetry in England halted, for complex developmental reasons, there were plenty who put verse to the service of courtesy, culture, manners, chivalry. Hewe Rodes (Hugh Rhodes) compiled, between 1450 and 1480 (but not published until 1577), his *Boke of Nurture* for the boys of Edward IV's court. Between 1440 and 1450 John Russell, steward to Humphrey Duke of Gloucester who collected a splendid library, wrote *The Babees' Boke*. It was published in 1475. Russell's ' Babees ' were pages between seven and fourteen years of age, children of noble birth receiving courtly training in the Duke of Gloucester's household. Russell instructed them how to behave, at mealtimes, before their lord, at joust: ' Babees ' were not to quarrel, not to use coarse language, not to belch, ' claw ' their ' cods ', claw their heads after a louse, not to pick their teeth or noses, not to throw bones at each other or under the table, not to stick their tongues into food. They were to use the new hand-kerchiefs introduced by Richard II. The age of Norman chivalry was almost gone; traditional, knightly training lingered. We can hear the battle of discussion joined in the old-fashioned, alliterative verse of those books of courtesy which dealt with what Renaissance man was to be. In Britain he was to be citizen of the new Common-wealth. This word ' Commonwealth ' was used well before the days of Oliver Cromwell. The question grew: what was Virtue in a commonweal, in a healthy, reasonable society ? Among Romans virtue had meant manly strength, moral and physical. Was it now to become a veneer of manners only, such as *The Babees' Boke* taught, hiding a savage irrationality beneath the skin ? Virtue must surely be of the whole man. The studious, saintlike young Edward VI became one kind of example.

C

Francis Seager, translator of the Psalms, first published his *School of Vertue* in Edward's reign, the age of the English Reformation. It was many times reprinted after 1550. It is less physically forthright than the others, more homiletic; it does not subscribe to the crudely aristocratic tradition that ' All vyce be of vilanye '—that is, in the ignorant, the unfree, the slave. Instead, Seager propounds, with all the confidence of a member of a young nation, the doctrine associated with the name of Erasmus: that not wealth, or land, or brutal warring makes a man. Learning alone makes human beings fit to be virtuous members of an emerging Commonwealth:

For learnynge wyll leade thee Vice to subdue . . .

Experience doth teache   And shewe to thee playne
That many to honour   By learninge attayne
That were of byrthe   But symple and bace,—
Suche is the goodnes   Of Gods speciall grace,—[2]

But how was learning—in spite of the example of such as Chaucer's young squire—to be joined to physical valour in the many ? More practically, remembering Chaucer's ' pauvre scholar ', it had to be linked with the new, and apparently necessary, power of wealth, which often demanded the predator's cunning. Seager's concluding exhortation can only uphold traditional practice in piety; he accepts the chasm between rich and poor as intended by God.

Ye men of lawe,   in no wyse delaie
The cause of the poore   but helpe what ye maie.

Ye that be craftsmen   vse no disceite,
Geuing to all men   tale, measure and weighte.

Ye that be landlordes   and have housen to let,
At reasonable rentes   do them forth set . . .

Ye rych, whom god   hath goods vnto sente,
Releue the poore   and helpe the indigente.

[2] Quoted from F. J. Furnivall's reprint, Early English Text Society (Trubner, 1868), pp. 340, 346.

Ye that are poore,   with your state be contente,
Not hauinge wherwith   to lyve competente.[3]

Carols

This century and a half of change in many aspects of Britain and
not least in its language was the century of the greatest English and
Scots ballads, though ballads had begun much earlier. Caxton,
translator and indefatigable collector as well as printer at Westminster, made between eighty and a hundred books; to him we
are indebted for the preservation of the courtly works of Chaucer
and the *Morte Darthur* of Thomas Malory. But with no daily or
weekly press, no journalism, with, before 1485, war and rumours
of the brave and the loved dying in battle, with many men outlawed
for taking sides, people were avid for news, views, information.
Entertainment by wandering singers, minstrels, went on as before,
with some help from rudely printed broadsheets and ballads.
Singers and harpists improvised. Some poetical entertainers were
educated men. Richard Corbet, the son of a gardener who became
Bishop of Oxford, wrote ' Farewell to the Fairies ', to remind us
how puritans' minds were already banishing as rubbish nursery
rhymes and stories dealing with the Little People of Celtic Britain—
as more and more austerities were to banish ballads and eventually
to help close the theatres.

The troubled fifteenth century and the Reformation led to bloodshed over heresy in the sixteenth and seventeenth centuries. Carols
of that earlier century show the language making its own rhythms
(though not yet exploring them), through pressures of what had to
be said. At this level rhythm does not need or heed rules more than
vital, deep feeling and breath-phrasing. Carols like ' The Holly and
the Ivy ' and perhaps ' I Sing of a Maiden ' show the influence
which a young nation's ordinary people have on the evolution of
their language and of their poetry.

Scottish and English carols, like ballads, continue to be important
in this period. ' The Holly and the Ivy ', of older, pagan origin,
has a Christian overlay: the stiff, strong holly, a pagan masculine
symbol, and the clinging, feminine ivy, are praised equally with

[3] Ibid.

the chivalric joust and stag-hunting, and with the Christian organ and choir-music. This carol's pattern of a variable number of unaccented syllables in its lines foreshadows what Gerard Manley Hopkins, in the nineteenth century, called ' sprung rhythm '.

> The holly and the ivy,
>   When they are both full grown,
> Of all the trees that are in the wood,
>   The holly bears the crown:
>
>   The rising of the sun
>   And the running of the deer
>   The playing of the merry organ,
>   Sweet singing of the choir.[4]

Classical Welsh Poetry

Whilst England went through this period of change and con-solidation, Welsh poetry reached a pinnacle. The Welsh call the fifteenth century their classical phase. Since the heroic days of events from *The Book of Taliessin* in the sixth and seventh centuries, the Celtic language had stayed remarkably stable. Its written form in the tenth, eleventh and twelfth centuries preserved it from further flux. Its poetry had alliteration, end-line rhyme and what to an Anglo-Saxon ear sounds like consonantal sound pattern within each line—*cynghanedd*. In the fourteenth century Celtic verse-forms were classified into twenty-four strict measures. All were accompanied by *cynghanedd*. The poet Dafydd ab Edmwnd further tightened poetic rules to discourage the careless, the over-weaning and the half-trained. Gwyn Williams[5] tells us that the years from 600 to 1600 saw the rise and decline of Celtic poetry in these strict metres. After the latter date there was plenty of verse in freer forms, though the classical metres were, and are today at each *Eisteddfod* or poetic festival, still used.

Celtic poetry is not architectural in the way Anglo-Saxon poetry is. It feels less need for a beginning, a central point or climax,

---

[4] Text from *The Oxford Book of Carols* (1956).
[5] Foreword to *The Burning Tree*: *Poems from the First Thousand Years of Welsh Verse* (Faber & Faber, 1956).

and an end. It prefers to follow some idea-sense-sound of overall poetic pattern that is almost instinctive. Its themes contain what Matthew Arnold called Celtic magic. Often these themes hold a deeply imaginative linking of opposites, seen intellectually or philosophically as contradictory: death is present in the very scent and breath of Maytime; fighting is never far, in poem, deed or thought, from love-making; mead-drinking often preludes extinction. Up to the fourteenth century the Welsh, still in tribal families, were incessantly involved, like the Scots, in fighting for their lives, their freedoms, their land, their very existence.

In 1485, after the Battle of Bosworth Field, Henry Tudor, Earl of Richmond, established a half-Welsh line of kings on the English throne. Soon after, the great Elizabeth's great minister was a Welshman. Many Welsh flocked to England. English became the tongue of more and more of Wales. Yet the Celtic language remained, as today it remains in Welsh mountain communities, and certain Welsh poets write in it. Its classical, written form has, as has classical Arabic, remained almost unchanged for well over a thousand years. Some say it is sure, in time, to die. But this contention may well be premature. Most of us do not recall, unless we are asked to, that William Langland, John Donne, Henry Vaughan, William Collins, Thomas Gray, Gerard Manley Hopkins, Wilfred Owen, Alun Lewis, Edward Thomas, Dylan Thomas and Vernon Watkins were all, in greater or less degree, of Welsh blood. Because their work is in English, we tend to ignore their Welsh roots.

The host of Celtic poets in the Welsh classical period wrote in a language completely incomprehensible to Englishmen—as Welsh is today, but as Scots is *not*. Dafydd ab Gwilym was a wandering scholar-poet, a bard of the middle fourteenth century, and Dafydd ab Edmwnd lived in the fifteenth century. Dafydd ab Edmwnd (David, son of Edmund) wrote an elegy on the death of his harpist friend, Siôn Eos. Englished, this bard's name was John Nightingale. Eos lost his life in the time of Welsh participation in the Wars of the Roses, which wars ab Edmwnd managed to avoid. But in ab Edmwnd's lament, ' Marwnad Siôn Eos ' (The Death of John Nightingale), the bitterness of centuries between imaginative, more slowly advancing, Celtic Wales and aggressive, law-imposing Anglo-Saxon England resounds. However much, before and after the accession of the Welsh Henry Tudor to the throne, life was

enriched for both Welsh and English, and men were joined by
blood, memories of the past are long:

> O men, why isn't it better,
> if one is killed, not to kill two ?
> He took one enemy's blood,
> avenged our dual enmity.
> It was sad, the killing of two good men
> for such a little cause !
> He wounded, there's no denying,
> but never meant to kill the man.
> Somebody was at fault
> for striking back in a chance mêlée . . .
> and so one man was killed
> and vengeance takes the other . . .
> I hate the churlish law;
> The Chirk Lordship took a nightingale away . . .
> When they had put upon him
> the fulness of London's law,
> they would not, for his life's sake,
> lay bare a relic or cut a cross.
> And so they doomed to death
> the man who was father of music . . .
> Is there, now Nightingale's gone,
> his equal at playing a prelude,
> an improvisation and manly song. . . ?
> There is no angel or man
> who'd not weep at his harp-playing. . . .[6]

Here are the first ten lines of the Welsh:

> O wŷr, pam na bai orau,
> o lleddid un na lladd dau ?
> Dwyn ein gelynwaed a wnaeth,
> dial ein dwy elyniaeth.
> Oedd oer ladd y ddeuwr lân
> heb achos ond un bychan.
> Er briwio'r gŵr, heb air gwad,
> o'i farw ni bu fwriad.
> Yr oedd y diffyg ar rai
> am adladd mewn siawns medlai; . . .

---

[6] *The Burning Tree*, pp. 137-9.

Gaelic Ireland also had maintained a literary tradition since the landing of the first waves of the language-culture groups we call Celts. Gaels were a section of Celts. It is uncertain how many waves of these invaders there were, or how many different peoples there were in Ireland before the Celts. Celts are related to Gauls, and their culture may reach back towards Indo-European language times. They may have come from as far away as the Asian steppes, acquiring on their way to Northern Europe the horse-drawn chariots Caesar describes Gauls and British using, and iron swords from Hittites and Scythians.

Earliest Irish-Gaelic literature used prose for the epic and non-rhymed verse for the personal lyric. At the coming of St Patrick, who brought Christianity to Ireland in the fifth century, Gaelic was supplanted by Latin, and Ogham script (of Celt or pre-Celt?) was superseded. But the myths of such ancient people, their pantheon, legends and heroes mythical and historical, were too strong to go into oblivion. Under Christian learning they were crushed, but later allowed to be written down, though some of the vitality, greatness and grandeur of this earliest but one of European literatures was inevitably lost.

Four cycles of Gaelic sagas are preserved in manuscripts dating from the twelfth century: the Mythological Cycle concerns gods and the Other-world: no old age, grief, sickness or death plague those on that island in the Western Sea. This legend is thought to have inspired the French romances of the Grail. The second is the Ulster Cycle with Cuchulain in *The Cattle Raid of Cooley*, and with the oldest of medieval love stories (the origin of *Tristan and Iseult*?) in *The Exile of the Sons of Uisnech*. Myles Dillon in *Irish Sagas* (p. 15) suggests that this cycle is probably the greatest contribution of the Celts to world literature. The third cycle is the Fenian or Historical Cycle; and the fourth cycle is about kings of ancient Ireland.

The oldest manuscripts in Ireland are scriptural and in Latin. The sagas of *filidh* or poets were in Gaelic. But meanwhile Gaelic ballads, lyrics about love, death, feuds, bravery, were growing into a strong tradition. Irish ballads, like those in Scotland and England, have two forms. There is the popular or street ballad such as you may hear sung in the ballad-pubs of Ireland today. These are usually anonymous, and have therefore, probably, additions from the work of more than one poet. There is also the literary ballad; by the sixteenth century this was signed by a known author. Even whilst the spoken language was dying, ballad-makers used Gaelic turns of speech, ways of vision, rhythmic and phonic cross-rhyme, vowelling (*aicill*), in *amhran* metres for the *aisling* or vision-song type of ballad. The influence of Irish ballads and the influence of Irish usages on the English tongue can never be estimated.

The Norse invasion of Ireland of the ninth century and the Anglo-Norman invasion of a still disorganized Ireland by Henry II at the behest of Pope Adrian did not so much quench the Gaelic literary culture as allow it to affect Icelandic saga, and Norman and English romance. There were still Tudor penal oppression and the eighteenth-century Protestant ' ascendancy ' for the Irish to live through. In time the Gaelic language was pushed back to the island's western shore; and the strong Irish culture would await some possible renaissance.

Tudor Peace

In 1485 England moved into what was to be, for her, the Tudor age of relative peace, in union with Wales. But when, in 1603, the crown of England and Wales was united with that of Scotland under the Stuarts there were still strife and bloodshed to be endured; whilst Ireland has endured, under further repression, strife until today.

In England men did not cease to persecute and torture each other for belief as well as secular loyalty. Civil war in England only temporarily over, a central state and a strong line of monarchs had yet managed to wrest civil power from great barons and from ferocious rivals. Life in the English culture and newly felt nationhood surged, eager for maturity ahead. London grew as a rich, brilliant, if uncivilized capital, its housing barbarous, its daily life often overtly violent, busy and often quiet enough underneath. Trade flourished. Agriculture, after a fifteenth-century recession, began again to expand. Crafts were still slow, absorbing, domestic. Most parents and children worked as units from dawn to dusk. Ambitious elders strove more and more, through commerce and politics, to found and raise illustrious, cultured families. In the court circle and the great houses the chivalrous doings of earlier times were obstinately maintained, riding the ' great horse ', staghunting, hawking, music-making, dancing, courtly intrigue. But this life was for the few. The amusements of the many, and often, outside the capital, of rich and poor alike, were bull-baiting, bear-baiting, badger-baiting, cock-fighting, gambling, wrestling, country- and sword-dancing, watching interlude or pageant on craft-guild stage; applauding Morality or Mystery play at the religious festivals; gathering in crowds to watch public hangings; jibing at, or pelting with filth, mischief-makers set for public contempt, their feet clamped in the stocks.

The writing of poetry had fallen from the place it held in heroic days. The monarchs Henry V, Henry VI and Edward IV, with a few nobles and their ladies, were lovers of books; and a system of patronage, by which a writer dedicated in print, with hopes of advancement, his work to a man or woman of standing, was growing up.

Skelton

Into this kind of an England John Skelton was born about 1460. Skelton was educated at Oxford and Cambridge. At both he seems to have been called ' poet laureate ', a ' Delphic ' title, Edward Gibbon tells us, first taken by Petrarch. He was a scholar very much of his age—outspoken, full of dynamic vigour, within the Church. His output of poetry was vast. For a time he was tutor to handsome, dashing Prince Henry, who was to become the grossly cruel Henry VIII. In 1498 Skelton became Rector of Diss in Norfolk, where he remained until his death in 1529. He was a good Catholic and spoke against Martin Luther's Protests nailed on the door of Wittenberg Church in 1517. But in long satires Skelton raged against the corrupt magnificence of great churchmen—of Henry VIII's Cardinal Wolsey in particular. Skelton was one of the few men who dared to stand up to the autocratic Wolsey.

He shouted against that evil—not new—of power concentrated in the hands of one man; against unjust laws made; against taxes levied which brought public hardship. These shouting satires were ' Colyn Cloute ', ' Speke, Parot ', ' Why Come Ye Nat to Courte ' and ' The Bowge [Rewards] of Courte '. The last, in seven-line rhyme-royal, shows expectation in the very air of ' merry ' England, as well as Skelton's usual bodeful warnings:

> The sayle is up, Fortune ruleth our helme,
> We wante no wynde to passe now over all;
> Favoure we have tougher than ony elme,
> That wyll abyde and never from us fall:
> But under hony ofte tyme lyth bytter gall;
> For, as me thoughte, in our shyppe I dyde see
> Full subtyll persones, in nombre foure and three.[7]

Observe how his verse seems to stumble a little. Skelton was unsure in metrical if not in spoken pronunciation; but read aloud, his verse flows and ripples without faltering.

He wrote plays as well as poetry. A great deal has not survived. Some of it limps, as lines five and six limp in the above. When the evils Skelton wrote against are reconciled in history, he is remembered by a few lyrics and perhaps *The Boke of Phyllyp Sparowe*. This tells, apparently in imitation of the kind of poetry Catullus the Roman wrote, of a nun, Jane Scrope, and her grief for the death of her pet sparrow. It was still ' fashionable ' in poetry to imitate classical poems. English poetry took a long time to move beyond imitation and perhaps it gained from its slow advance. Skelton's attention to the small and insignificant, as in sorrow for a sparrow, has brought him contempt from some. To Jane Scrope Skelton also addressed ' The Commendations '; and again he shows a tenderly humorous praise of what lies within physical form, however small and unimportant:

> How often dyd I tote
> Upon her prety fote ?
> It raysed myne hert rote
> To se her treade the grounde
> With heles short and rounde.
> She is playnly expresse
> Egeria the goddesse,
> And lyke to her image
> Emportured with corage,
> A lovers pylgrimage;
> Ther is no beest savage,
> Ne no tyger so wood,
> But she wolde chaunge his mood,

---

[7] John Skelton, *Poems*, ed. Richard Hughes (Heinemann, 1924), pp. 69-70.

Such relucent grace
Is formed in her face;
For this most goodly floure,
This blossome of fresshe coloure,
So Jupiter me succour,
She flourissheth new and new
In beaute and vertew. . . .[8]

On a very different sort of being, Elynour Rummynge, in her red ' kyrtel ' and ' huke of Lyncole grene ', and all the motley crowd who came to trade with Elynour, Skelton wrote with equal zest, if equally shaky awareness of metre:

. . . this comely dame . . ,
She is a tonnish gyb;
The devyll and she be syb . . .
She breweth nappy ale. . . .[9]

Few poets and scholars agree, even now, about Skelton: here is an opportunity for readers to try making up their own minds. Caxton, his contemporary, praised him. Erasmus, the great Dutch Renaissance humanist who emphasized that learning alone gave nobleness and virtue to men, who twice lived in England under Henry VIII and who understood the country and the people's labour and travail for ' liberty ', called Skelton ' the only light and glory of English letters' of his day. Samuel Taylor Coleridge approved *Phyllyp Sparowe*. Robert Southey noted Skelton's ' pithy ' use of English. Alexander Pope damned him as ' beastly ' Skelton alongside Chaucer. Skelton himself wrote of his ' rude, rayling rimes '. Probably the English of his day, unstable still in respect of its use of Norman-French words, its altering plurals and verb-forms, was not yet capable of lyricism.

The short, rushing line, of ' Phyllyp Sparowe ', ' Elynour Rummynge ' and the lyric ' To Mistress Margaret Hussey', is not Skelton's invention. But what are now spoken of as Skeltonics helped to press Middle English into newer, spontaneous and, of course, more modern forms.

Skelton appreciated the ordinary men and woman and their popular poetry. He was aware—if only negatively and critically—

[8] Ibid., p. 92.
[9] Ibid., pp. 31, 42.

of great events; as he was but half-aware of his poetry's language. Scholar as he was he knew the value of folk poetry yet could not link popular and learned in that artistic, elusive, complex end-product poets call the great or the beautiful. He did not understand form and content as finally indivisible. Nor did he grasp that, though a poem will stand alone in its own right as poetry, neither form nor content is separable from the personality of the poet or writer. Skelton's huge output was diffuse. His character must contain part of the reason why he remains at most the only important link we now have between Chaucer and the first of the great Elizabethan poets.

In 1557 Thomas Tusser published another kind of popular poem—his *Hundreth Goode Pointes of Husbandrie*. It sold so well that Tusser expanded it to *Five Hundreth Pointes of Goode Husbandrie united to as many of Goode Huswifery*. But none of it rises, as none of the then current books of nurture or courtesy rose, above rhymed verse of a finely practical kind. The great age of English prose arising from the Reformation was at hand.

Early Elizabethan Poets

In that same year, 1557, Richard Tottel printed *A Miscellany of Uncertain Authors*—to be reissued seven times before 1584. In this were poems by Henry Howard, Earl of Surrey, John Heywood, Nicholas Grimald, Edward Somerset and Thomas Wyatt. Thomas Wyatt wrote:

> Forget not yet the tried intent
> Of such a truth as I have meant;
> My great travail so gladly spent,
>   Forget not yet !
>
> Forget not yet the great assays,
> The cruel wrong, the scornful ways,
> The painful patience in delays,
>   Forget not yet !

> Forget not! O, forget not this!
> How long ago hath been, and is,
> The mind that never meant amiss—
> > Forget not yet!

This poem shows at once that English poetry had made a great leap forward. It had done this, after a century and a half of germination, almost overnight. Every young scholar, certainly every ' gentleman of letters ', in the ferment of the Renaissance was soon to be trying his hand at a lyric, a sonnet, a play. These two knights, Wyatt and Surrey, may be said to have sparked off a burst of lyric poetry which ushered in the Elizabethan age of poetry and drama. Yet the two were still imitators, not of Chaucer, but of French, Italian and classical poets. We owe the introduction into England of the exacting, beautiful sonnet form to their translations of Petrarch in his sonnet series to Laura.

English poetry, having abandoned stressed metre, relied on classical syllables, short and long in often complex stanza forms.

A sonnet has fourteen ten-syllable, iambic lines in two parts, octet and sestet (or sextet). The first eight and the last six lines form a unity both of idea and of metre. Wyatt translated ten sonnets of Petrarch in the Petrarchan sonnet form. In others he used variations of that form. But the need for precision and economy in any sonnet helped to fix fluctuating English pronunciation and rhythm. Listen to four lines of the elder poet, Wyatt, in his version of Petrarch:

> The longe love, that in my thought I harber,
> And in my hart doth kepe his residence,
> Into my face preaseth with bold pretence,
> And there campeth, displaying his banner. . . .[10]

Wyatt did not follow Chaucer's method over final ' e ' consistently: probably he had not, as Skelton had not, understood it. He accents ' preaseth ', ' residence ' and ' banner ' on the last syllables as in Norman French pronunciation. His fourth line halts in our ears. Surrey's translation of the same sonnet a little later avoids these pitfalls:

[10] Text from *The Cambridge History of English Literature*, Vol. III, p. 169.

Love that liveth, and reigneth in my thought,
That built his seat within my captive brest,
Clad in the armes, wherin with me he fought,
Oft in my face he doth his banner rest. . . .[11]

Surrey uses the rhythms that were evolving in English. His stresses on words of more than one syllable usually fall on the penultimate syllables, which sounds ' right ' to us, and this makes him seem more assured than Wyatt.

Both these poets are remembered together (though not much is known whether or how they influenced each other). Both experimented with the ballad or hymn quatrain. This ' common ' measure, four lines of six, six, eight, six, syllables, rhyming in the second and fourth final ones, is deeply, anciently lyrical; its snare is that it can easily, as does use of rhyme itself, degenerate into jingle.

The chivalric ideal of knightly love, begun in the eleventh century about the same time as the cult of the Virgin (both attempts to heal an emotional breach in our nature), was passing. Wyatt and Surrey brought the theme of romantic personal love in poetry to Britain. If both were imitators, this did not take from their poems an underlying glimmer of direct feeling. Our debt to them is the bringing of the sonnet form, the modernizing of accent and of rhythm, and the theme of faithful, civilized love. After them Spenser wrote his sonnet series, *Amoretti*; Philip Sidney wrote *Astrophel and Stella*, an eloquent but occasionally artificial series of love-sonnets. And from the early 1590s William Shakespeare was writing the greatest of all English sonnet sequences, built on no Petrarchan model but each of the 154 sonnets in the form of four quatrains with a final rhymed couplet. Shakespeare's sonnets were printed in 1609.

One thing more we owe to Surrey. He translated the *Aeneid* of Virgil into English verse: Surrey used a ten-syllabled, unrhymed metre (iambic pentameter), with great possibilities in variety, for the first time in English. We now call this blank verse. He wrote, too, an elegy on the death of his childhood friend, the Duke of Richmond, which gives a picture of the England of the early sixteenth century. Surrey was confined at Windsor Castle in 1539, when *Songs and Sonnettes* were first issued—for smiting a fellow-poet. He was beheaded in 1547, when he was just thirty years old.

[11] Ibid., p. 176.

Robert Southwell wrote 'Saint Peter's Complaint' and 'The Burning Babe'.[12] No prosodist, he used chiefly the four-line hymn stanza. 'The Burning Babe', appealing to a puritan strain in Anglo-Saxons, was much read. Southwell was new in that he harrowed his readers with a sense of personal responsibility for the world's corruption. A brave Jesuit he sought to convert; and his utter gloom must be understood within the memory of Queen Mary's zealous Catholic cruelty. Intolerance towards outspoken rebels was part of the age. Southwell was imprisoned, racked many times; finally he was publicly hanged, drawn and quartered, in Elizabeth's reign. He is important because, in the days of Sidney's and Spenser's 'golden' love poetry, he turned poets' thoughts to divine subjects, so foreshadowing the religious poets of the next century.

George Gascoigne wrote the first long English satirical poem, *The Steele Glas*, in 1576. Thomas Sackville, first Earl of Dorset, wrote *The Complaint of Buckingham* for what must surely be the last of the leisurely, moral, long-winded, medieval poems—*A Mirror for Magistrates*. This was twenty stories by different authors, compiled by George Ferrers and William Baldwin, and licenced for publication in 1559. Its fourteen hundred pages were intended as 'a mirrour for al men as well nobles as others to shewe the slipery deceiptes of the wavering lady, and the due rewarde of all kinde of vices'.

Wandering poets and minstrels had almost all gone. The Renaissance was flooding into Britain. After Wyatt and Surrey poets of learning increased in number. They translated Virgil, Ovid, Cicero, Plutarch, Dante, Tasso, Ariosto, Boccaccio, and Petrarch. Peace and prosperity were in the offing and a national sense of greatness flew in the air. The time was propitious for a man of strong gifts who would dedicate himself to poetry.

Spenser

Edmund Spenser was such a poet. Born in 1552 of a noble family, educated at Pembroke Hall, Cambridge, he early came under the influence of the Fellow, Gabriel Harvey, of Philip Sidney, the Earl of Essex and of Sir Walter Ralegh. All these encouraged his brilliant

[12] See Robert Southwell, *Complete Poems*, ed. Alexander B. Grosart (London, 1872).

and receptive mind, fostering his fervent ambition and his devotion to learning. These men put him in touch with the religious movements of Protestantism, Lutheran and Calvinistic, and with the masters of literature, Greek, Roman, French, Italian, as well as of his own English. With an almost imperial confidence Spenser seems to have seen his aim extraordinarily early. *The Shepheard's Calendar* was published in 1579. In Spenser's dedication to Master Gabriel Harvey, speaking as ' E.K.' and asking patronage for ' the new poet ', the young aspirant's sense of himself, his mission, his poet's lineage and his language are all sublimely assured:

> Uncouth, unkist, said the old famous poet Chaucer: whom for his excellency and wonderful skill in making, his scholar Lydgate, a worthy scholar of so excellent a master, calleth the loadstar of our language: . . . so . . . this our new poet, who for that he is uncouth (as said Chaucer) is unkist, and unknown to most men, is regarded but of few. But I doubt not, so soon as his name shall come into the knowledge of men, and his worthiness be sounded in the trump of fame, but that he shall be not only kist, but also beloved of all, embraced of the most, and wondered at of the best . . . in my opinion it is one special praise of many, which are due to this poet, that he hath laboured to restore, as to their rightful heritage, such good and natural English words, as have been long time out of use, and almost clean disinherited. Which is the only cause, that our mother tongue, which truly of itself is both full enough for prose, and stately enough for verse, hath long time been counted most bare and barren of both. Which default whenas some endeavoured to salve and recure, they . . . made of our English tongue a gallimaufry, or hodgepodge of all other speeches. . . . In regard whereof, I scorn and spue out the rascally rout of our ragged rhymers. . . . So finally flieth this our new poet as a bird whose principals be scarce grown out, but yet as one that in time shall be able to keep wing with the best. . . . With this high regard for his own tongue, and strong desire for praise.[13]

Spenser put *The Shepheard's Calendar* into the form of twelve short eclogues. Again we have the inspired imitation. Not even he could see beyond that. This time the poem was after the manner of Virgil and Theocritus. But the rich pattern of Spenser's eclogues, each named after a month and devised as talk between shepherds and goatherds, does in one respect what the poet says he will do: it

[13] Text from Everyman Library edn (1949), p. 3.

restores the ' rightful heritage ' of ' good and natural English '. Yet Spenser uses words even in his own day archaic. He gives a gloss after each month, as if he were attempting to restore words and forms rapidly going out of use. He continued in this effort to find, in the changing speech of five million people, a poetic diction, in his greatest poem *The Faerie Queene*.

As Theocritus' *Idylls* were, so Spenser's *Calendar* is—because of this making of shepherds and goatherds into symbolic talkers on subjects such as poetry, love, worldly success—artificial. Why did Spenser use this pastoral convention, which Philip Sidney used in his prose *Arcadia* and which English poets were to return to, again and again ? Arcadia was a part of ancient Greece inhabited by the earliest of Greek herdsmen. Spenser knew the overwhelming need for poetry to be clearly and directly in touch with the deep sources of our nature; at the same time he knew the poetic art's need to advance intellectually. Poetry could not stand still or it was lost. Ballads had been able to be generic by being anonymous. They had achieved this by stark use of human drama, direct feelings and the portrayal of instincts that were understood by all. But for Spenser there could be no advance for poetry merely through knowledge of generic feelings and using only the ' common ' ballad metre. Expression of human emotion must grow ever more complex. A poet's feeling must be linked both with past truth and with his present culture and self.

Spenser had a great poet's ear for the subtlest tone-patterns and phonetic melodies and harmonies we sometimes, not very accurately, call word-music. He had a deep appreciation of both the countryside of classical Greece and the countryside which helps to make Britain what she is. In the twelve ' months ' of the *Calendar* he used thirteen different metres (three in August). Some of the eclogues are about Platonic love, and about youthful love's pains and disappointments. But though Spenser might let ' Colin Clout ' his mouthpiece declare in ' June ', ' I play to please myself ', Tomalin, another shepherd, is made to argue in ' July ' what not many authentic countrymen knew, but what Spenser knew well:

> . . . they that con of Muses' skill
> .   .   .   .   .   .   dwell
> (As goatherds wont) upon a hill,
> Beside a learned well.

The hill was Parnassus. The well was the bottomless Castalian spring of the desire for knowledge. Goatherds were not shepherds; they were not contented, quiet men. For all the pastoral-artificial sadness of shepherd Colin at the loss of his ' Rosalind ', this ' peerless poesy ' was Spenser's love, to write it was his restless aim. Ambition that his ' curious skill ' would make of him a great poet was in him boundless. It was so great that he is said to have remained dissatisfied throughout his life with the rewards he received. In the *Calendar* argument for ' October ', although Cuddie later exclaims that his poetry, ' so little good hath got, and much less gain ', Spenser states vauntingly that poetry is:

A divine gift and heavenly instinct not to be gotten by labour and learning, but adorned by both.

Spenser knew that poetry's potential might be in all men, but few make great poetry. Nor could poetry any longer, as in heroic days, be sure of princes' rewards:

O ! trustless state of earthly things, and slipper hope
Of mortal men, that swink and sweat for nought,
And, shooting wide, do miss the markéd scope;
Now have I learned (a lesson dearly bought)
That nis on earth assurance to be sought;[14]

Still, publication in 1579 of *The Shepheard's Calendar* made Spenser the first poet in England. It did not bring him the wealth and standing his sense of himself may have desired. He was an idealist. He hated the Irish when later he was sent to work among them. He longed to be a perfect knight like his friend Sidney. Instead he went on to write six books, of a projected twelve, of a vast, allegorical poem in the vein of Ariosto. This, *The Faerie Queene*, its first three books published in 1589, its second three in 1596, has a rich tapestry of often archaic word-patterns, and a new nine-line rhymed stanza; with a resounding Alexandrine at the close of eight iambic pentameters, this stanza is named after its originator. Glorious in coloured scenes, *The Faerie Queene* offered an imagined world which was endowed with the ideals and the learning of pagan, religious, classical and medieval times, and of Spenser's own era. In it Pan

---

[14] Ibid., p. 91.

may signify Christ—or the Pope. The world of *The Faerie Queen* is not that in which Martin Frobisher discovered the North West Passage in 1576, Francis Drake sailed round the world in 1580 and Britain beat off the Spanish Armada in 1588. Spenser the idealist had little sympathy with what Edmund Burke later called the age of sophisters, economists and calculators, which succeeded the age of chivalry.

He dedicated *The Faerie Queene* to ' the most excellent and glorious person of our Soveraine the Queene, and her kingdome in Faeryland ', Queen Elizabeth. Even this seems not to have brought Spenser what he sought. He died, disappointed, it is sometimes said, in 1599, only five years after his marriage. He wrote in *Colin Clout's Come Home Again* (1591):

> Cause have I none, of cank'red will
> To' quite them ill, that me demeaned so well:
> But self-regard of private good or ill
> Moves me of each, so as I found, to tell
> And eke to warn young shepherds' wandering wit,
> Which, through report of that life's painted bliss,
> Abandon quiet home to seek for it,
> And leave their lambs to loss.[15]

He was warning about the conflict between the self-dedication necessary for a poet and a poet's need for communication and reward. Spenser's own quickening spirit helped to set—did set— English poetry on its widening path towards a richly coloured future.

Sixteenth-Century Prose

Not quite yet, after all those centuries, was English prose liberated from Latin. But it was almost free. After all, to Latin, Greek and French, English owes one-third of its word-roots and derivations, as well as much of its depth and width of content. In Henry VII's, Henry VIII's, Edward VI's, Mary's and Elizabeth's reigns translators from Greek, Latin, French and Italian multiplied. The

[15] Ibid., p. 263.

number of historians, chroniclers and antiquaries grew. In a nation exuberantly and recklessly ready for experiment of all kinds, mental and physical, Camden, North, Stow, Hakluyt, Hall, Holinshed, Harrison and others all delved into Britain's past and present on sea and land. They set about describing and charting this ' Anglia '. Map-making is as ancient as Babylon; it had been done in days before steel engraving in England. Now Edward Wright adapted Mercator's projection; Dee, Norden and Speed made maps which fostered the growing national consciousness.

Historians and topographers varied greatly in accuracy. Facts are elusive. Some social descriptions were rife with locally collected gossip and with superstitions of many queer kinds.

Sir Thomas More wrote his *Utopia* (1515/16) in Latin. Utopia was an island where social abuses were remedied—in More's way. After More was beheaded by his master Henry VIII, *Utopia* was put into the Latinized English then current; in such the book remains. A brave Catholic and a man of wit and generosity, More is said to have written, in English, a *History of King Richard the thirde*. More likely this book which sealed Richard, the last king of the Wars of the Roses, in Tudor and later memory as an almost totally evil hunchback, the murderer of the boy princes in the Tower of London and of many other people, was written (as George Buck, the seventeenth-century historian, states) by John Morton, benefactor and Archbishop of Canterbury. Some later historians have refuted this denigration of Richard's moral character and physical appearance. This classic case reveals the morass that can develop around historic ' facts '; and how ' truth ' about historic persons can warp as well as straighten in time's passage.

John Foxe dedicated in 1563 to Queen Elizabeth seventeen hundred folio pages—*The Actes and Monuments of the Church*. This book is better known as Foxe's *Book of Martyrs*. It was a voluminous ' history ', up to Foxe's own perilous days, of martyrs famous and not famous in the Prostestant cause, and it was widely read for at least three centuries. Queen Mary's savagery in the name of Faith was well within Foxe's lacerated memory. Even as he wrote, Anglican persecuted Catholic, Catholic Protestant; Protestant reformers persecuted Catholics. Foxe attempted to set down his ' facts ' from sources such as Bede, Eusebius and other Christian Fathers. A second dedication of his book to ' The Persecutors of God's truth commonly called Papists ' shows a not wholly disinterested recorder. In days when freedom of what Press there was was not in being, when tolerance for each other's beliefs was struggling to be born, Foxe goaded himself to describe in inexorable detail man's ferocity to man, as he collected it from British and European sources. He wore out his life in service to this harrowing ideal. Foxe's *Book of Martyrs* gives an authentic glimpse into the English sixteenth-century ambience and way of life. Bravery under torture, racking, beheading, disembowelling and burning alive, all are described at times with a certain masochistic relish. Elizabethans, for all their good humour, were rough and violent and wished to die heroically.

Hugh Latimer, reformer and Bishop of Worcester, was burned at Oxford in 1555 with Ridley, Bishop of London. Latimer had preached fiery, vivid, emphatic sermons, most of them lost now and unrecorded. Yet anybody who cares can read Latimer's *Sermon of the Plough*;[16] and his last reported words linger in the memory:

> Be of good comfort, maister Ridley, and play the man: We shall this day light such a candle by God's grace in England, as (I trust) shall never be put out.

Richard Hooker was also a bishop. In his *Laws of Ecclesiastical Polity* Hooker used persuasive arguments for reason without dogmatism, which are half a world away from Foxe's book or from Hugh Latimer's sermons. Hooker first pleaded, in eloquent English, for broadmindedness when self-interest clashes with the interests of others.

In 1518 the College of Physicians was established in Britain. But blood-letting, emetics and purging as prime nostrums, chains, whipping and solitary confinement in dark dungeons for the neuropsychotic and the criminal, went on some three centuries after this. There were Dietaries and Herbals—Hill's, Parkinson's and others'. Hill began the study of Britain's flora—in Latin. John Gerard took, it seems, his well-known *General Historie of Plantes* from the Frenchman Dodoens, and that without proper acknowledgement. There were bestiaries, jestbooks, religious homilies, tracts of many kinds. Censorship lay with the Lord Chancellor. Pamphlets were often acrimonious. In the theological turmoil of the Reformation, con-

[16] Ed. Edward Arber (Constable, 1903).

sciences, lacerated, turned morbid. Witchcraft, sorcery and magic were still deeply feared. In 1541 Henry VIII became the first English monarch to legislate against these. Often there was perse-cution of the old, the poor, the ugly or deformed, the eccentric; but worst of all was the torture meted out to the religious ' heretic '. This age in Europe became monstrous in its terrors and consequent cruelties. Britain was only slightly less terrible than the Continent. Reginald Scott's *Discoverie of Witchcraft* appeared in 1584. James I, so learned and so unwise, wrote on *Demonology*.

Books on education grew in number; they had not yet ousted books on courtesy. Roger Ascham, the unfortunate Lady Jane Grey's ' so jentle a scholemaster ', tutor to the Princess Elizabeth, and then Latin secretary to Queen Mary, wrote *The Scholemaster*. This was published posthumously in 1570. Camden in the *Annales* (1568) wrote of Ascham's addiction to dicing and cock-fighting.

Sir Thomas Elyot had put out his book, *The Governour*, in 1531. Both—Elyot in Latinized language, Ascham in fine and simple English—were for teaching by ' gentleness ' rather than with the lash. That instrument, both writers thought, was what caused boys to hate learning. Both pressed for the use of the indigenous language to be learnt in school and used in all books. Both thought a know-ledge of Greek and Latin imperative only for scholars. Both believed strongly in the benefits of physical education.

Many graduates from the medievally established universities of Oxford and Cambridge flocked to growing London to become men of letters there. *The Anatomy of Wyt* (1578), the first part of the young John Lyly's *Euphues*, was the first attempt to make the writing of English prose into a learned art. Much talked about, the second part, *Euphues and his England*, of 1580, had five editions in six years. Robert Greene, down from Oxford and Cambridge to make a living by writing, and to roister and drink with London thieves, pimps and tavern-haunters, wrote witty, naturalistic accounts of this kind of life as well as court romances. Among these last was *Pandosto*, on which Shakespeare drew for *The Winter's Tale*. Greene's *The Blacke Bookes Messenger*, *Cuthbert Conny-Catcher* and *The Defence of Conny-Catching*, all belonging to 1591 and 1592, are a fairly amusing string of tales about foolish ' coneys ', dupes who allowed themselves to be tricked by pick-purses, harlots, whore-mongers and other ' Rufflers ' in great cities. But it is Greene's lyric, ' Weep not, my wanton, smile upon my knee,/When thou art old there's grief enough for thee ', as well as his last letter to his wife, recorded in *A Groats-worth of Witte bought with a Million of Repentance* (1592), which, like Hugh Latimer's words as fire licked round him, linger obstinately in the mind. Greene's words are not intrepid: they merely indicate what a human being, dying in penury, can ask— and receive—from another:

> Sweet Wife, as ever there was any good will or friendship betweene thee and mee, see this bearer (my Host) satisfied of his debt, I owe him tenne pound and but for him I had perished in the streetes. . . .[17]

Philip Sidney's *Arcadia* and Thomas Lodge's *Rosalynde* were about the idyllic country life which growing numbers of English men and women were leaving. Spenser had applauded it in *The Calendar*. Artificial because too imitative of the pastoral genre in the same way that Spenser's *Calendar* was artificial, they advocated escape from the undiminished vanities of the city.

Thomas Dekker was no university man but a Londoner, no imitator but a rebel. Ben Jonson denounced him as vagabond, plagiarist, ignoramus; but Dekker was none of these, though he spent seven years in prison. Dekker's *The Wonderful Yeare* (1603), is a mocking but freshly realistic picture of a London sick of the plague; *The Gul's Horne-Booke* (1609) foreshadows a modern journalism dedicated to the fascination of ' realism '. Dekker, Greene, Nashe and Peele, young playwrights as well as prose writers, were contemporaries, rivals and admirers of Shakespeare. Thomas Nashe, another able rebel, forcefully attacked city fashions, moneylenders, superstition and rogues, in what is sometimes called England's ' first historical novel ', *The Unfortunate Traveller* (1594). Nashe's *Terrors of the Night* also appeared in 1594. Before he died at the age of thirty-four his comedy, *The Isle of Dogs* (1597), a tirade against both court and state injustice, not surprisingly now lost, had landed him in gaol.

Thomas Deloney, with his Irish name but first heard of in the silk-weaving trade at Norwich, was known in his early days as a

---

[17] *Groats-worth of Witte* (Bodley Head, 1932), p. 32. There is another version, the whereabouts of which I do not know, which seems, by some turn of style, to be more moving than the above: ' Doll, I charge thee, by the love of our youth and by my soul's rest, that thou wilt see this man paid: for if he and his wife had not succoured me I had died in the streets.'

ballad-maker. Moved to London Deloney wrote, with no imitation of Spanish picaresque, three lively prose tales of the new English trading classes: *Thomas of Reading*, on the clothier's craft, *Jack of Newbury*, a master weaver, and *The Gentle Craft*, of Simon Eyre, a shoemaker who became Lord Mayor, were all written between 1596 and 1600. London audiences could not hear enough of themselves from realist writers such as Greene, Nashe, Dekker and Deloney. Such demand shows the beginnings of a reading audience; and realism was advancing a new art form, the novel.

Literary criticism began in England too. Stephen Gosson wrote, among many other books, *The Schoole of Abuse* (1579). Gosson was among the first to write against the theatre. *The Schoole of Abuse* contains invective against ' Poets, Pipers, Plaiers, Jesters, and such like Caterpillars of a Commonwealth '. Gosson thought poets the ' fathers of lyes '. He voiced a fear which all tradition denies, that poetry makes a nation effeminate. The courteous Philip Sidney was provoked to reply in *The Apologie for Poetrie* or *Defence of Poesie*, but this was not printed until 1595. Mildly Sidney propounded that a poet should have a standing comparable with that of the Roman *vates*, the Celtic bard and *filé*, the Anglo-Saxon *scôp* or shaper of words, of man's heroic days. Sidney had not much to say for the drama in the 1590s; but that was because English drama of the 1580s and 1590s had begun not to heed the classical unities of time, place and plot.

Bacon

Modern science may be said to have begun in Britain in Elizabeth I's and James I's days. Francis Bacon was James's Chancellor. In his *Advancement of Learning* (1605), his analysis of his method in *Novum Organum* (1620) and the amplification of the *Advancement* in *De Augmentis Scientiarum* (1623) Bacon propounded the deduction of scientific laws from carefully examined and compared examples. He believed in the unity and the unifying of all knowledge; he saw man as a master of wisdom. He made no new departure in his emphasis of the importance of scientific philosophy inherited from Aristotle; but he helped to set science and empiric philosophy on their modern road.

Later, Bacon was accused and convicted of bribery and corruption. He is also said, on insufficient evidence, to have been the author of Shakespeare's plays. His character was subtle, enigmatic, but not base. He reveals himself clearly enough in the *Essays* he published, first in 1597, and again in 1612 and 1625.

We owe the essay form itself to Bacon; his short, personal pieces on such subjects as Truth, Revenge, Envy, Cunning, Friendship, Gardens, Praise, Vain Glory, Marriage and Single Life, Goodness, Love, Atheism, Usury, Anger, make fascinating reading. Bacon's opening for his essay ' Of Truth ' is by now a catch-phrase, the author of which we don't bother to call to mind, and the meaning of which is still often misinterpreted: ' What is truth ? said jesting Pilate; and would not stay for an answer.' He continues:

. . . it is not only the difficulty and labour which men take in finding out of truth; nor again, that when it is found, it imposeth on men's thoughts, that doth bring lies in favour; but a natural though corrupt love of the lie itself.

Sent from office for taking bribes in that violent, valorous, piratical, corrupt age, he concluded, in his essay on ' Truth ', with a touching prescience, concerning truth's opposite: ' There is no vice that doth so cover a man with shame as to be found false and perfidious.'

The Book of Common Prayer and the Bible

When the movement which turned England Protestant was under way, in days when a visitor from the Continent was struck by the piety of the ordinary people in Britain as well as by their harshness to children, the demand for a Prayer Book in the vernacular grew. The Primers of 1539 and 1545, and the Prayer Books of 1549, 1552 and 1571, whilst owing much to Archbishop Cranmer's scholarship, also owed much to English speech-ryhthms. They in turn have influenced language and idiom a great deal, though some of their substance may have grown out of date as sources of enlightenment.

The most important translation of that age of translations was that of the Greek and Latin Bibles, the Septuagint and the Vulgate, into English. John Wyclif had first set in being English translations of parts of both New and Old Testaments, with a second, improved version in 1388. By 1525 the pamphleteering, outspoken William Tyndale, inspired by the great Dutchman Erasmus, began to translate the New Testament from Greek and Latin, and, later, part of the Old Testament. Tyndale was burned as a heretic at Vilvorde in Holland in 1536, his work unfinished. Miles Coverdale, afterwards Bishop of Exeter, completed and published the first English Bible from European translations in 1535, a modified version being issued in 1537(?). These Bibles were printed in Europe. Archbishop Cranmer, afterwards burnt at the stake— recanting and then obliterating cowardice at the last minute by denying his recantations—brought out the ' Great Bible ' in 1539 under Henry VIII's auspices.

By 1611 a group of forty-seven scholars and churchmen at Westminster and Cambridge, convened by James I, completed two issues of the Authorised Version. This was based on Tyndale's Bible with some help from Wyclif's.

In 1947 a new translation of the Bible into modern English was begun. This is known as the New English Bible and was undertaken by members of all denominations in the British Isles except the Roman Catholic. It was published in 1961.

The Old Testament is an inclusive attempt to explain the mystery of our being here under one all-powerful, Creator-God. In another respect the Old Testament, the Pentateuch (the first five books), the Law, the Prophets and the Writings, are the earliest history of the development of the social and moral laws of Western man. In yet another respect the Old Testament is the history of a tribe, who were among the first to use writing and iron weapons, and their survival against Babylon, Assyria and Egypt. But in the first and most important aspect the Old Testament concerns man's advance from his wandering days when he believed that spirits inhabited fire, rock, water, air, earth and wood; from the practice of human sacrifice, if not of cannibalism, to belief in a God of mercy. The Old Testament's parts were written between 1200 and 250 B.C.

The New Testament is the account of the life, death and actual or symbolic conquest of physical death of Jesus of Nazareth, and of the growth and spread of the sect which followed Jesus's teaching. The story of his conquest of death symbolizes the way Good may supersede Evil. The idea of Good and Evil owes something to ancient Egyptian, Accadian, Zoroastrian and Buddhist teachings. The New Testament was written in Hellenistic—or popular— Greek. The English Tyndale used, the basis for the Authorised Version, was not learned or complex. It has the most uncomplicated, but not therefore the most easily understandable, sentences. It contains many difficulties, not least of meanings obscured by time, background and translation. Designed for the ordinarily intelligent many, Coverdale's Bible of 1535, and Tyndale's earlier one, did much to make stable a growing, moving language. Wyclif's, Tyndale's, Coverdale's, the Great Bible and the Authorised Version of 1611 all set a standard in English prose and poetic speech-rhythms. Clear, direct, yet with all the complexity of vision, much of the Bible is sometimes called poetry, and sometimes poetic prose. What is poetry and what is poetic prose and the often almost invisible line between these is a subject requiring knowledge of the poetry and prose of the ancient and the classical worlds and of thought and language outside these.

The unit of the English Bible's translation is a short paragraph or verse of variable length. The Authorised Version cut Tyndale's prose into these ' verses '. Biblical style belongs to days before dictionaries, speech-rules or grammars, and is in live, supple, often ordinary, English. It evidences what the language owes to Jewish prose and poetry, to Greek, and perhaps it reveals something of English character.

The Beginnings of Drama

The third great flowering in sixteenth- and early seventeenth-century English literature, besides those in lyric poetry and in prose, was in drama. The beginnings of drama are lost to us. Early minstrels, Celtic bard, Gaelic *filé* and Anglo-Saxon *scôp*, popular and courtly, had been in no sense dramatic. They were individual, musical tellers of stories about ancestors and founders of tribes; singers of praise to and for heroes. More significant for drama's beginnings, both on the Continent and in Britain, were primitive, pagan festivals of the seasons, with communal, ritual songs and dances. These were in many ways similar to what we can see in many parts of Asia, Africa and South America today. With their action, mime and costume, such songs and masked dances contained the germ of character presentation, dramatic happening and imagined scene. The early Christian Church incorporated pagan occasions for fun and licence into their feasts of the religious year. The European Feast of Fools—the rejoicing at the close of the Old Year and the beginning of a New Year—was joined to the Feast of Christ's circumcision; and the second curbed the sexual licence of the Saturnalia or New Year Games of pagan Rome. Most early peoples combine occasions for relaxation and release with artistic enjoyment. Masked and disguised, sometimes frighteningly, leaders of revelry (strangely comparable to masked, present-day *Egwugwu* of Eastern Nigeria) originated medieval ' mummers ' plays.

It is usually said that the conquering Normans introduced into England the religious play as it was known in Catholic Europe. Performances were in churches or churchyards; these places then were not only sacred but were the social centres of both town and village life in early Britain. But church plays were to instruct by amusing; they were not to condone licence or to air social grievance.

Pope Urban IV instituted the festival of *Corpus Christi* (Trinity Sunday, the Sunday after Whitsuntide) in 1264. On that day the triumphant Church held its most splendid procession. In time in Britain companies of tradesmen and craftsmen who formed themselves into guilds joined the processions of this day; they emulated each other in costume. They performed plays as the Church did. But guild plays were on a movable stage on wheels. Pageantry became sumptuous. For a time plays remained under the control of the Church and were performed only on Good Friday, Easter Day, Christmas Day and Saints' Days. However, as they grew in popularity, slowly they gained the interest of civic or lay actors.

These claimed more and more freedom to create and to perform. Mystery, Miracle, and Morality plays, from soon after the Norman conquest up to Elizabeth's day, sprang from this Church-secular, common source.

Mysteries were founded on Bible stories. The Wakefield Mysteries in the Towneley MSS. include thirty-two short plays from ' The Creation ' to ' The Judgment '. Underlying themes are chiefly of the rewards of obedience to God's laws and the fruits of disobedience. ' Cain and Abel ' fascinatingly explores from the mid-fifteenth century the human survival motif of cunning and greed in money-getting, leading to war between brothers.

Miracles were based on legends and lives of saints. Girls and women did not act. Female parts were taken by boys. Miracles and Mysteries were played either at one spot in a town from may-time dawn to dusk out of doors, or else guild players moved from place to place on their wagons throughout Whitsun week. The Cornish Miracle plays, the Chester plays, the Towneley plays, the Coventry plays, the Norwich plays, and the York Cycle, have all come down to us, and some occasionally are performed today. They have a combination of broad, horse-play comedy and solemnity, as everyday life often has. This mixture of farce and moral seriousness distinguishes them from early European plays. It accounts for the later mingling of tragedy and comedy called tragicomedy in English drama.

Drama in Britain did not develop as French drama developed, along the Greek and Roman lines of pure comedy and pure tragedy. Nor did English drama from the start preserve the Greek ' unities ' of time and place: the action was not forced to take place within the time of actual performance, and in the one scene.

Morality plays began in Edward III's reign and continued up to the fifteenth and early sixteenth century. They were serio-comic, human portrayals of abstract vices and virtues. They bore such astonishing titles as *The Castle of Constancy* and *Spirit, Will and Under-standing*. But when in the 1530s Henry VIII suppressed the monas-teries and made himself head of the Church in England he forbade plays about religious subjects lest they stirred up controversy. Pageants and splendidly luxurious Interludes were performed. Elizabeth, in 1559, instructed her magistrates, sheriffs, justices of the peace and other local law-defenders not to allow plays which touched questions of religion or government. But both Henry VIII and Elizabeth supported drama.

Plays were overwhelmingly popular with the ordinary Eliza-bethan. A play was the *spoken* word. Everyone not deaf could under-stand something. The written word was still barred to most. The young university men in London seized on this fact and on the thirst for entertainment and knowledge. Freedom in drama might be hampered, as freedom was in all writing and much think-ing at that time. But there are always ways round or through non-voluntary restrictions.

Scores of plays appeared. John Heywood contributed Interludes between 1520 and 1540. One was *The Four P's* [Prentices] (1545 ?). A Palmer, a Pardoner, a Potecary [*sic*] and a Pedlar competed to see who could tell the most thumping lie. In 1561 *Gorboduc*, known as the first English tragedy, was acted. Its first three acts were written by Thomas Norton and its last two by Thomas Sackville. Parts of *Gorboduc* might surely be construed as political dialogue, but Queen Elizabeth, before whom it was acted, does not seem to have taken exception to it. *Gorboduc* is said to imitate the Roman tragedian Seneca's work. It has real beginnings of that interest in human follies, sorrows and contradictions which was to make Elizabethan and Jacobean tragedy profound. Heywood's work and Sackville's and Norton's *Gorboduc* were a further advance in that they contained unexpected action and involvement which we think of as drama. They had wit too. In comedy *Ralph Roister Doister* was written by Nicholas Udall (*c.* 1553; printed *c.* 1567) for his boys at Westminster School to act. This is said to imitate Plautus and Terence of Roman comedy and is about the foolish Ralph seeking to marry Custance for her money when Custance is in love with somebody else. None of these plays betrays yet any deep, tender or very sensitive or sympathetic knowledge of human nature.

Many plays translated or imitated from the early classical writers, in the mid-sixteenth century, were, with all their merits, but a prelude to what was to come—curtain-raisers to the essentially English drama. The group of young prose writers previously mentioned, some raffish, trained at the universities of Oxford or Cambridge, wrote and translated plays with incredible industry: John Lyly, Thomas Nashe, George Peele, Robert Greene and Thomas Lodge. In the drama Lyly helped to develop plot and a certain grace and delicacy of language. English drama needed this last sorely. It had, in Miracles and Mysteries, been crude, coarse, unsubtle. Peele was ingenious and satirical. Greene, in drama, contributed to plot, and his charactization of women foreshadows some of Shakespeare's heroines. Nashe called Greene a master of his craft in the matter of plot. In all these men's plays there was new poetry and there were exquisite lyrics or songs. But in none did personality and human character work from within with the inevitability of drama as now we understand character and drama.

Marlowe

Christopher Marlowe too held a Cambridge degree. Marlowe's six plays set him above the group of ' university wits '. His four chief plays are *Tamburlaine the Great* (1587), *The Tragicall History of Dr. Faustus* (1588), *The Jew of Malta* (1592) and *Edward the second* (1592). Before the end of 1593 Marlowe, said to have been a Secret Service double agent, lay dead after a tavern quarrel. He had made the ten-syllable, unrhymed lines we call blank verse (which Surrey had introduced into England) the vehicle of the English drama.

In each of his four chief plays Marlowe gives us one character, great, rich or ambitious, yet as greatly flawed. He rushes his hero through powerful action to death or to doom. We watch the vaunting fourteenth-century conqueror, Tamburlaine, strut, rant and die. This play made Marlowe popular. We read of the villainies of Barabas, the rich Jew of Malta, aware from the end of the second act that we are but in on a blood-and-thunder confrontation of Turk, Jew and Christian. Christians are sure to be the most triumphantly, ' righteously ' cunning of the three.

Many of us have heard of Marlowe's ' mighty line '; and in *Edward the second* and *Tamburlaine* we listen to it swinging along grandly, sometimes grandiloquently, seriously, pitilessly, humourlessly. It is the emblem of action rather than of feeling or thought. But in *Faustus* it is almost the perfected instrument which Marlowe bequeathed to Shakespeare. English blank verse, succeeding alliterative metre, end-line-stopped, with a pause (the caesura) usually in the middle foot, the third. Marlowe used the most supple variations on the line's five iambic stresses. He varied the place of the mid-line breath- or sense-pause; he interposed a broken, short line; he left out the initial unstressed syllable; so that some lines begin strongly on a stressed syllable; sometimes he adds an eleventh syllable ; but not, as John Fletcher added this eleventh syllable in *The Faithful Shepherdess*, to make the line light, ' feminine '. Marlowe makes the line support the heaviest weight of tragic, powerful, heroic action. At the close of *Faustus*, when the clock strikes eleven, when Faustus can only wait the expiation of his selling of his soul to the Devil, the verse rises to a varied magnificence that might be Shakespeare's own, but for a certain quality of making characters larger than life, such as that greater dramatist did not even in his greatest plays permit himself:

(The clock strikes eleven)

FAUSTUS:
  Ah Faustus,
  Now hast thou but one bare hour to live,
  And then thou must be damn'd perpetually !
  Stand still, you ever-moving spheres of heaven,
  That time may cease and midnight never come;
  Fair Nature's eye, rise, rise again, and make
  Perpetual day; or let this hour be but
  A year, a month, a week, a natural day,
  That Faustus may repent and save his soul !
  O lente, lente currite, noctis equi !
  The stars move still, time runs, the clock will strike,
  The devil will come, and Faustus must be damn'd.
  O, I'll leap up to my God !—Who pulls me down ?—
  See, See, where Christ's blood streams in the firmament !
  One drop would save my soul, half a drop: ah, my Christ !—
  Ah, rend not my heart for naming of my Christ !
  Yet will I call on him:—

Shakespeare

The man to whom Marlowe is said to have bequeathed this ' mighty line ' of blank verse, William Shakespeare, was born in the same year as Marlowe—1564. By the time Marlowe was lost to us in that tavern brawl, Shakespeare was, at the age of twenty-nine, already well known in the London theatres. He had been in the metropolis since he was twenty-two.

We know little, except through his plays, about Shakespeare's personality and character. The portraits we have are problematic. We know little of his looks or his life. We know he was born at Stratford-upon-Avon in the English Midlands. He spoke naturally the London dialect which had almost become standard English. We know that his father was John Shakespeare, a town burgess, glover, wool-dealer and butcher, and that his mother, Mary Arden, was the daughter of a well-to-do farmer. We do not know for certain whether Shakespeare's wife was 'Anne Hathaway' or 'Anne Whateley'. We know little about his education. It was not a university one. A successful playwright in London between 1586 and 1609, he left London for good in 1613, to live again in Stratford. By then he had made enough money to buy the biggest house in the small market-town. We do not know the dates when many of his plays were written. What Shakespeare is remembered for is that in the thirty-six plays, the 154 sonnets, and the longer poems, *Venus and Adonis*, *The Rape of Lucrece*, *The Passionate Pilgrim* and *A Lover's Complaint*, he has put so much of the innocence, grace, beauty, ambition, greed, treachery, lust, folly, moods and passions of men and women great and small.

When Shakespeare arrived in London there were but two theatres. He joined the actor Burbage's, moving later to the Black-friars Theatre, and then to the Globe. In days when lighting was by tallow or rushes, plays began at 3 o'clock in the afternoon. The stage was open to the weather. Nobles, ladies and patrons sat on stools on the circular stage itself. The audience stood. A blanket or sometimes a more elaborate drape made the curtain, and a board told where the scene was being played. There were a few towers and balconies, but little scenery aided the imagination.

Shakespeare was soon known and perhaps envied by writers such as Greene, Peele, Marlowe and the younger, brilliant Ben Jonson. At first he refurbished older plays. Not from first to last did Shakespeare bother to invent his own plots. All his plays except one rely on known stories, on chronicles and histories such as Holinshed's, Hall's and North's. *Hamlet*, published, imperfectly at first, in 1603, was based on an earlier play, now lost, of the same name, but the story is also in Saxo Grammaticus (author of *Gesta Danorum*) and elsewhere. *The Winter's Tale*, produced in 1609-10 but not printed until the folio of 1623, was based on Robert Greene's *Pandosto*, a prose romance published in 1588. *As You Like It* owes its theme to Lodge's *Rosalynde*, a prose pastoral interspersed with sonnets and eclogues and in turn indebted to Lyly's *Euphues*, published in 1590. The characters Jaques and Touchstone are found in Shakespeare only. *King Lear*, first performed in 1606 and printed in 1608, resembles an older play, *The True Chronicle History of King Lear*, said to have been 'lately' acted in 1605, but the story is also found in Geoffrey of Monmouth and Holinshed, and the origin of the name

D

'Lear' is 'Llyr', which was the name of a Gaelic or pre-Celtic sea-god.

Soon Shakespeare's work was patronized by Queen Elizabeth. He became the friend of the Earls of Essex, Southampton and Pembroke. He and his work were successful, admired.

Usually Shakespeare's working life is divided into five periods: the early period from 1586 to 1596; the second from 1596 to 1601; the third the early 1600s; the fourth 1608; and the fifth from 1608 to 1613. To the first period most scholars would allot: *Titus Andronicus*, a retouched play the source of which is unknown; Part I of *Henry VI*, the first historical or patriotic drama; *Love's Labour's Lost*, in which Shakespeare surpassed John Lyly in euphuistic, word-spinning wit; the even more intellectual *A Comedy of Errors*; the poetic *A Midsummer Night's Dream*, with the fates of fairies and mortals intriguingly enmeshed; the Italian story *Two Gentlemen of Verona*; the first passionate tragedy of young love, *Romeo and Juliet*; *Richard II* and *Richard III*; *Henry VI*, Parts II and III; and *King John*.

His second period is usually thought to include: *The Merchant of Venice*, his first mature play, a tragicomedy; *The Taming of the Shrew*; *Henry IV*, Parts I and II; *The Merry Wives of Windsor*; the last historical play, *Henry V*; *Much Ado About Nothing*; *As You Like It*; *Twelfth Night*; *All's Well That Ends Well*; and the *Sonnets*, printed in 1609.

A fourth period contains the great tragedies: *Julius Caesar*; *Hamlet*; *Othello*; *Macbeth*; *King Lear*; *Antony and Cleopatra*; *Coriolanus*; and *Timon of Athens*.

His fifth period contains plays of human reconciliation after the great tragedies: *Pericles*; *Cymbeline*; *The Tempest*; and *The Winter's Tale*. For three years Shakespeare was silent. He died in 1616, aged fifty-two.

If one were given the superlatively difficult task of pointing out in a few sentences wherein Shakespeare's strength as both dramatist and poet lies, one would be tempted to say that it is in his capacity to create so many varied characters of men, women and children so richly and movingly individual that he seems to write from ten men's experience. This, of itself, sets him above all other English dramatists and poets. But there is one thing more: not only does he give us the whole gamut of human life in his plays, first of heedless, innocent, passionate youth, then of the portrayal of 'mature' men's folly, treachery and often tragic deaths, and finally, of some men's and women's outgoing harmony in their later years; not only did he write plays which stated a still young nation's confident patriotism, but he contrived to mirror, in a way which pleased and inspired in his contemporaries their own ebullient ambitions, joys and griefs. He did all this without in the very least narrowing, debasing or even confining any human values.

In *Henry V* Shakespeare gives us the battle exploits of a young hero-king. The story had come down for nearly two hundred years well romanticized, with Henry's actual cruelties to some of his own people forgotten. At the start of the play the great churchmen Canterbury and Ely quote scripture to support the young King's unethical, and (as events proved) madly impractical, desire to unwind his ' bloody flag ' against France. Their arguments are specious, flimsy in the extreme. But we cannot lift any play, not even Shakespeare's, out of the contexts of time and place. The whole story ministers to men's (not only Englishmen's) admiration and craving for the kind of reckless valour that, in 1415, had won at Agincourt for Henry's six thousand longbowmen a victory against some forty thousand Frenchmen in their own country. At the same time, though clearly delighting in his portrayal of the dashing Henry, dead at thirty-four and a mediocre sovereign at home, Shakespeare contrives to indicate something about a greatness beyond.

In *Julius Caesar* he discloses what can happen when men, in their primitive adulation of leaders, actually help to produce a dictator. That theme, important then, is highly relevant today.

T. S. Eliot thought *Hamlet* a failure as a work of art. In it Shakespeare poses problems: metaphysical, philosophical and of the abundantly human kind often overlooked; human dilemmas such as the hiatus between thought and action, between chastity and faithfulness, between loyalty and treachery, between a kind of irrational majority-sanity and a madness that has its own distorted reason. Revenge was the chief theme of Kyd's *Spanish Tragedy*, printed in 1594, as it was of Cyril Tourneur's *The Revenger's Tragedy* (1607), and of Webster's *The White Divel* [*sic*] (1608), as well as of *The Duchess of Malfi* (*c.* 1614); revenge was a primitive obligation or moral law the sixteenth century was striving to outgrow. All Shakespeare wrote on this problem has lost no relevance because, though revenge is no longer a duty, an innate leaning to it is still deep in us. Hamlet's ' madness ' and Ophelia's loss of ' sanity ' are interesting in the light of modern psychological interpretations of mental states.

King Lear concerns the changing relationship between parents and children, between older and younger generations. The critic William Hazlitt thought it Shakespeare's ' best ' play. It is the one in which he seems most passionately committed. The grown-up, cold-hearted children of Lear are Regan and Goneril; the ill-treated, illegitimate Edmund is driven to brutal crime; the filial children are Cordelia and Edgar. The aged fathers, Lear and Gloster, have learnt little wisdom. The play's background is neither Christian nor pagan: it is wholly outside time or convention. Dame Helen Gardner has said in a discussion of the play that ' the mingling of a terrible pathos with an awful absurdity in Lear himself ' is what makes us feel compassionately for Lear.[18] That is, if we accept with enlightenment the pathetic irrationality of the old we must love them.

In the tragicomedy, *The Merchant of Venice*, as in the tragedy *Othello, the Moor of Venice*, Shakespeare dared to outline to a touchy, nationalistic England raw controversies in their midst which yet refer to all time. Jews came to Britain with the Norman conquerors. They were a necessary means of wealth to monarchs such as John, and even to stronger kings. They had been protected by law against the envious hatred of the people. Money-lending or usury at exorbitant interest, begun long before and stepped up in the economic growth of the eleventh century, had by the sixteenth become a question for much heated debate in Elizabethan and Jacobean London. Demanding an impossible pound of flesh as payment for bad debts was probably sensational myth but was familiar enough to be hated. Portia's remedy might also be known. But how many groundlings, or for that matter how many nobles, felt any sympathy for Shylock as they watched his ruin ? Nobody could feel a qualm for Marlowe's completely inhuman Barabas, the Jew of Malta. And how many theatre-goers either at the Globe or the Mermaid or at Stratford today feel that the Christians in *The Merchant of Venice* do not come out too well ? Yet the case *for* Shylock, as the case against him, are both there, set forth plainly yet with brilliantly unobtrusive irony. When Shylock thinks he can win he is merciless. But the Christians, with the possible exception of Portia, are revealed as being sanctimonious rather than generous.

---

[18] Helen Gardner, *King Lear* (John Coffin Memorial Lecture, 1966), p. 9.

The Jew's evil has been safely thwarted. He has not compassed Antonio's death. Anglo-Saxon and Elizabethan civil justice, whatever the practices of Venetian justice, did not always demand a man's life for plotting unsuccessfully against another's. Antonio's prime folly in accepting Shylock's bond stands outside conventions of the time. For all their high-mindedness the Christians do not show outstanding human mercy:

PORTIA:
> Tarry, Jew:
> The law hath yet another hold on you.
> It is enacted in the laws of Venice,
> If it be proved against an alien,
> That, by direct or indirect attempts,
> He seek the life of any citizen,
> The party, 'gainst the which he doth contrive,
> Shall seize one half his goods: the other half
> Comes to the privy coffer of the state;
> And the offender's life lies at the mercy
> Of the duke only, 'gainst all other voice.
> In which predicament, I say, thou standest. . . .
> Down, therefore, and beg mercy of the duke.

GRATIANO:
> Beg, that thou may'st have leave to hang thyself:
> And yet, thy wealth being forfeit to the state,
> Thou hast not left the value of a cord;
> Therefore thou must be hang'd at the state's charge.

DUKE:
> That thou shalt see the difference of our spirits,
> I pardon thee thy life before thou ask it.
> For half thy wealth, it is Antonio's;
> The other half comes to the general state,
> Which humbleness may drive into a fine.

PORTIA:
> Ay, for the state; not for Antonio.

SHYLOCK:
> Nay, take my life and all; pardon not that:
> You take my house when you do take the prop
> That doth sustain my house; you take my life
> When you do take the means whereby I live.

PORTIA:
> What mercy can you render him, Antonio?

GRATIANO:
  A halter gratis; nothing else, for God's sake !
ANTONIO:
  So please my lord the duke, and all the court,
  To quit the fine for one half of his goods,
  I am content; so he will let me have
  The other half in use, to render it,
  Upon his death unto the gentleman
  That lately stole his daughter:
  Two things provided more, that, for this favour,
  He presently become a Christian. . . .

There would seem to have been three halves to the Jew's wealth, which might be seized; and to some readers at least the good Antonio's demand that the Jew become Christian is as insensitive as Shylock's aim at fleshly outrage.

The tragedy of *Othello* is on a subject which today has earthly peace in jeopardy. Enslavement of dark peoples by their own chiefs and white dealers was just beginning to be lucrative when Shakespeare wrote. Awareness of the inhumanity involved, however minimal such awareness, must also have been present. Whatever his nationality, the Moor Othello was a dark-skinned man. Othello is variously seen as ' noble ', ' brave ', ' credulous ', ' jealous ', ' not easily jealous '. That there can be such difference of opinion about Othello is some proof of Shakespeare's subtlety of presentation. Whichever view of Othello Shakespeare intended, Othello's mind is no match for the mental sophistication of the cold, astute, white Iago.

In an early play of Shakespeare's—*Love's Labour's Lost*—Shakespeare aired one of the questions of the day, the relations between young men and women. In *Romeo and Juliet* he showed the young as less vindictive than some parents; but the result he presented as tragedy. Now in *Othello* Shakespeare aired the sixteenth-century subject of the marriage of a girl, against her father's consent, to a dark stranger from a less ' civilized ' background. Othello's marriage with Desdemona came about, despite the fact that he was cutting her off from her father. A girl in Shakespeare's day, a piece of property, was bound by obedience, in law, to her father. Yet the *mores* of the day were changing.

We are to assume that Othello's and Desdemona's union was

good, since the father had resigned himself to it. Their marriage and their lives might have been safe had it not been for the envy, physical and professional, which has been called ' motiveless malignity ', of Iago. But it was not motiveless. It came, if from no other source, from deep irrationality, carefully hidden, even then.

That Shakespeare dared to treat of this subject, as well as the subject of the Jew, three and a half centuries ago, is part of what makes him far more than an Elizabethan or a national dramatist. Shakespeare is cosmopolitan—for all times and many ages, and for many peoples.

IV

The Seventeenth Century

1616 - 1702

The personal names of *scôp*, *scald*, bard, singer, entertainer and poet had in ancient days almost invariably died with their owners. Since Caedmon in the seventh century, Cynewulf in the eighth or ninth, Chaucer and Gower in the fourteenth, British poets' and prose-writers' names began to be remembered. The sixteenth century saw men of letters of many kinds. In the seventeenth names became more and more numerous.

Poets and writers of the seventeenth century were most often comfortably off, sons of the wealthy, or themselves country gentle-men. Only a few at first came from the rising industrial and commercial class. When a writer was intent on making a name or money by his writing he went to the capital. By a new system of patronage a writer dedicated his work to a particular nobleman or to a member of the royal circle and received in return money and help. By the second half of the century such a system made for sycophancy, a tendency towards political writing, or for writing to be used politically by literary aspirants.

Caedmon had been a herder of animals. The greatest of British poets, son of a plain burgess in a small town, was known in the seventeenth century to have made only a modest fortune by his plays. Some of Shakespeare's contemporaries were poor men like Dekker or squandered their money as Greene did. The seventeenth century produced Ben Jonson, nine years younger than Shakespeare and Shakespeare's friend and admirer. Jonson's stepfather was a bricklayer. As a youth Benjamin ran away from his brick-laying apprenticeship to make a career by writing plays. The century also brought other impecunious writers—John Bunyan, the tinker, and the ' Water Poet ' John Taylor, the Thames ferryman: enough to prove that the new society set on a path towards riches

104

through hard trade and seafaring held some freedom of reward for aesthetic endeavour.

An outspoken Royalist, Taylor wrote a good deal of both prose and verse. He had a facile pen, a seventeenth-century species of crude, but very rarely coarse, humour, a poet's delight in playing with words and a certain amount of book knowledge. He may even have had a little Latin and Greek. His *Wit and Mirth* (1635) is a book of jests:

> chargeably collected Ovt of Taverns, Ordinaries, Innes, Bowling-Greenes and Allyes, Alehouses, Tobacco-shops, Highwayes, and Water-passages. Made vp, and fashioned into Cliches, Bulls, Quirkes, Yerkes, Quips, and Jerkes.

Taylor's *Pennylesse Pilgrimage* (1618), *A Common Whore* (1622), *Sense upon Nonsense, Wit and Mirth* and *A Journey to Wales* were printed in 1630 in a ' collective ' edition. This was reprinted by the Spenser Society (1868-78).

Women began to write. Exceptional, such females were soon nicknamed ' Blue-Stockings ', from the French *bas-bleus*. Girls' education in Britain at that time was domestic for the poor, ornamental or concerning management of houses and servants for the well-to-do. The first was carried on at home. Usually, in the second, the girl was sent to a richer friend's house to learn; as boys still went from home to learn the manly arts of knighthood. Girls could be betrothed when five years old, particularly among the wealthy. It happened frequently that a girl was married at twelve. Dowries, the bride-wealth of more primitive days, were still arranged among some parents. Education for girls, in spite of Queen Elizabeth and of Anglo-Saxon traditions of women's learning and independence, was currently thought, by many Puritans and many Catholics, unbecoming or needless.

The earlier half of the seventeenth century was torn by both religious and civil conflict. After Mary's Catholic persecutions and Elizabeth's Protestantism, Catholic still worked against Protestant under the first Stuart king James I. Under James's son, Charles I, gay cavalier had little tolerance for grave and sober Puritan. The differences became aggravated into monarchism and parliamentarianism under the ' Divine Right ' assumptions of Charles I between 1625 and 1645. Civil war then slashed the land in two.

Again father might be against son, or brother against brother, in the Puritan fight to bring to earth ' The Kingdom of the Saints '. How difficult knowing where loyalty lay must have been. How intrepid to hold to any sense of truth or honesty, in days when for criticism, religious or social, one might be branded, imprisoned, racked, have one's ears shorn off, or hanged, drawn and quartered, or have one's heart torn out.

The seventeenth century, the Puritan régime and what came after, can be seen as holding the end of one poetic, dramatic and prose age, and the initial direction in all three in the succeeding age. The period between 1611 and 1702 holds extraordinary change in poetry, drama and prose. Each development is an integral part of national thought, aims, ambitions, ideals, illusions and lost illusions of the day.

Drama

By his historical drama and in his revelation of human character Shakespeare had helped to create British national theatre. In the early part of Shakespeare's London life national drama had also been popular drama. Much later than the distinction between popular lyric poetry and literary lyric after the ballads, popular drama was not yet separate from literary drama. Saying this is saying much more than that British popular drama had not yet acquired the standards of literature. Playgoing was still one of the most enjoyed and favoured of social recreations of all classes in Elizabethan and the Stuarts' London.

But most dramatists, though prodigious workers, had little or no thought for the preservation of their plays. In the year 1623, when the Folio edition of Shakespeare's plays came out, a step was made towards the making of British drama as literature. Jealous, ambitious, astute Ben Jonson had a first Folio volume of his plays securely published by 1616. But men like Marston, Thomas Heywood and Dekker took no such measures. Writing for the stage was the best way of earning a literary livelihood; but it was a scramble. Poverty overtook Ben Jonson again in his later years; and penury was never far from Thomas Heywood and Dekker, as it had not been from the earlier university young men, Greene, Peele and Nashe.

New theatres continued to be built. These were covered, not open to the sky. In them ' groundling ' audiences, chiefly but not wholly men, stood and shouted applause or derision. After 1603 the Stuarts, not parsimonious as Elizabeth had been, encouraged sumptuous pageants and court masques celebrating birthdays and other state occasions. By the seventeenth century pageant and masque were no longer part of popular entertainment. In 1604, when the rights of nobles to patronize a troupe of players were revoked, theatres became places of Crown entertainment. Plays were being raised to higher social standing. The old kind of poor travelling player and popular entertainer could even be classed as vagrants; and under the change from subsistence economy to industrial competitive improvement vagrants increased in number.

Playwrights who were writing after Shakespeare's partial retirement to Stratford include Ben Jonson, George Chapman, Francis Beaumont, John Fletcher, Thomas Heywood, Thomas Dekker, John Webster, Cyril Tourneur, William Rowley, Thomas Middleton, John Ford, Philip Massinger, John Marston and James Shirley. As the new theatres had costume but still no scenery, dramatists' dependence on theme, action and language to hold their audiences' attention grew. The theme interesting to a rapidly developing society was morality within the elements of violence—the old question, in a changing form, of how a knight and a stout English yeoman came to be in days of growing education a *gentle*man, while remaining a ' compleat ' male.

In seventeenth-century Britain men were the dominant sex in society. Therefore Don Juanism (which today we see as a masculine attempt to prove manliness) interested playgoers. Fidelity of wives, who had brought land or money as dowry, was important for founding illustrious families. The subject of incest interested high and low. Incest was not very common, though it may have been commoner than we can know; the idea of it provoked instinctual fancy, as well as stirring moral austerity. Delineation of the means of getting wealth, including murder and cunning of all kinds, fascinated people, as it had drawn those who watched the ' Cain and Abel ' Mystery play. Revenge repelled yet attracted. The family vendetta in which revenge had been a sacred duty was not so far behind seventeenth-century memories. The Mosaic law of ' an eye for an eye ' was accepted; but the thin veneer of civilization was being pierced, as Marston's, Tourneur's, Webster's, Dekker's and

Ford's plays all show. Such agitation on ' eternal ' questions is often what literature is about.

The complex theme of lifelong fidelity in personal and family association concerned seventeenth-century people. Some parents were dismally despotic—as Elizabeth Tanfield's mother, who required her (it is said) to approach always on bended knees. Off-spring, especially girls, were expected to be docile parts of family possessions. Marriages could be legalized at home. ' Oliver's law ', as the diary of the countryman, Leonard Wheatcroft, discloses, demanded at last a service before a public ' Justice of Peace '. (Our present religious ceremony of marriage only became legally neces-sary later.) A young man and woman could actually ' plight their troth ' without consulting their elders. The whole question of the choice regarding marriage partners, in seventeenth-century Britain, was being put to the test. The idea of faithful love is far, far older than the medieval, artificial ideals of romance and chivalry.

Often superstitious, seventeenth-century playgoers and people in general were enthralled by spirits, fairies, ghosts and witches, the last two almost always of evil intent. Jacobean dramatists borrowed plots, with all these kinds of themes, as Shakespeare borrowed his plots, from Latin and Greek stories, from Renaissance and con-temporary Italian stories, from French, Spanish, Germanic and Scandinavian sources. Playwrights collaborated with each other, Beaumont with Fletcher, Rowley with Middleton, Dekker with Thomas Heywood, Jonson with Marston and Chapman. When they collaborated they were often expert mutual critics. They so erased each other's defects that we are still not sure sometimes who wrote what. They borrowed from Shakespeare, as occasionally he borrowed from them. Most of them rose, if only on occasion, to powerful or beautiful verse—Tourneur in *The Atheist's Tragedie* (1611), Jonson in *The Sad Shepherd* (in the folio of 1641), Chapman in *Bussy D'Ambois* (1613), Fletcher in his pastoral, undramatic *The Faithful Shepherdess* (1610), Ford (whom Charles Lamb admired but T. S. Eliot misunderstood) in *The Broken Heart* (1633), Thomas Heywood, though in completely different vein, in *A Woman Kilde with Kindnesse* (performed 1603; printed 1607) and Thomas Dekker in *The Honest Whore* (Pt I 1604; Pt II 1630). Charles Lamb called Dekker a ' prose Shakespeare '. All these playwrights tell much about their society rather than create individual characters.

All of them delighted, as did their audiences, often with

boisterously confident revelry, satire, but serious ambition, in the great future as a nation they saw for themselves. They were absorbed by the human adventure of the seething life in their capital. They reflect their time in important ways.

European plays featured brothels and lewdness quite openly. Anglo-Saxon dramatists followed their example. They presented spectacles of gallants, wantons, dupes, coneys, cozeners, murderers, great and small villains of many kinds. But, compared with the characters of Shakespeare's plays—Hamlet, Lear, King Richard II, Portia, Othello, Shylock, Falstaff, Perdita, Miranda, Imogen— the people in the plays of the other dramatists of the early seventeenth century are not ' compounded of many simples '; they have not virtue and vice, strength and weakness, greatness and stupidity combining and conflicting, as Shakespeare showed, and as human beings have. Creators other than Shakespeare seem narrow in vision, a little what Chapman might have called ' soul-blind ', including himself. Ben Jonson's Subtle, Sir Epicure Mammon and Doll Common in *The Alchemist* (1610), Massinger's Maleforts and Sir Giles Overreach in *The Unnatural Combat* (1639) and *A New Way to pay Old Debts* (1633), Tourneur's atheist D'Amville in *The Atheist's Tragedie*, Chapman's Sir Gyles Goosecappe, Dekker's and Middleton's Moll Cutpurse in *The Roaring Girle* (1611)—all these by their very names tell that their owners are symbols but little removed from personifications of human frailties rather than people in their own right. In a young civilization, Jacobean dramatists explored, first, social situations. Exploration of intricate individual characters and mutual misunderstandings came later (except by Shakespeare) in the working out of literary forms.

Middleton, Jonson and Ford used overdone horror to give point to attitudes of their age. Jonson satirized heavily. His early comedies include *Every Man in his Humour* (performed 1598) and *Every Man out of his Humour* (1599). The list of Jonson's plays is prodigious. This decamped stepson of a bricklayer grew into a learned man. One of his aims was to bring the ' classical ' unities into his plays. Few British playwrights had any wish so to bind their art as classical and French playwrights were binding theirs. Shakespeare did not bind his. But Jonson, Shakespeare's friend and admirer, wrote his brilliant, long-winded comedies and tragedies, on classical lines, with acid vigour, satirizing the faults and follies of his day as he saw them. These main traits of people Jonson called ' humours '. In his comedy, *Volpone, or The Fox* (performed 1605/6; printed 1607), for instance, Volpone is a rich, cunning, ageing but sensual miser who, by raising hopes in his acquaintances that he will favour them in his will, dupes them into all kinds of revolting ill-doings. Corvino (crow), a merchant, is prepared to allow his wife to sleep with Volpone. There is little fun in Jonson's comedies. They are full of action, plot and counter-plot, the whole so vigorously overdone as to be beyond reality, amusing in that sense. Volpone—long speeches pared—complete with dwarfs and eunuch, became farcically amusing when televised by the BBC. Jonson is often coarse, as in his *Epigrams* (1616); the times were coarse.

Cyril Tourneur and John Webster are remembered chiefly for their gloom, their tragic outlook on people's lives and actions. In *The Revenger's Tragedy* (1607) Tourneur portrayed human violence resulting in horror. The play's tone is a strange combination: whilst a family vendetta for a second marriage made independently by a young countess is clearly condemned, Tourneur does not evoke sympathy for her and her lover. The play is so equivocal that pity and horror in us are blurred. In *The Atheist's Tragedie* opposing sympathies are again so inwoven that we are left unmoved when the atheist has sufficient ' mercy ' shown for him to absolve his sins by taking his own life. Free thought (begun as long before as the days of Sophocles) was seen by both Puritan and Catholic as so evil as inevitably to accompany only the most utter depravity. In fact, free thinking as seen in the work of writers such as Abelard and Erasmus carried a very reverent outlook. Tourneur's remorseless showing of vindictive human beings trapped by their own harsh non-sympathy is terrible in its warning, fascinating in its complexity.

Webster in *The White Divel* (printed 1612), and in *The Duchess of Malfi* (*c.* 1614), portrayed horrifying human baseness; yet Webster endowed the White Divel herself, the courtesan Vittoria Corombona, with a movingly heroic defiance towards her enemies; while the Duchess of Malfi's courage and dignity under torment excite pity and admiration. Both Tourneur and Webster were beset by memories of civilization's more savage days: as Ford in *The Broken Heart* (1633) was concerned to glorify Spartan courage under the personal tragedy of enforced marriage.

Middleton, Marston, Rowley, Chapman, Massinger and Ford were all fettered by, or at least tied to, their emergent society's problems. All wrote plays of violence, grossness or satiric morality. Thus, their plays are not for all time but belong to their age. Shakespeare's human compassion and hope were what alleviated savagery in some of his plays, freeing them from being merely of their day. In the murder of Lady Macduff and her son, the child's courage seems to pay for all. The only instance in his work of that inhuman violence which Jacobean dramatists such as Webster and Tourneur portrayed occurs if we accept Shakespeare as responsible for *Titus Andronicus*. Its primitive raping and cutting off of hands may have been historically actual, since the story is Roman. But the extent of Shakespeare's share in its authorship is not known. Richard III's deformity, though dubious as historical fact, does offer some sort of cause for the bloodthirstiness of Richard's portrayal. Yet even Richard Shakespeare saw as conscience-troubled, rendered sleeplessly clear-sighted by dreams:

> Guilty ! Guilty !
> I shall despair:—There is no creature loves me.
> And if I die no soul shall pity me.

Iago's evil in *Othello* and Goneril's and Regan's in *King Lear* are unalleviated. But in *Lear* the two unfilial daughters are offset by the loving Cordelia; and in *Othello* Shakespeare was revealing a universal prejudice and inhumanity.

This portrayal of human violence, blood-lust, vindictiveness and their resulting miseries is a perennial problem for dramatic art. The difficulty in showing any of them through satiric characters or unrelievedly harshly is that readers often do not know whether the violence or vice are to be seen as normal or abnormal; whether the author means what he says or whether he means the opposite. After 350 years this problem of presenting violence and vice in drama is very much with us.

Dekker and Thomas Heywood have little violence in their plays. These two began what may be called domestic drama. Shakespeare's, Marlowe's and most dramatic heroes and heroines had so far been mostly from the great, the public, the ' noble '. Jonson's ' characters ' were usually from the middle classes, the wealthy, the commercially aspiring and their servile, often cunning hangers-on and servants. In *The Shoemaker's Holiday* (1600) Dekker portrayed Nashe's Simon Eyre, the humorous, convivial, London shoemaker who supplied the Lord Mayor with shoes and became Lord Mayor himself. He filled many scenes with apprentices, tradesmen, aldermen, together with wives, daughters and suitors. Dekker offered the hurly-burly, not alarmingly crude or violent, of city life which he knew and liked. The day-to-day lives of the ordinary have always been less violent and freer from certain conventions than the lives of the publicly great. Whether they are therefore duller is not certain. In *The Honest Whore* Dekker portrayed in Part I a harlot, Bellafront, who returns to virtue and the difficulties of marriage. Dekker has a sense of human decency rather than of sin. Webster, an expert playwright himself, put Dekker, as Lamb perhaps overgenerously did, beside Shakespeare. Profligate with an impetuous talent, Dekker is said to have written his works with the bailiff and the printer's devil always at his elbow.

Thomas Heywood, an immensely industrious Londoner, both actor and playwright, also loved his city. In his directly moral writings he saw little in his surroundings, from 'prentices to Puritans, to satirize. Beaumont and Fletcher's farce, *The Knight of the Burning Pestle* (1609; printed 1613), ridiculed the citizens' approach to culture presented in Heywood's *The Four P's*. Heywood's *A Woman Kilde with Kindness* presents a faithless wife who, though forgiven by her husband, was yet banished by him to die in loneliness of a ' broken heart '. Today we do not see this wife as overwhelmed by kindness; if anything she was killed by her husband's inability to forgive in any real sense. But clearly Heywood felt that he was, in his brawling, lusty, changing age, pressing home the point about fidelity with the erring wife's death; yet it is gently done.

Strict censorship, the Star Chamber court after Elizabeth's decrees, threat of prison or pillory, made seventeenth-century dramatists wary of contemporary political criticism. In outspokenness on social matters they did as Elizabethan prose-writers had done. Most, as Middleton and Rowley in *The Changeling*, were careful to asset moral intent:

> justice hath so right
> The Guilty hit, that innocence is quit
> By proclamation, and may joy again;

Ben Jonson in *Volpone* identified himself patriotically with the state in upholding right: ' Stern justice still maintains her upright cause.' Whether satirically, tragically, harsh, or mild and uncondemning, Jacobean dramatists, apart from Shakespeare, were, for all their sophistication, by no means emancipated from the tradition of earlier Morality plays.

Yet as early as 1579 the stage in England was being accused of licence and frivolity. Watchful civic authorities who thought beggars and wandering players immoral could now act against them. As Puritans became the anti-court party, so accusations against the morals of the theatre grew. And as this happened, less and less was playgoing social enjoyment for all. Discussion raged. Books and tracts defended or attacked. Before the mid-century Puritan rule had closed the London theatres. At the death of Cromwell the Protector in 1658 hope sprang in many members of a young and impetuous nation weary of austerity. People longed for a monarch for England, Scotland and Wales, united since 1603. In 1660 Charles II returned from exile in France. He gathered round him a dignified, exquisite, voluptuous court. Integllient, gay, dissolute, Charles kept his word to friend or enemy no more than many kings had done. Yet by 1662 Charles had founded the Royal Society. He encouraged science by helping the opening of libraries: the nucleus of what would later be the British Museum Library; in Oxford Thomas Bodley's Bodleian had been opened in 1602 and endowed under James I. Printed books multiplied.

In 1660 the London theatres, often shut for health reasons and closed for eighteen years under the Puritans, opened to welcome gay—and far more elegant—crowds. Women acted for the first time.

Restoration playwrights after 1660 included John Dryden, William Congreve, William Wycherley, John Vanbrugh, George Etherege and George Farquhar. All these portrayed—still no individual characters, but cardboard marionettes that were types of libertines—jealous husbands, fashionable beaux and dames of all ages, usually staged seeking and arranging marriages, wenching, carding, cuckolding. Their dialogue can grow wearisome; but it shows what subjects and licences rise to the surface when a culture first grows luxurious and allows more general sexual liberty after restrictive fears. Today we do not see Restoration comedies, safely in the past, as seriously immoral. Their impact is distanced. Congreve's *Love for Love* (1695) and *The Way of the World* (1700), Farquhar's *The Beaux' Stratagem* (1707) and Wycherley's *The*

Country Wife (staged 1672/3; printed 1675), when exquisitely produced, are witty and funny; and underneath the trivial, worldly talk there is almost always a refreshing edge of something more than coy or entirely flippant immorality. ' Is it not a frank age ? ' Sparkish laughs in *The Country Wife*. ' Am I not a frank person ? ' What still bothered them was whether the ' gallant ' who easily seduced girls ' of low degree ' and then, as Dryden put it, ' kills his Man ' was, even then, the ' compleat male '.[1] Underneath their artificiality these comedies were suggesting characters ready to take their places in a competitive, commercial, increasingly sophisticated society.

In 1698 moralist wrath—this time not Puritan but that of the high Anglican, non-juring bishop, Jeremy Collier—descended on the Restoration stage again. Charles II had died. The bloodless revolution of 1688 deposed his brother James after two years and accepted James's daughter Mary and her Dutch husband, William of Orange. Theatre audiences were more and more socially aspiring, commercially wealthy or intellectual. The cleavage we saw overtake lyric poetry after the heyday of the ballads now overtook drama. London's plays were no longer for all citizens. And until this twentieth century, when a few young dramatists began to strive to alter the schism and heal this grievous breach, hiatus has remained.

Prose

In prose, after the Authorised Version of the Bible in 1611 had set a majestic simplicity and a poetic beauty in style, writers of prose in the seventeenth century experimented. Individualism began to flower. Prose had to communicate on an increasing number of fronts. It had to be the vehicle for the scientific, anti-Aristotelian philosophy Francis Bacon had helped to set in motion for politics, for philosophy, for criticism of many kinds, for increasing knowledge and learning, as well as for religion, religious controversy and the arts. Each writer explored, and sought, as a writer must seek, his own personal way to say what he wanted to say.

Walter Ralegh's *History of the World* (1614), written whilst that ' well-read rover ' was imprisoned for thirteen years by King James

[1] See Dryden's Prologue to *The Wild Gallant*.

in the Tower of London, and undertaken for his captor's promising young son Henry, perhaps belongs to the previous age. Sir Thomas Overbury's *Characters*, the first edition of which appeared in 1614, might be said to mark, in prose, the seventeenth century's growing interest in individual personality. Of a similar kind of writing were Izaak Walton's *Lives*—those of *Donne* (1640), *Wotton* (1651), *Hooker* (1665) and *Herbert* (1670). Better known is Walton's book on fishing, *The Compleat Angler* (1653). Other biographies were Thomas Fuller's *Worthies of England* (1662), John Aubrey's *Lives*, full of lively, if occasionally apocryphal stories (not published until 1813), the Puritan Lucy Hutchinson's biography of her husband, *Memoirs of the Life of Colonel Hutchinson* (written after 1664; published 1806), and Margaret Duchess of Newcastle's *Life* of her husband the Duke. Dorothy Osborne's *Letters* of between 1652 and 1654 to William Temple give a fascinating picture of two young people who met in France, were determined to marry—and did marry, despite combined family opposition.

Leonard Wheatcroft, a country tailor and husbandman, left a diary. Another countryman, young Roger Lowe, left a diary of the years between 1663 and 1674. These records of the lives of two unknowns strike a balance between national events and life as it was lived by the majority. But they have been reprinted very rarely. They are not easy to find. Far better known is Samuel Pepys's *Diary*. Pepys kept this social and intimate record between the years 1660 and 1669. It is useful as commentary on its times but also for its self-aware honesty. Written in a private shorthand, it was not deciphered and published until 1825. John Evelyn, a wealthy and careful Royalist, published in 1661 *Fumifugium or The inconvenience of the Air and Smoke of London dissipated*, which, in our pollution-troubled era, has a prophetic ring about it. Evelyn's *Diary* (1818), covering the years 1640 to 1706, reveals the external, cautious social life of many prominent people. The Anglican Thomas Traherne's *Centuries of Meditations*, a collection of prose sketches, shows a seventeenth-century Celtic, pantheistic devotion. Traherne's book is a moving record of osmotic sensations; it conveys emotional oneness with earthly phenomena as part of spiritual oneness: 'You never enjoy the world aright, till the sea itself floweth in your veins, till you are clothed with the heavens, and crowned with the stars.' The manuscript of *Centuries of Meditations* was not discovered until the beginning of the twentieth century and was first published in 1908.

There were learned books such as Robert Burton's *The Anatomy of Melancholy* (1621), an exhaustive study revealing how long men have suffered from the burden of consciousness. Sir Thomas Browne's *Religio Medici* (1642) and *Hydriotaphia or Urn Burial* (1658) were also recondite in content and not simple in style. There were theological lectures, later printed, such as Samuel Clarke's *A Demonstration of the Being and Attributes of God* (1704), *A Discourse concerning the Unchangeable Obligations of National Religion* (1705) and the *Truth and Certainty of the Christian Revelation* (1632). Dr Clarke, later the friend of Isaac Newton, was answering Hobbes, whom he called an ' atheist '. Dr Clarke's arguments are meticulous, closed-circle theology ones. He was also answering the ' new ' philosophy of the age which, as John Donne wrote, ' calls all in doubt '.

On most cottage shelves in Britain for the next two centuries there might have been found Jeremy Taylor's *Holy Living* and *Holy Dying* (1650-1). There is little that is dismal in this Irish bishop's kindly, simple severities which comforted John Keats before his untimely death, and must have played a small part in the long progress of civilized man.

> Remedies against Anger. Of all passions it endeavours most to make reason useless. . . . If it proceeds from a great cause it turns to fury; if from a small cause it is peevishness; and so is always either terrible or ridiculous. It makes a man's body, monstrous, deformed, and contemptible; the voice horrid; the eyes cruel; the face pale or fiery; the gait fierce; the speech clamorous and loud. It is neither manly nor ingenuous. It proceeds from softness of spirit and pusillanimity.

Thomas Hobbes, secretary to Francis Bacon for a time, began the written science of Government with *The Leviathan* (1651). That book killed for all time the theory of ' Divine Right ' which had helped slay Charles I. Hobbes argued that the aim and end of Government is the good of the State, the many, the people, the Commonwealth. But, having entrusted power to Government, the people, Hobbes held, cannot take power away again.

John Locke, in his *Essay concerning Human Understanding* (1690) argued that power *can* be taken from the Government by the people. Both Hobbes's and Locke's books, coming two centuries before parliamentary reform gave ordinary people any real voice in Government, are important in the slow evolution of democracy.

The seventeenth century has the first woman professional writer, Mrs Aphra Behn. Forgotten now, this coarse court playwright and poet advanced, after Deloney, Greene and Nashe, the novel as art-form with *Oroonoko, or the History of the Royal Slave* (*c.* 1678). Over-done, yet clear-eyed, *Oroonoko* is the first writing on the discredit of racialism and the horror of buying and selling our own kind.

This century saw the end of the long thraldom of the English language to Latin. John Selden's *Table Talk* came in 1689. and Isaac Newton's *Principia Mathematica Philosophiae Naturalis* (1687) was among the last important books in Latin. Newton restated Pythagoras', Copernicus', Kepler's and Galileo's theory of the universe against Ptolemy's of about 140 B.C. The Roman Church had long upheld Ptolemy's. Newton's *Principia* gave us his own theory of gravitation; but it has no place in the history of English prose.

John Bunyan, whilst in prison for preaching the independent, nonconformist Baptist faith, wrote *Pilgrim's Progress* (1678). Two friends, Christian and Hopeful, leave their homes and set out for the Celestial City. They meet many strange people—Mr Worldly Wiseman, Ignorant from the City of Conceit, Pliable, Talkative. They pass through the Valley of the Shadow of Death, through a bog called the Slough of Despond. They lose their way and fall into the clutches of Giant Despair of Doubting Castle. These, and many more adventures before the two arrive, make *Pilgrim's Progress* a prime story for young and old.

Poetry

Lyric poetry, going back in origin to crises of personal joy and grief, births, betrothals, marriages and deaths, is, through all its changes, happy or sorrowful, praising, elegiac, or scornful. Elizabethan, ' golden ' lyrics that have come down to us were mostly gay yet serious love poems of men such as Sidney, Marlowe, Lodge, Lyly. Lyric poetry of the seventeenth century became far less optimistic. Its makers include Jonson, John Donne, Andrew Marvell, George

Herbert, Henry Vaughan, Richard Crashaw, Thomas Carew, Henry King, Henry Wotton, John Suckling, Richard Lovelace, Abraham Cowley. The most influential poet, writer and critic, Dryden, called these (except Suckling, Lovelace and Carew) ' metaphysical ' poets; he named their similes ' conceits '. He meant that the poets did not separate the non-physical from the physical; they enriched their lyrics by illustrating the eternal by the immediate here and now, as Donne's:

> *Go and catch a falling star,*
> > *Get with child a mandrake root*
> Tell me where all past years are,
> > Or who cleft the Devil's foot;
> Teach me to hear mermaids singing,
> Or to keep off envy's stinging,
> > > And find
> > > What wind,
> Serves to advance an honest mind.

Marvell's:

> *Annihilating all that's made*
> *To a green thought* in a green shade;

Or:

> . . . at my back I always hear
> *Time's winged chariot* hurrying near,

Herbert's:

> When God at first made Man
> Having *a glass of blessings* standing by—

and his:

> ' *You must sit down,*' *says Love,* ' *and taste my meat.*'
> *So I did sit and eat.*

Vaughan's:

> But ah ! *my soul* with too much stay
> *Is drunk, and staggers in the way.*

John Donne is said to have influenced most strongly this literary 'metaphysical' poetry diverging so far from popular balladry and contrasting with Elizabethan poetry. Its direct ancestors were classical poets and Dante. Donne, after a tempestuous youth in which he wrote witty satires and highly individual love poetry, was imprisoned for marrying without parental consent, freed and left to regret. The passionate intellectual, brought up a Catholic, turned to the Anglican Church. He became one of that Church's great orators. We remember from Donne's *Devotions* (1624), if only because of Ernest Hemingway's novel *For Whom the Bell Tolls* (1940), Donne's sense of men's need for unity:

> any man's death diminishes me, because I am involved in mankind, and therefore never send to know for whom the bell tolls; it tolls for thee.

In his love poems, his religious lyrics and his satiric poems Donne is the most versatile of his group.

Poets of Britain have never been able for long to forget the countryside. Andrew Marvell wrote both of love and nature. Only after the Restoration and poetry's complete swing to the satirical did Marvell turn to satire. Herbert dressed the most sacred matters in the homeliest of phrase and simile. Vaughan is more mystical, an Anglican a little less at home on earth. The Catholic Crashaw's 'conceits' contain the enthusiasm and wild, if narrower, joy of the convert.

Carew—of 'He that loves a rosy cheek,/Or a coral lip admires'— was a gallant at the court of Charles I. Wotton, a courtier too, a diplomat and a lawyer, was the author of 'A Hymn to My God in a Night of My Late Sicknesse'.

Rich, gay, generous, popular, Sir John Suckling, who fought in Europe as well as at home, was involved in a plot to rescue Lord Strafford from the Tower. Suckling died in exile. It is said he died by his own hand, depressed after some earlier torture. He was thirty-three. A Cavalier and man of action, his lyrics were tossed off in leisure hours. We think of Richard Lovelace together with Suckling. Lovelace was another Cavalier—gay and dissipated. The verse of these two, more than that of Edmund Waller (of divided loyalties), is light-hearted yet holds depths, though without the studied metrics of religious poets. Suckling and Lovelace helped

to change the course of the seventeenth-century English lyric.
Suckling's best known verses are ' The Constant Lover ':

> Out upon it, I have loved
>   Three whole days together
> And am like to love three more
>   If it prove fair weather . . .

and ' Why So Pale and Wan ? ':

> Why so pale and wan, fond lover ?
>   Prithee, why so pale ?
> Will, when looking well can't move her,
>   Looking ill prevail ?
>   Prithee, why so pale ? . . .

Lovelace's best-known lines are ' To Lucasta, Going to the
Wars ' and ' To Althea, from Prison ':

> When Love with unconfinèd wings
>   Hovers within my gates,
> And my divine Althea brings
>   To whisper at the grates ;
> When I lie tangled in her hair
>   And fetter'd to her eye,
> The birds that wanton in the air
>   Know no such liberty.
>
> When flowing cups run swiftly round
>   With no allaying Thames,
> Our careless heads with roses bound,
>   Our hearts with loyal flames ;
> When thirsty grief in wine we steep,
>   When healths and draughts go free—
> Fishes that tipple in the deep
>   Know no such liberty.
>
> When, like committed linnets, I
>   With shriller throat shall sing
> The sweetness, mercy, majesty,
>   And glories of my King ;
> When I shall voice aloud how good
>   He is, how great should be,

Enlargèd winds, that curl the flood,
Know no such liberty.

Stone walls do not a prison make,
Nor iron bars a cage;
Minds innocent and quiet take
That for an hermitage;
If I have freedom in my love
And in my soul am free,
Angels alone, that soar above,
Enjoy such liberty.

Abraham Cowley was turned out of his university for joining the Royalist cause. Cowley wrote loyal odes after the 1660 Restoration and he became the last of the so-called metaphysical poets. In his odes Cowley frankly imitated the rhymed metrics of the Greek Anacreon and the Roman Horace. Some of Cowley's ' conceits ' are so far-fetched they do not seem part of the verse.

Other poets continuing in that age, or of it, include Thomas Campion, Samuel Daniel, William Drummond of Hawthornden, Michael Drayton, George Wither and John Denham. Drayton's long *Poly-Olbion* described in patriotic alexandrines England's mountains, rivers, birds and beasts. Denham's *Cooper's Hill* is also a descriptive poem, the description localized.

Robert Herrick was a Royalist Devon parson whose religious cares sat lightly on him. Herrick wrote *The Hesperides* and *Noble Numbers*—a great quantity of almost paganly pious lyrics, love poems and country poems:

Gather ye rosebuds while ye may
Old Time is still a-flying;
And that same flower that smiles today
Tomorrow will be dying.

One poet who at this point was to concentrate on the greatness of epic poetry was John Milton. Born in 1608, eight years before Shakespeare's death, Milton, son of a scrivener and music composer, was dedicated almost from birth to piety and to poetry. From the age of twelve he ' spent '—ruined—his eyesight reading until the small hours by candle- or rushlight. He was studious, reserved and, during his seven years as a young man at Cambridge, apart from his fellows. When he was twenty-one he wrote the ' Ode on the Morning of Christ's Nativity '.

For six more years the young Milton steeped himself in scholarship at home. He wrote the pastoral masque, *Comus*, and in 1634 it was performed at Ludlow Castle. But in a more and more urban society the *genre* of masque was going out of fashion. Milton wrote the poems ' L'Allegro ' (the cheerful man), ' Il Penseroso ' (the contemplative man), and the lyrical lament for his friend, Edward King, ' Lycidas '. In all three he used the ancient pastoral convention. As still further preparation for a high task as yet unknown to him he travelled in France and Italy, meeting Galileo and other scholars in Florence. Returning to a house of his own he tutored—domineeringly, it is said—a few boys there. When he was thirty-five he married the seventeen-year-old daughter of a Royalist; but within a few months Mary Powell had fled home. Milton reaccepted her later, and she bore him three daughters before dying in childbirth at twenty-six.

Since his early lyrics Milton had forsaken poetry. He had published pamphlet after pamphlet, *Of Reformation touching Church Discipline in England* (1641), *The Doctrine and Discipline of Divorce* (1643), *Of Education* (1644), and also in 1644 the courageous *Areopagitica; a Speech for the Liberty of Unlicenc'd Printing, to the Parlament of England*:

> . . . who kills a man kills a reasonable creature, God's Image; but he who destroys a good book, kills reason itself, kills the Image of God, as it were in the eye. Many a man lives a burden to the earth; but a good book is the precious life-blood of a master spirit.

A staunch Puritan, Milton became the Commonwealth's Latin or Foreign Secretary up to the Restoration of 1660. That event not being unduly bloodthirsty, he escaped death and persecution; but he lost his post.

Blind, over fifty years old, respected for his forthright courage, he turned to completing a long poem he had begun in 1658 and had had the idea for since his return from Florence. This was the epic *Paradise Lost*. In ten books, it was published in 1667 and revised in twelve books in 1674. *Paradise Regained*, and his last work, the tragedy *Samson Agonistes*, were printed in 1671.

A poet is often a lonely person; he must spend time in solitude, in the ' red-rock wilderness '. In an age when the freedom of writers was in danger from the government Milton was an example of integrity much as Boris Pasternak was in twentieth-century Russia.

Confident in his powers a poet must also be; and confidence may be seen from Milton's aim in *Paradise Lost*:

> That to the highth of this great Arguement
> I may assert Eternal Providence,
> And justifie the wayes of God to men.

The poem tells of the rebellion of Satan—Lucifer—against God, of the temptation of Eve, of Eve's temptation of Adam, of their fall, and of their punishment. *Paradise Lost* is the epic of man's setting out on what Loren Eiseley calls his Immense Journey through the lonely way of knowledge down the centuries. On this journey

> The world is its own place and in itself
> Can make a Heav'n of Hell, a Hell of Heav'n.

Punished, Adam and Eve must leave the innocence of the Garden:

> Som natural tears they drop'd, but wip'd them soon;
> The World was all before them, where to choose
> Thir place of rest, and Providence thir guide:
> They hand in hand with wand'ring steps and slow,
> Through Eden took their solitarie way.[2]

Whether, now, we accept Milton's theology or not, most people acknowledge *Paradise Lost* a poem of grandeur and a great epic. T. S. Eliot called its verse 'grandiloquent' rather than grand. Milton used blank verse, forgoing what he wrote of as the ' troublesome and modern bondage of rimeing '. But rhyme had never yet belonged to epic poetry. Milton's vocabulary and his style are influenced by the scholar's adherence to the Latin from which the English language had such difficulty in escaping.

Paradise Lost has no hero; most epics have one. The most alive figure is the rebel Satan. Satan's arrogant strength derived straight from the proud, lonely selfhood of the author. Though stressing the doctrine of submission to divine authority Milton was yet an

[2] Text from *Complete Poetical Works of John Milton* (Oxford Univ. Press, 1921).

unbowing dissenter himself. Strong, perhaps not very compassionate, he was an interesting companion, as some who knew him have
testified.

Another poet, born in 1631, was to carry English poetry into an
entirely different course from Milton's lyricism and blank verse and
from ' metaphysical ' poetry. John Dryden, the son of a vicar of
Aldwinkle All Saints in Northamptonshire, was educated at Cam-
bridge as Milton was, and like Milton he took time to ponder his
art of poetry before embarking on composition. In 1659 he wrote
' Stanzas Consecrated to the Glorious Memory of His Serene and
Renouned Highness Oliver ', and in 1660 ' A Poem on the Happy
Restoration and Return of His Sacred Majesty Charles the Second '.
The following year, after a ' Panegyrick ' on Charles's coronation,
Dryden was made Poet Laureate—a public post dating back to
before Chaucer. Intent on becoming an influence in letters Dryden
wrote much for the stage between 1660 and 1680. He ' modernized ', bringing what he saw as the ' rougher ' language of earlier
poets into line with the understanding of his day, Marlowe's *Tamburlaine the Great*, Shakespeare's *The Tempest, Troilus and Cressida* and
Antony and Cleopatra (as *All for Love*). Whilst London theatres were
closed on account of the Great Plague and Great Fire of 1665 and
1666 Dryden turned to criticism in an essay ' On Dramatick Poesie '.
This contained his theory for a totally new poetry: the epic was to
be written in ' heroic couplets '—lines rhyming in pairs, each line
with ten strict syllables (not stresses).

    In 1667 he produced the long *Annus Mirabilis*, ' the glorious
year ', about British success in the rather futile naval war with the
Dutch. Then, determined to put epic satire on a pinnacle, Dryden
produced in 1681 *Absalom and Achitophel*. This contained character
sketches of, among others, already fallen favourites of the King,
the Earl of Shaftesbury and the Duke of Buckingham. Next year
came *The Medall. A Satyre against Sedition*; *MacFlecknoe* was a
crushingly clever diatribe against the dramatist and minor poet
Shadwell, once Dryden's friend. Shadwell had dared attack him
in *The Medal of John Bayes* (1682). Just before Catholic James II
came to the throne, Dryden, having turned to the Church of Rome,
wrote the lyric, ' A Song for Saint Cecilia's Day ', printed in 1687.
Religio Laici (A Layman's Faith) followed in 1682, *The Hind and the*

Panther in 1687, many elegies on the great, and *Fables Ancient and Modern*; these were translations from Homer, Ovid, Boccaccio and Chaucer; and ' in our own language, as it is now refined ' he wrote a secular masque, *The Pilgrim*.

Dryden, whose sincerity as a writer is sometimes called in doubt, wrote of Charles II as ' the God-like David '. Yet his portrait of a minister already arraigned is saved (as not all the word-portraits in his work are saved) by a fine balance in his disparaging wit:

> Of these the false Achitophel was first:
> A name to all succeeding Ages curst.
> For close Designs, and crooked Counsels fit;
> Sagacious, Bold, and Turbulent of wit: . . .
> A fiery Soul, which working out its way,
> Fretted the Pigmy Body to decay:
> And o'r inform'd the Tenement of Clay.[3]

This same poet writes:

Chorus:

> Then our Age was in it's Prime,
> Free from Rage, and free from Crime,
> A very Merry, Dancing, Drinking,
> Laughing, Quaffing, and unthinking Time.[4]

and:

> All all, of a piece throughout;
> The Chase had a Beast in View;
> The Wars brought nothing about;
> The Lovers were all untrue.
> 'Tis well an Old Age is out,
> And time to begin a New.[5]

' The true end of Satyre ,' Dryden wrote in his Preface to *Absalom and Achitophel*, ' is the amendment of vices by correction. And he who writes honestly, is no more an enemy to the Offendour, than the Physician to the Patient .'

A. E. Housman has written of Dryden's deliberate change to

[3] Text from Dryden, *Poems and Fables* (Oxford Univ. Press, 1967).
[4] Ibid.
[5] Ibid.

satire in English poetry as a ' self-corrupted taste and the false guidance of his ambition '. Matthew Arnold has noted the ' touch of frost ' on Dryden's imagination. It is true that satire, however intellectually clear-eyed, works negatively. Its very strength is in some way connected with what can only be called ' spiritual ' disillusion.

Dryden, also remembered as ' the father of English prose ', wrote prose that is clear and flexible. But English prose was begotten long before and by much more mixed ancestry than one father—Deloney, Greene, Tyndale, the forty-seven translators and revisers of the Authorised Version of the Bible, Dorothy Osborne, Bunyan, Locke, Jeremy Taylor and many others came before him.

T. S. Eliot affirmed that Dryden had a ' commonplace ' mind. But of Dryden's poetry, as distinct from what he judged of Dryden's mind, Eliot wrote: ' Dryden set standards for English verse which it is desperate to ignore.'

Neither Milton nor Dryden cared whether poetry reached a great number of people. They were concerned with necessary standards and the intellectual development of verse. By the close of the seventeenth century epic poetry, as well as drama and lyric poetry, had become the literary interest of the few. They were not yet a part of the humanity of a nation, as, in barbaric days, ritual poetry and prose had been part of people's daily life.

V

The Eighteenth Century

1702 - 1798

The Rise of Journalism

From the close of the seventeenth century until almost the middle of the eighteenth there was no overtly spectacular change in the literary style of British poets. Dryden died in 1700. Alexander Pope, born in 1688, followed Dryden in maintaining standards of ' wit ' or intellectual brilliance in the continued use of the rhymed, ten-syllable lines we call the heroic couplet. But change and development went on, quietly, often subterraneously.

The eighteenth century has more prose than poetry, and new uses for prose start at the very outset of the age. Queen Anne's London, from 1702 to 1714, was a society that was growing more and more self-conscious and therefore capable of self-scrutiny and self-criticism. Coffee-houses had been a feature of London begun under Protector Cromwell in a sack- and ale-drinking public that was turning to gin. Now coffee-houses multiplied. They housed professional poets and men of letters, and attracted others. Given to talk, interested in ideas and in each other's personalities, these coffee-house haunters were the new literary men. They were intent on fostering what had originated with Dryden—the idea of a great literature.

Religious dissension and discussion remained in Britain after religious persecution diminished. Ferocious political rivalries replaced persecution; though pillorying and imprisonment for political and religious offences, as for debt, persisted.

The names Whig and Tory, indicating those who wished for improvement through change and those who sought to preserve the *status quo*, came into being. Beneath a comparatively few leaders, of wealth and title, the mass of the islanders stayed poor, often ill-housed and ill-educated. But the need for spreading news, information, and so improvement had, following the religious pamphleteering of the previous century, increased. Printers, booksellers, bookshops, were multiplying; and since the first sheets of foreign news of 1622, factual bulletins were much in demand. The first news journal, *The London Gazette* (at first *The Oxford Gazette*), was soon followed by many papers and periodicals.

The man we think of as among the first of British journalists was the son of a London butcher, Daniel Defoe. Little is known of Defoe's life until he produced, in 1701, *The True-Born Englishman*. *The True-Born Englishman* supported William of Orange. Defoe had to work secretly because of the dangers inherent in what he was attempting to do. Ignominiously set in the pillory in 1703, and again in 1707, on the first occasion Defoe was pelted and insulted by a howling mob. On the second, he was acclaimed a hero. In 1704 he began *The Review*. Its aim was a liberal balance of more informed opinion. Defoe is thought to have written most of *The Review* himself, working steadily for the Union of the Scottish and English parliaments, which came about in 1707. Later he employed assistants. He was imprisoned a second time in 1713. After that, he was more cautious and secret than ever, chary of pillory and prison. He seems even more deliberately to have cloaked his movements whilst being political agent for Queen Anne's two ministers, Godolphin and Oxford. Yet he brought out *Mercator*, one of the first trade journals, and a liberal one. The amazing thing is the man's untiring versatility: in pamphlet after pamphlet, book after book.

What most of us remember best is Defoe's desert-island story. Not until he was nearly sixty, in 1719, did he produce *Robinson Crusoe*. It is a symbolic story of man's resourcefulness when stripped of almost everything. Crusoe's candid correction of his first, ignorant estimate of Man Friday is moving and revealing in the context of today. Defoe's prose is vivid and forthright.

In 1722 came *Moll Flanders*. Scholars find some evidence that Moll was a real woman Defoe could well have known. The book has that quality essential to the novel: its creator's capacity to identify with and speak through the mouths of very different characters. Defoe's novels are a great advance on Nashe's or Deloney's.

1722 also saw Defoe's *Journal of the Plague Year*. He had been four at the time that disaster killed at least a hundred thousand Londoners; but he recorded events with a detached yet vivid pen. In

1724 he produced *The Fortunate Mistress*, its title later changed to *Roxana*, the story of a high-class prostitute.

Only at his death in 1731 did Defoe's astounding output cease. A complete edition of his work is still to come. Whether he was a patriot of genius, or a first-class literary mercenary, is still being argued about. He could well have been both.

Political writing, under undeveloped parliamentary rule and in a country unsettled after the quarrels of the preceding century, remained largely scurrilous. A movement to correct literary involvement with political parties was stirring. Once dire religious and political punishments were abolished, this balancing element sought to improve social *mores* by laughing out of existence crudities and intolerance of many kinds.

The names we associate with this tolerance in the making are Richard Steele and Joseph Addison. Steele, a convivial, restless, ex-captain of the Coldstream Guards, was a light-hearted Irishman with some knowledge of the classics. He produced *The Christian Hero* in 1701. Eight years later he hit on a better way of reaching a wider audience, a way more effective than the occasional pamphlet days of sparser print had allowed. In 1709 Steele began the weekly journal, *The Tatler*; in 1711 he and Joseph Addison launched *The Spectator*. In both these, at their beginnings, essays were short. Citizens' foibles lurked in portraits meant to inform and correct, not by theological threat or vitriolic satire, but by gentle irony and good humour.

Comedies

Steele wrote for the stage. His comedies are superficial, at once less ' exquisite ' and less febrile than Restoration plays. Drama in the new century was not memorable. *The Beggar's Opera* (1728) of John Gay temporarily brought populace and high society together again by its success in London and Bath. Polly Peachum's songs were sung in and outside the capital; the atmosphere of the opera appealed to the youth of the nation and brings to mind Gay's own epitaph in Westminster Abbey: ' Life is a jest and all things show it./I thought so once, and now I know it ! '

The comedy writers Oliver Goldsmith and Richard Brinsley

Sheridan were both Irishmen. Goldsmith's *The Good-natured Man*
was produced in 1768 and *She Stoops to Conquer* in 1773. Sheridan's
The Rivals came in 1775, *The School for Scandal* two years later, and
his farce *The Critic* in 1779. These plays are not reports on universal
or individual human nature. They do not come from any deep
strata of experience. They are concerned, as the century was, with
outward dignities and decencies.

Poetry

The eighteenth century has been called, variously, the age of
manners, the golden age of prose, the age of reason, the classical
age, the Augustan age, the age of corruption, the age of urbanity,
and the age of elegance. Two distinct layers of poetry remained.
One kept the satiric mode carried over from Dryden and the
seventeenth century that we associate with the literary centre in
London. The other layer was much less overt, less heard in the
capital. This second layer strengthens towards the century's close.
It strengthens amid the social changes until a completely new
poetic form emerges.

In an age when verbal violence sought, however vainly or
prematurely, to temper physical force, satire was a useful weapon
for poetry. Alexander Pope is the eighteenth century's satirical
poet. Frail and deformed, educated at home and largely by his own
reading, from the age of twelve Pope had a faculty for metre and
rhyme which he developed long and patiently.

Pope invented no new form for poetry. He took Dryden's satiric
mode and Dryden's rhymed couplet as his models. Ill-health,
ambition, an urge to excel, sensitivity, self-awareness, a need to
while away ' that long disease my life ', were what guided him. He
was a more polished poet than his mentor. His dancing epigrams
and stately verse were composed with strict regard for the poetic
conventions of the day. Pope believed in Dryden's ' poetic diction ':
only certain subjects could in themselves be poetic; therefore
certain attitudes and words only might be used in metrical composition. Meadows must be ' flowery meads '; wood paths were
most frequently ' bosky glades '; girls were almost always ' nymphs ';
hours were, with a non-English frequency, ' rosy-bosomed '.

It can be said that this kind of thinking leads straight to artificiality in poetry. Dryden and Pope both ordered and ornamented
poetry as in the seventeenth century Browne and Burton ordered
and ornamented their prose. Yet Dryden and Pope believed in
unending effort towards honesty in poetry: ' First follow Nature,
and your judgment frame/By her just standard '; ' A *little learning*
is a dang'rous thing '; ' True Wit is Nature to advantage dress'd ';
' Be thou the first true merit to befriend '. But: ' Blunt truths more
mischief than nice falsehoods do '. All these maxims are from Pope's
Essay on Criticism. Detesting ' false eloquence ' he relied on ' taste '
(often in the sense of ' tact '), on judgment and learning; he thought
these could be acquired by ' rules ', laws of ' good breeding '.
' Wit ', with intellectual balance, and satire not ' base' or ' obscene ',
saved ' immortal ' poetry from the worst pitfall of ' dullness '.

Living near London, intent on becoming known, Pope at sixteen
was writing pastoral verse. By 1711 he was known for his *Essay on
Criticism*. Soon after *The Rape of the Lock*, first published in 1712, he
was famous beyond London. *The Rape* is sometimes said to be the
perfect satiric poem. According to William Hazlitt, Charles Lamb
declared that he could read it over and over again. Pope wrote this
story of how a ' gallant ' snipped a lock from a society ' nymph's '
hair and the two families quarrelled over the incident. Replete with
fays, elves, fairies and spirits, the artificial and the sentimental in
the poem are both allayed by a superb balance of satirical wit; this
is akin to that ' touch of frost ' Matthew Arnold felt in Dryden.
Whether or not one dotes on card parties, this poem delights by its
verbal brilliance.

Again following Dryden, Pope turned to translation. No Greek
scholar, he rendered Homer's *Iliad* and *Odyssey* into the fashionable
' heroic couplets '. For this he received some £8,000 and alleviated
further fear of poverty or neglect.

But, surveying the poetic scene around him, Pope's rigorous
standards were not satisfied. Booksellers and publishers were, he
deemed, forcing poets to hack-work from which the dreaded ' dullness ' resulted. In 1728 in *The Dunciad* Pope ridiculed less secure
poets, as Dryden had ridiculed some of his contemporaries in
MacFlecknoe. *The Dunciad* is dexterous but not good-natured, not
really disinterested or detached. It is brilliant, balanced verse, but
its subject is a past cause now, interesting chiefly to literary scholars.
Its historical interest outweighs it as poetry. Pope's deformity and

continued ill-health often turned into resentment of his fellows. However much he strove consciously to transmute resentment into the most careful art, *The Dunciad* will not ' stand alone ', as poetry should; it needs this reference to its creator's circumstances.

By 1734 Pope had published four parts of *An Essay on Man* in one volume. This contains four Epistles to Henry St John, Viscount Bolingbroke, for whom, as a man if not as a poet, Pope had a curious admiration. The Epistles treat of ' Man and the Universe ', ' Man as an Individual ', ' Man and Society ' and ' Man with Respect to Happiness '.

Edward Young is essentially an eighteenth-century poet. The nine cantos of his *Complaint, or Night Thoughts on Life, Death, and Immortality*, which came out in parts between 1742 and 1745, had a wide popularity difficult to understand today. Yet some of his lines are familiar enough:

> Procrastination is the thief of time, . . .
> At thirty man suspects himself a fool;
> Knows it at forty, and reforms his plan;
> At fifty chides his infamous delay,
> Pushes his prudent purpose to resolve;
> In all the magnanimity of thought
> Resolves; and re-resolves; then, dies the same.

Robert Blair's one and only poem, *The Grave*, was published in 1743. This poem is not satiric and, despite its title, not very dismal. Blair tells what he owed to friendship:

> Oh ! when my friend and I
> In some thick wood have wandered heedless on . . . ,
> Oh ! then the longest summer's day
> Seemed too, too much in haste; still the full heart
> Had not imparted half: 'twas happiness
> Too exquisite to last.

Prose

The most prolific writer of prose satire in the eighteenth century was Jonathan Swift. Born in Dublin of English parents in 1667, Swift was early left fatherless. During all his childhood and youth he was dependent on the charity of relatives. Sir William Temple's wife, Dorothy Osborne, and Dryden, were his relatives. Reading in the Temples' library, Swift, destined for the Church, began to write at an early age. ' Cousin Swift, you will never be a poet,' Dryden warned him.

Two prose satires from Swift's pen in 1704, *A Tale of a Tub* and *The Battle of the Books*, published anonymously, brought him recognition. They did not bring the preferment in the Church Swift desired. *A Tale of a Tub* is about Peter, Martin and Jack, who represent the Catholic, Lutheran and Anglican quarrels of Swift's day. *The Battle of the Books* is on classical versus ' modern ' learning. Both these subjects are causes long dead, and few but scholars and students read either satire today. Until 1727, Swift, Chaplain to the Lord Deputy of Ireland, visited London regularly; regularly he attacked the Whigs in satirical pamphlets, wondering why Queen Anne disliked him. At her death in 1714 he was given the deanery of St Patrick's, Dublin.

He published *Gulliver's Travels* in 1726. Captain Lemuel Gulliver voyages to remote islands—to Lilliput where the people are six inches high, to Brobdingnag where they are as tall as church-steeples, to Laputa and to the island inhabited by the reasonable horses, Houyhnhnms, with their slaves the revolting Yahoos. This bitter satire, originally written for adults, nevertheless has a simplicity which has captivated generations of the young.

Swift was ever conscious of the plight of the Irish, of their devastating poverty. His *Drapier's Letters* (1724), published under the pseudonym M. B. Drapier (Drapier=Draper), was written to incite the Irish against a new coinage, ' Wood's half-pence ', and a reward of £300 was offered for betraying its author's identity. This was well known, but proof was not forthcoming from Swift's loyal Irish admirers. Among his more celebrated minor prose satires was *A Modest Proposal for preventing the Children of the Poor from being a Burden to their Parents or the Country* (1729), mysteriously published as most of his writings were. Here the savage irony speaks for itself:

. . . I have been assured by a very knowing *American* of my acquaintance in *London*, that a young healthy Child well Nursed is at a year Old a most delicious, nourishing, and wholesome Food, whether *Stewed, Roasted, Baked,* or *Boyled,* and I make no doubt that it will equally serve in a *Fricasie,* or a *Ragoust.*

I do therefore humbly offer it to *publick* consideration, that of the hundred and twenty thousand Children, already computed, twenty thousand may be reserved for Breed . . . and . . . That the remaining hundred thousand may at a year Old be offered in Sale to the *persons of Quality*, and *Fortune*, throughout the Kingdom, always advising the Mother to let them Suck plentifully in the last Month, so as to render them Plump, and Fat for a good Table.[1]

Horrifying human conditions sometimes demand cutting descriptions, designed to shock. This approach no doubt opened a few eyes to a misery for which, over centuries, the English were largely responsible.

Swift himself, for all his satiric strength, was not temperamentally robust. He seems, for instance, to have had a repugnance for the physical aspect in relationships. His love for Hester Vanhomrigh produced ' Cadenus and Vanessa '. Of his long relationship with Esther Johnson, reflected in *Journal to Stella* (1766/8),[2] he wrote how much more satisfying he found friendship than love. His ' Verses on the Death of Dr S. Written by Himself, November, 1731 ' foretell his tragic end:

> Perhaps I may allow the Dean
> Had too much Satyr in his Vein;
> And seem'd determin'd not to starve it,
> Because no age could more deserve it.
> Yet Malice never was his aim; . . .
>
> He gave the little wealth he had
> To build a house for fools and mad;
> And shewed by one satirick touch
> No nation wanted it so much.[3]

The figure of Samuel Johnson dominated the mid-eighteenth-century literary scene in London. The last Stuart monarch, with her war-loving, fortune-gathering Marlborough, had given place

---

[1] Text from *Swift*, ed. John Hayward (Nonesuch Press, 1949).
[2] A series of letters written for Esther Johnson. Letters 1 and 41-65 were published in Hawkesworth's edn of Swift's works in 1766; Letters 2-40 in Deane Swift's edn in 1768. G. A. Aitken's annotated edn appeared in 1901.
[3] Text from *Swift*, ed. John Hayward, pp. 823-4.

to the first Georges, the settled German dynasty of the Hanoverians, ancestors of the Windsors. Robert Walpole, a master of finance, was in office as Prime Minister between 1721 and 1742. Until 1739, when war with Spain was declared against his wish, Walpole controlled British policy. He enjoyed bottle and table, but not books, and he encouraged peace and free trade. He made a fortune larger than Marlborough's but gagged no opponent. The older aristocratic families were still dominant in both the House of Commons and the House of Lords and enjoyed their country estates. They had growing commercial interests, too, in coal and iron.

Gradually new men of commerce appeared. Profits were increasing—from what is now seen as exploitation, as any book on the slave trade abroad and industrial conditions at home will disclose. Overseas plantations were developed. Through vigour and by astute trading with poorer peoples, the British Empire began. As has occurred many times before in history, civilization—this time British—by trade and conquest, travelled to remote parts of the earth which might otherwise have remained uninfluenced by change for much longer. In Britain, beneath relatively few holders of wealth, the growing mass of people continued uneducated and often ill-housed; and thus only with infinite slowness did they grow more capable of thinking beyond the narrow content of everyday lives.

After Walpole, who could administer peace but not war, William Pitt the elder, ' the great commoner ' who became Earl of Chatham, prosecuted the Seven Years' War with determination and courage whilst jointly leading a coalition with Lord Newcastle. William Pitt the younger, the elder Pitt's second son, became Prime Minister in 1783 when he was only twenty-four years old. Pitt the younger sought to maintain peace but died in 1806, in the middle of the war against Napoleon. Coal, steam and factory inventions were beginning to make obsolete home and cottage industries, and so to alter the lives and occupations of many people in Britain. The Industrial Revolution was in its initial stages. In the succeeding century, ocean-going steamships would help consolidate the empire the first Pitt worked to set in being.

In 1776 the American colonies seized their independence from the empire. In 1789 France's Revolution set up the idealistic but unforgettable cry against oppression: *Liberté, Egalité, Fraternité*. Then came the disillusioning Terror, followed by the dictatorship of Napoleon. Though the younger Pitt was for peace, the great Irish orator, Edmund Burke, was not. There was war between France and Britain from 1793 until Wellington's victory at Waterloo in 1815.

The second half of the eighteenth century is sometimes said to have begun the modern age. Dare one say the modern age holds a wider tolerance of man for man? If either of these statements has any validity, we should see and hear something of this humanity and sympathy in what Johnson did and what he said. Born in 1709, the son of a Lichfield bookseller, Johnson knew books, that world within this world, almost from his cradle. He went up to Oxford and came down without a degree but with a great deal of knowledge. He married and went to London when he was twenty-eight. Convinced a living could be made out of writing he endured poverty for a time. He wrote for *The Gentleman's Magazine* and began a periodical, *The Rambler*. In 1765 he published an edition of Shakespeare. At length, through essays that were learned yet had profound moral sense, in a more successful periodical, *The Idler*, but also through a readiness to help any friend in distress, Johnson became known and loved by many.

This huge, ugly, carelessly dressed man with the capacious memory, a ' hardened and shameless Tea-drinker ', was also a coffee-house talker. He spoke little about himself; he invited people to clear their minds of cant; and he was ready to pronounce, even indomitably to lay down the law, or propound his prejudices, on most other matters. Hear him on the confinement of one of his poet acquaintances, Christopher Smart, in a madhouse:

> I did not think he ought to be shut up. His infirmities were not noxious to society. He insisted on people praying with him; and I'd as lief pray with Kit Smart as with any one else. Another charge was, that he did not love clean linen; and I have no passion for it.[4]

Two pensioners lived in Johnson's house many years; when one of them, the aged Robert Levett, ' a practiser in Physic ', died, Johnson wrote with shrewd but affectionate regard:

[4] James Boswell, *Life of Samuel Johnson* (selections), ed. R. W. Chapman (Oxford: Clarendon Press, 1919), p. 39.

Obscurely wise and coarsely kind . . .
His virtues walk'd their narrow round,
Nor made a pause, nor left a void;
And sure th' Eternal Master found
The single talent well employ'd.

Most men of letters in the eighteenth century could compose a verse; Johnson's ' The Vanity of Human Wishes ', in the rhymed couplet, reminds us of what our perpetual hunt for ' happiness ' ignores; there is fear, hope, wisdom, power, war; but as Johnson— determined like most eighteenth-century writers not to see beyond what so obviously *was*—does not hide:

In Life's last Scene what prodigies surprise,
Fears of the Brave, and Follies of the Wise !
From Marlborough's Eyes the Streams of Dotage flow,
And Swift expires a Driv'ler and a Show.

Johnson's prose story, or short novel, *Rasselas*, is about a Prince of Abyssinia who set out to find the elusive happiness. In a great continent of simpler life, of astonishing beauty and variety, happiness might be glimpsed but never captured. *Rasselas* has been much translated. It suffers as little from being translated as by being over two hundred years old.

In spite of the slowness with which education spread in Britain more and more people did read for pleasure, as if the legacy of knowledge could not be suppressed. Miscellanies of information multiplied. The great daily papers came into being: *The Times, The Morning Post*. There had been vocabularies in plenty. Johnson turned to what he had been thinking of a long time, a full *Dictionary of the English Language*. He was convinced the pronunciation of our language should be ' fixed ', brought under rule and law. He espied a great need concerning our ' unsettled spelling '. English spelling *was* unsettled. It was still left almost to individual choice. Johnson's gigantic task took him eight years. By the time it was finished he had learnt that, even whilst his book was hastening to press, ' some words are budding, and some falling away '. His *Dictionary* was not perfect, as he had meant it to be. A ' living language ' could not be ' fixed '. Johnson's work has long been superseded; but his love of words and of defining meanings makes it still a fascinating book.

When he was sixty-seven he undertook another enormous enterprise. This was *Lives of the Poets*. Johnson had been going to write on Shakespeare who, after being thought of as belonging to a barbarous past, was just beginning to be admired. Shakespeare is not inincluded in *Lives of the Poets*. Nor is Chaucer. The work was undertaken for booksellers who made their stipulations. It begins at Abraham Cowley and includes fifty-two poets. Johnson grew so interested in his task that it became much longer than he intended. His method is to give facts of a poet's life first and then to discuss and criticize the poetry. He does not insist that a poet's life and his poetry are closely linked, but personal character clearly interested him. He is true to his eighteenth-century justice of balance, and when he does not like a poet, as in the case of Milton, he is careful to praise after giving damning facts on Milton's arrogance. Of Swift, from whose ' depravity of intellect ' he thought ' every other mind shrinks with disgust ', he closed his account with the words of one of Swift's admirers. Perhaps it is Johnson's concept of tolerance that is modern.

In 1763, James Boswell, the son of the Scottish laird of Auchinleck, met Johnson and became so great an admirer that he set about noting down the conversation of the ' great moralist ' and Man of Letters. Boswell's *Life of Samuel Johnson* came out in 1791, seven years after Johnson's death. It is one of the first of full-length biographies, and it is still one of the best. Boswell explains how, ' wrapt in admiration of (Johnson's) extraordinary colloquial talents':

> when my mind was, as it were, *strongly impregnated with the Johnsonian aether*, I could, with much facility and exactness, carry it in my memory and commit to paper the exuberant variety of his wisdom and wit.

The Rise of the Novel

In the eighteenth century letters went by messenger, on foot or on horseback; there was no postal delivery; travel was by horse-drawn coach; there were no police; brawls and duels were not infrequent; unlighted thoroughfares, roads deep in mud, streets with refuse cast about, and highways and byways infested by thieves and footpads were common. Clearly there was a need for reading matter at home. Press, pamphlets, plays and handwritten missives were not enough for an age of increasing literacy.

In 1740, in a two-volume edition written in the form of letters, a bookseller named Samuel Richardson put out the first full-length novel, *Pamela*. In 1741 a second, larger part was added. Two years later a lawyer, Henry Fielding, wrote a satiric, masculine counterblast, *Joseph Andrews*. Fielding's *Tom Jones*, in 1749, and his *Amelia*, in 1751, made him known. Richardson's second novel, *Clarissa Harlowe*, was published in two volumes in 1747 and in five in 1748. Its immense length indicates the amount of leisure then enjoyed by the well-to-do. Women, from the first greater readers of fiction than men, were Richardson's audience.

The exploration of character and character motive in *Clarissa Harlowe* pointed a way the novel could advance. It is a story of the property marriage then usual among ambitious families. Arranged marriages had been discarded among the unillustrious, though girls still received and listened to practical advice from parents and friends. Clarissa, an intelligent, beautiful, pious girl of eighteen, was to be forced by parents, elder brother and uncles into marriage with a much older, illiterate but wealthy man: this arrangement was to gain money and lands, and a chance for her elder brother of a coveted title. Rather than marry a man she cannot love, Clarissa flees from home. Another suitor, a wealthy rake who has declared his devotion, betrays her when she seeks his protection: not believing in her ignorance of the world, and enraged by her steady refusal to marry him, he rapes her. Clarissa dies of a ' broken heart ', alone.

Summed up thus, *Clarissa* would perhaps be no more than a ' tedious lamentation ', as Horace Walpole described it. But besides its well-drawn individual characters, it is a stinging indictment of the material snobberies of the time; on a third plane, and unlike *Pamela*, it is a tragedy illustrating moral weaknesses inextricable from human strengths; it echoes well beyond its age.

Reading of novels caught on. Tobias Smollett (whom George Orwell thought Scotland's best novelist) published *Peregrine Pickle* in 1751 and *Humphry Clinker* in 1771. These with Laurence Sterne's nine-volume *The Life and Opinions of Tristram Shandy, Gentleman* (1760-7), were similar to *Tom Jones* in their long ramblings of often only slightly related incidents and their many digressions. All reveal the outspokenness and lusty directness which existed side by side with eighteenth-century attempts at refined elegance. Digressions came straight from the author. This technique was recognition of the artificial character of fiction. Not until the twentieth century was a sustained illusion of reality thought necessary for the novel to be effective as art.

Sterne also wrote *A Sentimental Journey* (1768); *The Bramine's Journal* (to Mrs Eliza Draper) and his *Letters of Yorick to Eliza* were printed in 1775. He was a country parson, and his volumes of *Sermons* are undogmatic and clear-sighted. There has been much controversy about his writing and character since *Tristram Shandy* was denounced as immoral by Dr Johnson, Richardson, Horace Walpole, Goldsmith, and later by Thackeray. Yet it was very much read. Sterne advanced the novel by his joining of realism to character and humour and to what has been called sentimentality. Dickens owed much to him. Perhaps one of the central facts about this parson-novelist who suffered from ill-health and a wife who went insane, is that his humane compassion was balanced by a reliance on sensual humour.

Fanny Burney, daughter of Dr Burney, who wrote a *History of Music*, and a favourite of Dr Johnson, published the serio-comic *Evelina, or the History of a Young Lady's Entrance Into the World* anonymously in 1778, and *Cecilia* in 1782. She married a French refugee and her *Early Diaries* of 1768-78 (published in 1889) contain sketches of Johnson and Garrick. Thomas Macaulay in the nineteenth century thought *Evelina* ' the first tale written by a woman . . . that deserved to live '.

Oliver Goldsmith further advanced the possibilities of the novel with *The Vicar of Wakefield* in 1766. An important feature of this story is the fact that it does not consist, as Thomas Deloney's *Jack of Newbury* does, and as Smollett's and Fielding's novels tend to do, of a string of incidents and digressions. *The Vicar of Wakefield* has logical sequence and a unity of event. Ordinary as these events are, they allow a related group of engaging characters to grow in the inevitable way people do grow under life's experiences. Our insatiable curiosity in each other is what lies at the root of all novels. Oliver Goldsmith contrives to satisfy and delight this curiosity in a novel—with a plot—one-quarter the length of *Clarissa Harlowe*.

Philosophy, History and Natural History

This century of prose almost naturally saw an advance in social philosophy. Yet another Irishman, the genial bishop George Berkeley, introduced in 1710, in his *Treatise Concerning the Principles of Human Knowledge*, the theory that from our senses' perception of material things we make our mental images and so our ideas. David Hume, a Scotsman, wrote a *Treatise on Human Nature* (1739-40). Hume's *Inquiry Concerning the Principles of Morals* of 1751 in part recast the earlier work. Religious persecution in Britain had gone; but fear-based, physical and mental ill-treatment of the young, the poor, the insane, the social offender and some still accused of sorcery remained. Torture for daring to think independently about religion was in the past; but harrowing questions of faith and doubt persisted. Hume placed reason above faith. He set this reason against superstition which, he argued, could not but belittle blind faith. The mystic, William Law, in *A Serious Call* and *The Case of Reason, An Appeal to all that Doubt*, pointed out, in opposition, a possible incapacity of reason to convince some vital, invisible part of our make-up. Bishop William Paley also defended faith against this reasoning common sense.

Edward Gibbon recalled admiration for imperial Rome with his history, *The Decline and Fall of the Roman Empire*. In 1789 Gilbert White, a country parson, of Selborne in Hampshire, drew the attention of an increasingly town-loving society to the wealth of plants, birds and animals of which so little was known. Culpepper and other early herbalists had valued flowers and plants chiefly for their uses in disease or as food. In the eighteenth century Linnaeus the Swede showed that all earth's plants and animals belonged within great families and could be systematically classified. Plants and creatures could be known for their own complexity and beauty. White's *Natural History and Antiquities of Selborne* is a series of country letters to Daines Barrington and to a younger, Welsh zoologist, Thomas Pennant, touching a wealth of country matters as well as on then unsolved puzzles such as what swallows do in winter. Pennant's *British Zoology*, *A History of Quadrupeds* and *Arctic Zoology* are excellent in that, as Johnson said, Pennant ' observes more things than any one else does '.

Personal letters were an important way to lighten solitude in days when life was often very cut off and when people needed to be self-reliant. Horace Walpole, the son of the Prime Minister, wrote letters all his life. Staunch admirer of his father, refined and reserved and frail where the elder Walpole was rough and blunt and robust, these two show how personality can change from one generation to another. Dryden's wenching ' wild gallant ' who ' killed his man ' was fading still further into the past in Horace Walpole's generation. Walpole's ' conversations upon paper ' are as readable to those who prefer reality to fiction as they are important to scholars.

Walpole declared he set no store by his literary work; but he thought Fielding so coarse, Richardson so domestically senti-mental and Sterne so immoral that, in 1765, he ' dashed off ' a novel, *The Castle of Otranto*. His intention was to write a story free from both coarseness and sentimentality. The background he hit upon was the ' miraculous '. He found this in old romance. Walpole started modern ' blood-curdling ' stories of the supernatural. To us, now, *The Castle of Otranto* seems elementary, clumsy, artificial. You wonder how the poet Gray could, after reading it, have been ' afraid to go to bed o' nights' or Walter Scott have felt either pity or fear. But Byron, too, praised it.

Walpole also examined the accusations against Richard III. He did not search sources sufficiently to free Richard from all the guilt heaped on him in Tudor days; but most today would agree with the need Walpole saw to re-examine fixed historical judgments.

The third Earl of Chesterfield's *Letters* reveal more eighteenth-century attitudes. Among the wealthy, zealously strict laws on legitimacy protected lands and possessions. Chesterfield's *Letters* are mostly to his illegitimate son, Philip Stanhope, with a few to his nephew, the Earl having no heir. They were meant for no eyes but the boys'. They begin when Philip Stanhope was five. As early as that Chesterfield was exhorting the boy to seek ' knowledge '; but, above all, to get ' manners ', to become a ' gentleman '. Philip turned out intelligent enough but no great lover of books. As a growing boy he played unruly practical jokes. Almost obsessively his father urged him to be ' frank '. Critics have pointed to Chester-field's lack of moral depth—a deficiency of the age. In fact, in these *Letters*, of a father to an illegitimate son, the father tries persistently to make amends for an injustice of which he is clearly aware, a moral dilemma for which there is no remedy.

David Hume's countryman and friend, Adam Smith, held the Chair of Moral Philosophy in the University of Glasgow. Smith argued in *The Wealth of Nations* that the labourer was a hitherto unacknowledged part of the wealth of a community. Care of, and greater justice for, the wage-earning supporters of the new economy, Adam Smith propounded, could not fail to increase the wealth and, in the long run, the true welfare of a state. Smith's book of 1776, however much it has since been misinterpreted and parts of it ignored, set the subject of capital and labour on a scientific basis. Published at the time of the American Declaration of Independence, *The Wealth of Nations* advocated the representation of the colonies in the British Parliament. There had been rebels from below, before this. The rights of rule over the service of the majority had not been seriously questioned from above. Opposing such questioning as dangerous, Edmund Burke, the great Irish political orator, advocated at Westminster the older ideal of benevolence to the many and the indigent by wise rulers and leaders.

Censorship there had been in Britain since Elizabeth I's day. But somehow, though often belatedly, books got published. Thomas Paine's *The Rights of Man* (1791-2), the chief answer to Burke's condemnation of the Declaration of the Rights of Man of the French revolutionaries, was liberal yet dogmatic; it oversimplified complexities. It sold a million and a half copies. Its author, an excise officer who had fled to America over a question of a raise in excise men's pay, then fled to Paris to avoid legal action and possible prosecution. Blunt, tactless, Paine yet belongs to a line of international writers, in that he dared to speak out for what seemed to him elementary but imperative human justice. The short extracts below are taken from *The Rights of Man*:

. . . Reason and Ignorance, the opposite of each other, influence the great bulk of mankind. If either of these can be rendered extensive enough in a country, the machinery of Government goes easily on. Reason obeys itself; and Ignorance submits to whatever is dictated to it. . . .

Each Government accuses the other of perfidy, intrigue, and ambition, as a means of heating the imagination of their respective Nations, and incensing them to hostilities. Man is not the enemy of Man, but through the medium of a false system of Government. . . .

Mary Wollstonecraft Godwin wrote her *Vindication of the Rights of Women* in 1792 and also suffered opprobrium for her straight speaking on such matters as the British legal dependence of wives on husbands, the differing standard between masculine and feminine morals, and the right to ' free ' yet responsible love: the right of each individual to decide his own moral code, provided this code did no harm to others.

As the century continued, the passion—or fashion—for ' wit ' and ' reason ' in prose, and refinement, ' taste ', elegance and satire in poetry, wore out. Since the early decades the strong undercurrent mentioned earlier had been there. This movement among poets was against satire; quiet, direct feeling was preferred above hectic rivalries, heated political interests and intellectual dissensions, in a London where writers were often driven to literary hacking in Grub-street; country quiet was desired by some, more than town grandeurs and pressures.

Changing Poetry

In Isaac Watts's *Hymns and Spiritual Songs* (1707) and his *Divine Songs for Children* (1715) a fresh, if quaint, love of nature and understanding of the young are revealed. Anne Finch, Countess of Winchilsea, praised, in *The Spleen and Other Poems* (1709) some of the serenities of country retirement. James Thomson, in *The Seasons* (1726-30) and sitting at his town window, described country activities, though in language somewhat ' florid and luxuriant '. John Dyer's instructive long poem on ' A nation's wealth ' was titled *The Fleece*, about the wool industry. But fresher than *The Fleece* is Dyer's shorter poem describing the scene around picturesque ' Grongar Hill ' in Wales. Ambrose Philips's *Pastorals* quite needlessly excited the jealousy of Pope. Hardly less needlessly Thomas Tickell's translation of *The Iliad* did the same. Tickell's ballad ' Colin and Lucy ' Gray and Goldsmith thought one of the best in the language. Joseph Warton criticized the ' correct ' school of poetry, and in ' The Lover of Nature ' stated the case for escaping to a less artificial life:

O taste corrupt ! that luxury and pomp,
In specious names of polish'd manners veil'd,
Should proudly banish Nature's simple charms . . .

Oliver Goldsmith in *The Deserted Village* lamented a Lishoy
' where wealth accumulates and *men* decay '. Thomas Gray in
' The Bard ' told of the death of the last of the wandering poets of
early days; and in his *Elegy Written in a Country Churchyard* (1751)
praised those ' mute inglorious ' ones whose lives remain completely
unknown to more than a few. There were poets whose work, cheaply
printed, was—according to Dr Johnson—much more read than is
sometimes thought: up and down the country there were eager
readers. Among these poets were Tickell, Mallet, John Pomfret
(*The Choice*, 1700), Allan Ramsay (*The Gentle Shepherd*, 1725),
William Shenstone (*The Schoolmistress*, 1742), John Cunningham
(*Love in a Mist*, 1747), Mark Akenside (*The Pleasures of the Imagination*, 1757), and James Beattie (*The Minstrel*, 1771/4).

William Collins lived thirty-eight years, often saddened by
melancholy. But his ' Ode to Simplicity ' and his unrhymed ' Ode
to Evening ' plead strongly for a simpler sincerity that would
attempt to hold advancing urbanism at bay by keeping in touch,
both with a simpler, personal ethos and with the fruitful earth
from which all springs.

Thus, the early eighteenth century of Pope had been much
occupied with rules for manners, ceremony, property, heritage, rules
for poetry and prose, spelling and style. But the later part of the
century sought more freedom; poets turned to Britain's own traditions of the Middle Ages and of the so-called Dark Ages. Both
Chaucer, who had been thought uncouth, and Shakespeare, with
his passions and rude laughter, were at last transformed in literary
estimation from barbaric ancestors to great forerunners.

In 1765 Thomas Percy, the bishop son of a grocer, published
many years' gleanings of rapidly vanishing old ballads: *The Reliques
of Ancient English Poetry*, following Allan Ramsay's *The Evergreen*,
pioneer collection, of 1724, is a gateway through which to enter
Britain's past. Much is gone for ever. James Macpherson, a classical
scholar of Edinburgh University, undertook a journey through
the Highlands, detribalized only after the 1745 rebellion which
sought to put the last Stuart on the throne of Britain. Macpherson
went collecting vanishing Gaelic poetry, of which he acquired

considerable knowledge. He published a long prose-poem, *Fingal*, in 1762, and another, *Temora*, in 1763. *Fingal* recounts the vanquishing of Swaren and his ' sea-strangers ' by the Caledonian chief Fingal and other Gaelic heroes. Macpherson's claim was that Ossian the bard, Fingal's son, when lonely and old, had told these stories of the third century when Celtic hillmen were holding out against Roman-dominated conquest. Ossian's legends were written down, according to Macpherson, in Celtic verse. Their translation into English prose-poetry was what Macpherson claimed he had done. But Dr Johnson spoke against ' Caledonian bigotry and barbarism ', against ' fustian bombast '. Some charged Macpherson with compiling his long poems of chieftainship, of comradely loyalty and reckless valour from fragments only. He refused to produce what alone could have cleared him of the charge. Whilst decrying the legends of ancient Ireland, he compared Caledonian poetry with Homer's. The mystery in which both lay wrapped was similar. Ossian's background would have been of an heroic age; Macpherson's poems are tinged with the medieval and the romantic as well. Yet his talented enthusiasm roused the interest of Goethe and many others in Europe as well as of many in Britain. Once, Celt and Gael had spanned northern Europe; they may have originated farther south near the ancient Greeks and so have had ethnic connection with them. The rhythmic verse-prose of *Fingal*, *Temora*, *The Songs of Selma* and the rest of Macpherson's translations or adaptations, with their ' ringing of shield and spear ', their bloodshed, their praise of death in battle, their romantic loyalties, is stirring to read. But since Macpherson's death in 1796 the Ossianic poems have been little reprinted.

About a year or two after the publication of *Fingal* and *Temora*— later in the 1760s—a gifted boy born in 1752, Thomas Chatterton, was also delving in his country's past. Chatterton pretended to find, in the muniment room of the Abbey of St Mary Redcliffe at Bristol, some fifteenth-century poems by one Thomas Rowley, a monk. Inspired by Spenser and using a Chaucer gloss to hunt out rare old words, Chatterton, of the Percy-Macpherson breed, celebrated the traditional heritage of Britain rather than the legacy of her conquerors. Going to London to seek his literary fortune, Chatterton endured a few months of dire poverty in a garret there; but in 1770, at the age of seventeen, he took his own promising life in despair at poverty, the discouragement he faced, or from fear of sickness.

Only one poem by Rowley appeared in Chatterton's lifetime, ' Elinoure and Juga ', published in the *Town and Country Magazine* in 1769. ' Poems supposed to have been written . . . by Thomas Rowley ' were published in 1777 and 1778 and Chatterton's fraud exposed.

William Cowper, a shy and retiring poet, lived much of his adult life in the care of his friend Mrs Mary Unwin. Cowper wrote *The Diverting History of John Gilpin* (1782), hymns, and six books of *The Task* (1785)—' The Sofa ', ' The Time-piece ', ' The Garden ', ' The Winter Evening ', ' The Winter Walk ', ' The Winter Walk at Noon '. Cowper's hymns and all his verse point unobtrusively to the simpler, country-loving poetry soon to become general in Britain.

George Crabbe's long poems, *The Village* (1783), *The Parish Register* and *The Borough* (both 1810), clung determinedly to the rhymed couplets of Dryden, Pope and Johnson, as Crabbe clung to an eighteenth-century realism he thought in danger. He rejected the pastoral convention of Theocritus and Virgil decried by Johnson in Milton's ' Lycidas ' and revived in Crabbe's day by Goldsmith in *The Deserted Village*. Crabbe was resisting what he saw as a growing false sentiment about traditional peacefulness. Son of the sternest of fathers, as a village parson-poet Crabbe set out to expose the rude hardship of country life, as he saw it, and the sordid, uncouth manners of the rural ' clown '. The inhabitants of the scene where ' Nature's niggard hand/Gave a spare portion ' Crabbe described as ' . . . a wild, amphibious race,/With sullen woe displayed on every face '. They were ' bold, artful, surly, savage '. ' Some with feebler heads and fainter hearts/Deplore their fortune '.

Half of *The Village* is taken up with a dedication to the Duke of Rutland of the rather fulsome kind Johnson spoke against. But it makes clear Crabbe's desire to show the poor to the rich with as honest a balance as he knew:

> How would ye bear to draw your latest breath
> Where all that's wretched paves the way for death ?
> Such is that room which one rude beam divides,
> Where naked rafters form the sloping sides;
> Where the vile bands that bind the thatch are seen,
> And lath and mud are all that lie between;

Save one dull pane, that, coarsely patch'd, gives way
To the rude tempest, yet excludes the day:
Here, on a matted flock, with dust o'erspread,
The drooping wretch reclines his languid head;
For him no hand the cordial cup applies,
Or wipes the tear that stagnates in his eyes; . . .
　　But soon a loud and hasty summons calls,
Shakes the thin roof and echoes round the walls . . .
A potent quack, long versed in human ills,
Who first insults the victim whom he kills;
Whose murd'rous hand a drowsy Bench protect,
And whose most tender mercy is neglect. . . .

Whilst Crabbe was writing and well before the close of the century
a new way of seeing brought a totally different kind of poetry. John
Wesley was inspiring religious hope afresh. A lyric richness and a
ballad simplicity gave an impulse to defy poetic rules and eighteenth-
century intellectual wit. This did not despise Crabbe's harsh compassion, but it was itself less grim; owing more to emotion and feeling, its impulse at least was more generous.

Robert Burns was born in Ayrshire in 1759, of farming stock. His
' lallans ' or lowland Scottish poetry of laughing defiance—' Tam o'
Shanter ', ' Holy Willie's Prayer ', Address to the Deil ', ' To a
Mouse ', and his lyrics and love songs (many adapted from traditional folk songs)—burst like sunshine on the 1780s. Audaciously
they expressed and explored the completely new outlook, to become
in their turn traditional. ' Auld Lang Syne ' is still sung at the end
of convivial parties. Burns's best-known lyrics run to music, since
they were based on traditional songs. Such are ' My Luve is like a
Red, Red Rose ', ' John Anderson, my Jo ', ' The Rigs o' Barley '.
Burns was admired and influenced by his slightly older Scottish
contemporary, Robert Fergusson, who died at twenty-four in 1774.
The lyrical satire of, for instance, ' To a Louse; on seeing one on a
lady's bonnet at Church ' is strongly reminiscent of Fergusson's
' Braid Claith '.

More vehemently than Cowper, less harshly than Crabbe, more
solemnly than Burns, and whilst William Wordsworth was still a
boy on the fells mimicking owls, William Blake, in *Songs of Innocence*
(1789) and *Songs of Experience* (1794), also offered a new vision. A
new vision of life and humanity, Blake said, could arise only out of

poetry. But his poetry was steeped, as Kathleen Raine has shown, in medieval mysticism. The century of external manners, elegance, classical balance and beauty, and the rule of law, had clapped Johnson's friend, Christopher Smart, the poet of *A Song to David*, into a prison for the insane. It considered Wordsworth's ' marvellous boy ', Thomas Chatterton, as well as Savage, Collins and Cowper, mad. Jonathan Swift ended his life of protest against many kinds of civilized stupidity in the twilight of a broken mind. In spite of Johnson's impregnable humour and profoundly normal sense, he too suffered from a melancholy he said sometimes was near madness. Some of Blake's contemporaries did not fail, when his poetry began to reject the accepted moral, coercive order, to see Blake as an eccentric or even mad. However, his genius acknowledged by a few, such as Thomas Paine, William Godwin, Mary Wollstonecraft and the diarist Henry Crabb Robinson, Blake was content to live a retired, humble life.

He turned from what he wrote of in the Preface to his *Milton* as the ' Stolen and Perverted Writings of Homer and Ovid, of Plato and Cicero ' to the ' Sublime of the Bible '. Using the ballad quatrain in simplest form, his earliest book was *Poetical Sketches* (1783). Ideas of liberty, from the American and French revolutions, were in the air. Blake wrote *America* (1793) and *Europe* (1794) in long unrhymed lines of fourteen syllables. His prophetic books, *The Book of Urizen* (1794), *The Book of Ahania*, *The Book of Los* (1795), *Milton*, the long *Jerusalem*, and *Vala* (1797, later expanded to *The Four Zoas*), outline a philosophy compounded from his own titanic originality and his reading of medieval mystics—Swedenborg, William Law, Jacob Boehme and J. G. Herder.

Blake proclaimed that ' The Poetic Genius is the true Man ' and ' As all men are alike in outward form, so all are alike in the Poetic Genius.' He believed the physical world, the ' mundane shell ', to be ' a shadow of the world of eternity '. Eternal life could be here as well as after death. The ' poetic imagination ' Blake saw as the key to eternal, spiritual life. Two gigantic, multiple forces oppose and fight each other in Creation. The first is the poetic imagination which each one of us possesses; the second, for Blake, sterile, rigid materialism, caused by the principle of reason in religious, authoritarian, moral law. This second nullified for him the primal joy, Truth, and innocence in human beings who are part of the Divine being. True life, divine life, can only, he thought, be born of perfect liberty. In the Preface to *Jerusalem*:

> I know of no other Christianity and of no other Gospel than the liberty both of body and mind to exercise the Divine Arts of Imagination, Imagination, the real and eternal World of which this Vegetable Universe is but a faint shadow, and in which we shall live in our Eternal or Imaginative Bodies when these Vegetable Mortal Bodies are no more.

He lived his isolated, yet happy life to wage a ' mental ', a ' spiritual ' war. In the lyric which the late Dr Parry set to music, contained in his Preface to *Milton*, Blake touched on the new industrialism:

> And did the Countenance Divine
> Shine forth upon our clouded hills ?
> And was Jerusalem builded here
> Among these dark Satanic Mills ?

Then:

> I will not cease from Mental Fight,
> Nor shall my Sword sleep in my hand
> Till we have built Jerusalem,
> In England's green and pleasant land.

In a ' song ' most schoolchildren read, and many learn, ' Tyger ! Tyger ! ', he attempted to define the paradox of Good and Evil:

> What immortal hand or eye,
> Dare frame thy fearful symmetry ?

The supreme, Spiritual Mind who made the lamb, made also the lamb's devourer, the tiger. Life here on earth can continue only by one creature's preying on another, including, of course, man— the supreme predator.

In the *Prophetic Books* Blake's volcanic imagination continued to proliferate symbols, intractable antinomies such as the above. But in spite of the loneliness that must have arisen from his reversal of ' normal ' values of morals and reason, the essence of Blake's vision remained constant throughout his life and work. In *The Marriage of Heaven and Hell* (1790-3) ' Energy is Eternal Delight '. But into opposing forms, false cruelty and innocent goodness, he saw the God-given, human energy flowing. In a probably unfinished poem which he rejected for his *Songs of Experience*:

> Cruelty has a Human Heart,
> And Jealousy a Human Face;
> Terror the Human Form Divine,
> And Secrecy the Human Dress.[5]

Again, in the *Note-Book 1793*, Blake rejected false charity and abject peace, to reach a still more perplexing paradox:

> I heard an Angel singing
> When the day was springing,
> ' Mercy, Pity Peace
> Is the world's release.' . . .
>
> I heard a Devil curse
> Over the hills and the furze,
> ' Mercy could be no more
> If there was nobody poor;
>
> And pity no more could be
> If all were as happy as we.'
> At his curse the sun went down,
> And the heavens gave a frown . . .
>
> And Miseries' increase
> Is Mercy, Pity, Peace.[6]

In ' The Divine Image ' which he included in the *Songs of Innocence*:

> . . . Mercy has a human heart,
> Pity a human face,
> And Love, the human form divine,
> And Peace, the human dress . . .[7]

[5] ' A Divine Image ' and Poems from the *Note-Book 1793*, text from *Blake: Complete Writings*, ed. Geoffrey Keynes, Oxford Standard Authors (Oxford Univ. Press, 1966), p. 221.
[6] Ibid., p. 164.
[7] Ibid., p. 117.

Visionaries such as Blake help to bring change through deepening insight. Since every phenomenon here on earth is capable of containing at least some aspect of its own antithesis, and since every form is capable of being seen as ugly or beautiful, Blake's reversal of reasonable and moral values has existential as well as essential truth. If we reject Blake's belief in man's hermaphrodite beginnings as a fallen angel struggling through this ' vegetable ' existence, if we cannot see concrete reality as dream, with the invisible or spiritual as true reality, it is clear that Blake was not mad, as is even now occasionally suggested. If his doctrine of mutual forgiveness seems impractical except in a far future, his expression of it is unique in English poetry. He was centuries in advance of his time.

In 1798 two friends, William Wordsworth aged twenty-eight, and Samuel Taylor Coleridge two years younger, collaborated to state their new poetical outlook in the *Lyrical Ballads*. Wordsworth's Preface to this book explains the volte-face. Poetry, Wordsworth wrote, should be the simplest possible expression and should contain the most honest feelings the poet could attain to.   Its expression should be of the kind Blake had used in *Poetical Sketches* and the *Songs of Innocence and Experience*. It should avoid the gross, the harsh, the satiric, the violent. It must somehow concern itself with the decent dignity that belongs to all who travel between birth and death. Any human being, no matter how insignificant-seeming, is important. Poetry was to be so plain that it would approach the language of prose—' when prose is well written '.

Could this new way of seeing poetry's significance—Blake's and Wordsworth's—help to close the gap between popular and literary writing ? Poetry had come a long way from the days when Charms were prayers among rich and poor, taught and untaught alike, when singing or chanting them was thought to be able to influence health, weather, crops, friends, fate. Poetry belonged now to a few voices amid, since Dryden, a growing chorus of learned opinions. More and more richly it reflected past and present. It would also point to what poets thought might get forgotten in the future. The new poetry, Wordsworth added in his 1800 Preface to *Lyrical Ballads*, was to attempt something not tried before. It was not to be in carefully selected ' poetic diction '. It was to imitate, and, as far as possible to adopt, ' the very language of men '.

VI

The Nineteenth Century

1798 - 1914

From about the middle of the eighteenth century inventors had been originating, men of enterprise planning and workers building the factories, docks, trains, steamships and telegraph that meant modern industrialism. As the number who could read in Britain expanded, so printing and printed books became cheaper. By 1800, easily produced chapbooks kept alive what remained of popular traditional tales and rhymes from as far away as medieval sources. Hawkers, tinkers, chapmen sold these with ballads on penny broadsheets, in their boxes of cotton-reels, needles and pins slung from their shoulders. A sense persisted that written poetry and stories, as oral ballads and fables had been, were part of daily life. But as more and more printers catered for cheap productions, another assumption grew—that the inclination of untutored readers would be for sentimental or sensational reading. This assumption—still made today—is not now provable or disprovable. It is probably untrue.

Early Nineteenth-Century Poets

After *The Lyrical Ballads* of 1798, with their element of simplicity in depth, Wordsworth did not, in all his poems, uphold his intention to write in ' the very language of men '. His ' Michael ', ' Anecdote for Fathers ', ' The Idle Shepherd Boys ', ' The Affliction of Margaret ', ' There Was a Boy ', ' We Are Seven ', even ' The Idiot Boy ', simple as these are, are what almost every one of us would say—*if* we were ' well-nurtured ', as Keats put it, in our English tongue. They are successful poems; and they have wide appeal too.

They prove that the language of men can be poetry. Not to be fabricated out of good intention any more than hit upon by accident, poetry beautiful and valid is in them whilst they carry out Wordsworth's aim for poetry's language.

We know that ' We Are Seven ' was ' hawked about in penny ballads ' and that it ' met more popularity among the common people than all other songs English & Scottish put together '.[1] It reached remote villages as well as towns:

> ' Sisters and brothers, little maid,
> How many may you be ? '
> ' How many ? Seven in all,' she said,
> And wondering looked at me.
>
> ' And where are they ? I pray you tell.'
> She answered, ' Seven are we;
> And two of us at Conway dwell,
> And two are gone to sea.
>
> ' Two of us in the church-yard lie,
> My sister and my brother;
> And in the church-yard cottage, I
> Dwell near them with my mother.' . . .
>
> ' But they are dead; those two are dead !
> Their spirits are in heaven ! '
> 'Twas throwing words away; for still
> The little Maid would have her will,
> And said, ' Nay, we are seven ! '[2]

Little if any more of Wordsworth's poetry reached the destinations of ' We Are Seven '. In 1809 Byron, among his laughing jibes, in *MacFlecknoe* and *Dunciad* vein, in *English Bards and Scotch Reviewers*, declared that English poets were growing too ' refined '. There had been a cult of ' tuneful cobblers ' and of simplicity after the wide sale of Thomson's *Seasons* caught the 1730s' undercurrent of rural new fashion. The simplicity cult was not wholly to do with what poetry is; and by the beginning of the nineteenth century verse was, or is said to have been, much less bought. Twelve hours and more a day in factories undoubtedly stole leisure; repetitive work dulled

---

[1] Quoted from *The Prose of John Clare* (Routledge & Kegan Paul, 1951), p. 208.
[2] Text from Oxford Univ. Press edn (1920), p. 83.

spontaneity. But did these kill people's conscious and unconscious need for poetry ? The untutored could find, as now they can, only what was, and is, well distributed. They must buy only what is not time-consuming to search for.

In his youth Wordsworth had had an idealistic and ready sympathy for France's revolutionary struggle towards *Liberté, Egalité, Fraternité*. He saw poetry as ' the breath and finer spirit of all knowledge '. He had been ready to accept frugality as a poet writing ' the very language of men '. Later, in 1818, Shelley, in his Preface to *The Revolt of Islam*, recalled the

Panic which . . . seized upon all classes of men during the excesses consequent upon the French Revolution . . . because those who had been slaves for centuries were incapable of conducting themselves with the wisdom and tranquillity of freemen.

Disillusion rather than panic Wordsworth has described in himself in the tenth and eleventh books of his sustained *Prelude*, on the growth of a poet's mind, begun in 1799 and completed in its first version in 1805. Disillusion can also be traced in the *Ecclesiastical Sonnets* of 1822. It had been ' bliss '—' heaven '—to be alive before. What he finally saw in the Terror of the Revolution and the subsequent war—a little self-righteously and with a shade of that ' egotism, vanity and bigotry ' John Keats did not fail to mark in the ' great poet ' and ' poet of Nature '—was ' a terrific reservoir of guilt/And ignorance '.

The ode ' Intimations of Immortality from Recollections of Early Childhood ' also tells of the fading of Wordsworth's sympathy for the struggle towards an ideal: ' Shades of the prison-house begin to close/Upon the growing boy.' Between 1802 when the ode was probably begun and 1806 when it was completed the less inspired part after stanza five betrays again what Keats noted: it is a little difficult to understand how ' soothing ' thoughts can possibly ' spring/Out of human suffering '. Yet the final two stanzas show the acceptance, after those ' Blank misgivings of a Creature/Moving about in worlds not realised '. Lesser hopes seen in ' the light of common day ' may be necessary and inevitable for individual maturity. These are Wordsworth's ' thoughts that lie too deep for tears '.

By the time the ' Immortality ' ode was finished he was happily married and economically comfortable. His sister Dorothy in her *Journal* tells of their day-to-day life first in Dove Cottage and then at Rydal Mount, both in the Lake District. Deprived lives, simple yet somehow ' stately in the main ' under corrosive poverty and manifest hardship, offered Wordsworth examples of patience and indefeasible ' firmness of mind '. By such lives he measured his own longer perspectives of personal loss. This he described in ' Resolution and Independence ' or ' The Leech-gatherer '.

Until 1850 Wordsworth, succeeding Robert Southey as Poet Laureate, continued to write poems chiefly about country life. His long *Excursion*, published in 1814 and drastically revised as his liberal sympathy diminished, is of philosophic interest rather than satisfying as poetry. The poems of his to be remembered were all written by the time he was thirty-six. Yet, as he retreated further and further into a conservative narrowness, he continued to insist on serenity to be wrested again and again through love of Nature from time's corrosions and defeats.

Coleridge, who contributed *The Ancient Mariner* to the first edition of *Lyrical Ballads*, and to whose teeming, philosophic mind Wordsworth owed much, wrote, in *The Ancient Mariner*, a poem which should have appealed to a wide public and yet was ' great ' poetry. Later, Coleridge has himself disclosed how, to relieve pain and unhappiness, he turned to opium and soon found himself an addict. The second edition of *Lyrical Ballads* (1800) contained only Wordsworth's poems; *The Mariner* seems to have been left to scholars and the future. After his youth Coleridge became more a philosophical thinker and talker than a poet. After a long and courageous struggle, and with the help of Dr Gillman, he freed himself from the drug. His *Letters* and *Biographia Literaria* (1817), as also his *Anima Poetae* (not published until after his death), contain the most enduring parts of his prose. The ' caverns measureless to man ' of his ' Kubla Khan ', the insights of ' Frost at Midnight ', and his ' Dejection: an ode ', refuse to be forgotten:

> My genial spirits fail,
> And what can these avail
> To lift the smothering weight from off my breast ?

It were a vain endeavour,
Though I should gaze for ever
On that green light that lingers in the west:
I may not hope from outward forms to win
The passion and the life, whose fountains are within.

Blake, Burns, Wordsworth, Coleridge and the group of younger,
early nineteenth-century poets, Keats, Shelley, Clare and Byron,
were richly different from each other. Yet all agreed in the emphasis they gave in poetry to the feelings. By ' feeling ' Wordsworth and
Coleridge meant emotion; Keats meant the riches of the five
senses from which our emotions are fed. All except Byron rejected
satire. They relied on the inexplicable sense of beauty and pleasure
poetry gives. Poetry could offer the fulfilment which these early
nineteenth-century poets held was the spring of the fountain of joy;
and this fountain watered goodness and moral generosity; it helps
to make arid, vindictive areas of human nature more fertile.

John Keats had the years between 1795 and 1821 in which to
achieve the fame his ' clear spirit ' longed and worked for. Schooled
to the age of fourteen, in 1810 Keats was apprenticed to an apothe-
cary. Initially, he was expected to become a surgeon and by 1815
was working in Guy's Hospital. But he never joined the medical
profession. In poetry he was largely self-educated. By the time he
was twelve he had nursed his mother as she lay dying of tuberculosis. And in 1818 he nursed his younger brother Tom, who died
of the same disease. Keats's first book of poems appeared with
Shelley's help in 1817. *Endymion* was published in 1818 and savagely
criticized in *Blackwood's Edinburgh Magazine* and the *Quarterly
Review*. In 1820 *Lamia, Isabella, The Eve of St. Agnes and Other Poems*
was published and praised by Jeffrey in the *Edinburgh Review*.
Between 1818 and 1819 Keats wrote ' Hyperion '; but its two
versions remained incomplete.

Keats did not strive for simplicity in poetry. He sought for rich-
ness—to ' load every rift with ore '. He turned to Homer, Spenser,
Shakespeare and Milton for subjects, forms and inspiration. John
Gibson Lockhart in *Blackwood's* and John Wilson Croker in Gifford's
Quarterly Review condemned, from an intellectual, eighteenth-
century outlook, Keats's sensuous use of words. The emotive

symbols were described as ' witless meanderings '; the poet was advised to go back to ' pills and ointments '. Taking to heart only what he saw as near-truth in the criticisms, Keats composed ' The Eve of St. Agnes ' with the most careful, yet confident, craftsmanship. He began his long ' Hyperion ', on the rebellion against Heaven of the Titan of that name, but abandoned a first draft as too ' Miltonic '. In 1819 his five great odes were written: ' On a Grecian Urn ', ' To a Nightingale ', ' To Autumn ', ' On Melancholy ', ' On Indolence '. He began to rewrite ' Hyperion ' as ' The Fall of Hyperion '. It is in this, unfinished as it is, that Keats—his hopes of mortal fame almost gone, his medical knowledge having shown him death within sight—offers the ' veiled shadow's ' definition of what poets are. They are not idle dreamers, but ' those to whom the miseries of the world/Are misery, and will not let them rest '.

There lingers in some minds the question whether Keats was not almost as good a letter-writer as a poet. His letters contain so consistent and mature an outlook that only his humility would not call it philosophic. Yet his piercing sense of beauty within the transience all humanity sees as tragic makes him one of the most lyrical of English poets.

By 1820 illness forced poetry aside in him. By December of that year he was so grievously unwell that the painter Joseph Severn agreed to accompany him to Rome. Unsolaced by any firm religious belief and after much suffering, Keats died in Rome in February 1821.

On hearing Shelley wrote his lament for *Adonais*:

> . . . He has outsoared the shadow of our night;
> Envy and calumny and hate and pain,
> And that unrest which men miscall delight,
> Can touch him not and torture not again;
> From the contagion of the world's slow stain
> He is secure, and now can never mourn
> A heart grown cold, a head grown gray in vain;
> Nor, when the spirit's self has ceased to burn,
> With sparkless ashes load an unlamented urn. . . .

The One remains, the many change and pass;
Heaven's light forever shines, Earth's shadows fly;
Life, like a dome of many-coloured glass,
Stains the white radiance of Eternity,
Until Death tramples it to fragments.—Die,
If thou wouldst be with that which thou dost seek!
Follow where all is fled! . . .

What Mary Shelley meant in her note on *Prometheus Unbound*, that ' Shelley loved to idealize the real ', is clear from the second stanza above. In his Preface to twelve cantos of *Laon and Cythna*, later *The Revolt of Islam*, Shelley explained that his poem, though ' narrative, not didactic ' was to ' enlighten and improve mankind '. Again, according to his second wife, Shelley deliberated at one time whether he should dedicate himself to poetry or to metaphysics. Deciding on poetry he studied the ' poets of Greece, Italy, and England '. But he did not find conforming to social rule easy: he was sent down from Oxford for writing *The Necessity of Atheism*. His life after 1818 was spent in exile chiefly in Italy. His sustained poems, *Alastor*, *The Revolt of Islam*, ' Julian and Maddalo ', ' The Witch of Atlas ', the lyrical drama *The Cenci*, though alien in background, and perhaps emotionally fevered and grandiloquent, have something to say on men's need for liberty against the oppression Shelley saw as detestable. These poems were written in grim and threatening times; *The Mask of Anarchy* calls to mind dire happenings among the poor in Britain. If in *The Sensitive Plant* or *Prometheus Unbound* Shelley's distant vision will not transport us, his intrepidity may move: ' Gentleness, Virtue, Wisdom, and Endurance ' were his ' seals against destruction '. His determination was to hope ' till hopes creates/from its own wreck the thing it contemplates '. He did not stay for disillusion to overtake him. He was drowned sailing a small boat across the Gulf of Spezzia in 1822.

If we cannot believe that society will cleanse itself of imperfections through men's will, as Shelley sought to convince us it can, there are Shelley's shorter poems—' Mutability ', ' Ode to the West Wind ', ' To Night ', ' When the Lamp is Shatter'd ', ' Music, when Soft Voices Die ', ' Ozymandias ', or ' To a Skylark '—to remind us that the eighteenth century's concept of a finite universe, ordered, checked and balanced, was about to vanish for good.

Whether or not Shelley's discipline of love could take the place of oppression among the wider vistas he saw, is another matter:

> We look before and after,
>   And pine for what is not:
> Our sincerest laughter
>   With some pain is fraught;
> Our sweetest songs are those that tell of saddest thought.
>
> Yet if we could scorn
>   Hate, and pride, and fear;
> If we were things born
>   Not to shed a tear,
> I know not how thy joy we ever should come near.[3]

Whilst Keats died at twenty-six, and Shelley, at thirty, escaped from disillusion, John Clare, their contemporary, lived and wrote lyrics until he was over seventy, spending twenty-six years in places for the insane. Born in 1793, Clare's early life was lived during the most difficult period for rural workers and small-holders in Britain's long, perhaps necessary, but undoubtedly harsh, agricultural-industrial revolution.

Clare wrote prose with less trouble than he wrote verse; but in his prose autobiography, as well as in many poems, he tells in detail of an England predominantly agricultural not two centuries ago. Fairs and feast-days punctuated the year for the closely knit village community. Clare's father was a wrestling champion and a singer of ballads. His mother, like most village women then, knew many folk-tales. In the common fields goose-tending grannies sang to children when they were not at dame-school or church-vestry lessons. School for Clare finished when he was twelve. Like Keats he was self-tutored in the art of poetry.

His early poems identify, by almost becoming, the birds, creatures, plants and people described: ' The Blackcap ', ' The Wryneck ', ' The Yellow Wagtail's Nest ', ' Hares at Play ', ' Badger ', ' Marten Cat ', ' Water-lilies ', ' The Crab-tree ', ' Summer Amusements ', ' The Lout '. The later lyrics of this foremost of English ' country ' poets have a ' singing note ', as George Darley called it:

[3] From 'The Skylark'.

> Love lies beyond
> The tomb, the earth, the flowers, and dew,
> I love the fond,
> The faithful, young, and true.

It is in such as the above, in ' Hesperus ', in ' I am—yet what I am none cares or knows ' and ' I lost the love of heaven above ' that Clare's lyrical tone becomes the expression of power. This handful of lyrics, Geoffrey Grigson has said, is what pushes Clare ' over the border . . . into the great, however circumscribed his greatness '. Such capacity for joy, coupled with naturalist lore, under the sternest of fates, has also made Clare able, Edmund Blunden thinks, ' to make simplicity many times new '. This is not what all poets seek. Clare's account of his flight from his first asylum is one of the moving documents in English prose.

Byron has much closer ties than the rest of his contemporaries with the irony, satire, burlesque and rhetoric of the eighteenth century. Slightly lame, romantically handsome, the deserted son of titled, capricious parents, the young Byron made imperious demands for personal licence that conflicted with society's disciplines. In 1812, after two cantos of his long poem *Childe Harold's Pilgrimage* were published, he woke one morning to find himself in his own words, ' famous '. But his behaviour soon ostracized him, and he went to live in Venice, then Rome, then Genoa. *The Giaour* and *The Bride of Abydos* both appeared in 1813; *The Corsair* in 1814; *Manfred* in 1817; *Beppo* in 1818; and between 1822 and 1826 *Don Juan* was published. *Childe Harold* and *Don Juan* describe European, Mediterranean and Middle East scenes—Waterloo, the Drachenfels, Venice, the Apennines, Rome. All these were becoming, with increased trade and better communications, alluring to the island British. In poems such as *Childe Harold* and *Don Juan* Byron uses sometimes a spirited defiance, what Keats called ' hectoring ', sometimes a conversational irony deliberately emptied of the sentiment he distrusted in himself and in others, but which he could not entirely suppress. From *Childe Harold*, for example:

> I have not loved the world, nor the world me—
> But let us part fair foes; I do believe,

F

Though I have found them not, that there may be
Words which are things—hopes which will not deceive,
And virtues which are merciful, nor weave
Snares for the failing; I would also deem
O'er others' grief that some sincerely grieve;
That two, or one, are almost what they seem—
That goodness is no name, and happiness no dream. . . .[4]

' While stands the Coliseum, Rome shall stand;
When falls the Coliseum, Rome shall fall;
And when Rome falls—the World.' From our own land
Thus spake the pilgrims o'er this mighty wall
In Saxon times, which we are wont to call
Ancient; and these three mortal things are still
On their foundations, and unalter'd all;
Rome and her Ruin past Redemption's skill,
The World, the same wide den—of thieves, or what ye will.[5]

From *Don Juan*:

Sweet is a legacy, and passing sweet
    The unexpected death of some old lady
Or gentleman of seventy years complete,
    Who've made ' us youth ' wait too—too long already
For an estate, or cash, or country seat,
    Still breaking, but with stamina so steady
That all the Israelites are fit to mob its
Next owner for their double-damned post-obits.[6]

Byron wrote stirring poems on the liberty his age thought to be,
and in many places was—as it always has been—in jeopardy: ' The
Isles of Greece ', for instance. Lyrics of his such as ' So, we'll go no
more a-roving ' are free of the defiance, self-conflict and posturing
that so often cloaked and protected his loneliness of exile.

He died of fever at Missolonghi. His intention, which was frustrated, had been to fight for the Greeks in their bid for freedom
from Turkish dominion. He has had a strong influence on European
poetry and thought.

[4] Canto III, cxiv.
[5] Canto IV, cxlv.
[6] Canto I, cxxv.

These poets all made high claims for poetry. Even Byron, who thought poetry in Britain degenerate in his day, claimed his pen as ' nature's noblest gift '. Yet in a seafaring nation, setting out on a century of empire expansion to export her language, her religion, her way of life, along with her goods, to many parts of the earth, poets' voices were heard only mutedly. What they had to say held with other forces only the most tenuous balance.

Thomas Hood was a humorous and deeply compassionate London poet. His ' Song of the Shirt ' certainly had some share in waking public conscience about the growing distress of industrial workers under poor wages and bad conditions. Hood's ' Song of the Mid-summer Fairies ' deserves to be more readily available to children today. So do Coleridge's daughter Sara's ' Phantasmion ' and Hartley Coleridge's sonnets. Samuel Rogers, the banker—Byron's ' melodious Rogers '—is said to have been one of the few poets who (with Byron and Scott) made money out of poetry in the early nineteenth century. Rogers wrote *The Pleasures of Memory* in the ' poetic diction ' of the preceding age. Walter Scott wrote rousing stories in verse—*The Lady of the Lake, The Lay of the Last Minstrel, Marmion*—before he turned to novel-writing. Allan Cunningham is remembered for his patriotic ' A wet sheet and a flowing sea '; and we still sing Thomas Campbell's ' Ye mariners of England '. Tom Moore's Irish melodies, in his own day popular, include the well-known ' The Harp that once through Tara's Halls . . . .' George Darley was a gracefully expert lyricist, but not a well-known poet; James Hogg (the ' Ettrick Shepherd ') wrote the indigenous fairy-tale in verse, *Kilmeny* (1813). Hogg is also remembered in prose for *The Private Memoirs and Confessions of a Justified Sinner* (1824). Robert Bloomfield, a cobbler and maker of aeolian harps, wrote descriptive country verse. These last, and Stephen Duck the thresher, were the ' hireling bards ' Byron jibed about.

Essays and Criticism

Essayists and critics of the early nineteenth century include William Hazlitt and Thomas De Quincey, who wrote *Confessions of an English Opium Eater*; Leigh Hunt edited the outspoken, liberal

Examiner and went to prison for criticizing George IV. Despite all his political daring, Hunt could be trivial as a poet. Robert Southey was an industrious worker in verse and prose; Charles Lamb was one of those who, as Edmund Blunden has written in one of his many books of this period, ' helped to shape the speech of England '. Lamb's life was noble in the way Keats's was noble. Lamb worked as a clerk in a city office most of his life, caring for his sister Mary in her recurrent fits of insanity. In one of these, as a young girl, Mary had killed their sick and helpless mother. Lamb's punning *Letters* and his gay, humorous *Essays of Elia* are well worth reading. There were many excellent letter-writers of this period: Gray, Cowper, Keats, Coleridge.

As the century of scientific industrialism went on, cities continued to grow and people in Britain to move from the villages to the towns. Since the days of Sodom and Gomorrah, city life had been seen by some as evil because, perhaps, the city is the growing-point where new, untried activities begin. Five million gay, coarse, boisterous Elizabethans had undergone a sobering process. Their eighteenth-century satire has shown this. By 1837 there would be sixteen to twenty million Victorians. By 1900 there would be thirty-six millions. At the beginning of the century one hundred or more indictments—against stealing a turnip to murder—could still send some of them to death or transportation for life. And the gap between rich and poor was as great as it had been in all their history.

Earliest among the poets, William Blake had written his ' indignant page ' against ' Albion's treatment of her children '; against the ' mind-forg'd manacles ' of industry; against the appalling neglect and poverty in Britain's towns. Blake's voice was heard belatedly. Still, it was heard. The early Wordsworth influenced reformers, as we know from John Stuart Mill's *Autobiography*. Perhaps those bygone centuries of subjection to foreign conquest, those deadly civil wars, that slow, painful evolving towards representation in Parliament by the votes of the majority, helped—as writers like Langland, Chaucer, Shakespeare, Swift, Blake, Wordsworth and all the others helped—to form whatever built-in, imperfect sense of equity grew and fermented in the Britain of this time.

Reform

The century was to be one of reform, a ' march of improvement ':
to ' make the country worth living in '. A group of writers, mostly
women—Mrs Mary Sherwood, Anna Barbauld, Sarah Trimmer
and Hannah More—writing for the young, might cloak wretched-
ness by assuming that poverty, meekness and service were God's
dispensation for most of His people; that submissive patience would
have its reward in Heaven. But from the turn of the century there
were men who set their minds to practical problems of social
betterment. Among these was Jeremy Bentham. Bentham's books
include *Introduction to Principles of Morals and Legislation* (1789)
Punishments and Rewards (1811) and *Parliamentary Reform Catechism*
(1817). That grim parent, James Mill, was Bentham's staunch
supporter; Mill wrote *Elements of Political Economy*. These writers
on reform were called Utilitarians.

Bentham himself, a mild, hopeful prophet of simple happiness
for so many, was the son of an ambitious father. He had a thorough,
detailed, theoretic mind. Born in 1748, his way of thought belonged
far more to the eighteenth than to the nineteenth century. ' Utility ',
he insisted, was a principle that rests entirely on ' matter of fact '.
Pleasure and pain are what alone prompt people's doings. ' Quantity of pleasure being equal ', ' pushpin is as good as poetry '
Bentham further declared. To maintain that human beings had
' natural rights ' such as Thomas Paine had argued for was ' simple
nonsense '.[7] All rights, Bentham declared, were conferred by social
law. And since individual liberty could not coincide with all the
rights of the majority, legal liberty must always contain curtailment
of individual freedoms. But the aim of government should be the
greatest happiness (pleasure ?) of the greatest number of people.
Bentham did not accept that values behind pleasure and pain are
individual; that one person's pleasure can be pain to another: to
watch boxing, shoot pheasants or blackbirds gives pleasure to some
but misery to others. Bentham's deep-searching mind concerned
to find the exactest code of law for government, did not explore the
question that ' good ' itself must be a profound ' matter of fact '.
His style, Hazlitt said, needed translating into English.

[7] Quoted from *The Cambridge History of English Literature*, Vol. XI, p. 70.

Thomas Malthus, with his *Essay on the Principle of Population*, had caused a tide of discussion in 1798. In 1803 Malthus issued a more fully documented *Essay*. This reached a modified conclusion on what from ancient days men have feared: that food will run out on earth, as human numbers increase. Malthus recognized checks on population growth. His books influenced nineteenth-century thought, and technology has recently returned to this complex threat that is said to hang over our heads.

The self-educated William Cobbett was a more popular writer than Bentham and James Mill. He defended those whom G. K. Chesterton later called the ' Secret People '. These were the poor in revolt against the savagery of some landowners and industrialists and against the machines' takeover. His weekly newspaper, *Cobbett's Political Register*, appealed to farmers and small tradesmen. Cobbett began as a Tory and ended as a Liberal Radical. In 1810 he endured two years' prison for writing against the brutal flogging which, in army and navy, was a feature of those days when Britain feared invasion by Napoleon. Cobbett seems to have been allowed to continue his writing in prison. He came out almost ruined. But his hold on his public and his refusal of defeat restored his situation. He stood for Parliament but made no mark as a political speaker. He went about the country on horseback to observe what was needed ' to make the country worth living in '. The leisurely, down-to-earth sympathy and shrewd observation of his *Rural Rides*, begun in 1821, made him widely read, and so influenced both parliamentary reform and social thinking.

The Welshman Robert Owen was thoroughly nineteenth-century in outlook, practical yet having vision. Owen made a fortune in Manchester's first cotton mills and spent it carrying out schemes for the housing, care and education of his workers at his mills at New Lanark and elsewhere. In 1816, almost fifty years before Karl Marx sought refuge in London to construct his *Das Kapital* (1867-94) from overwhelming evidence of the British poor's squalor and misery, Owen offered his own brand of social justice in his *New Views of Society*. To Owen we owe the beginnings of trade unionism after the repeal in 1825 of the laws against combinations of workers. To Owen we owe the People's Charter. Owen saw that reading and writing, up to this time in the care of private philanthropists and religious bodies, must become public. The ' mob ', already feared by those in established power, could, Owen held, surely move beyond hot-headed, often impotent, violence, since a mob was but a phalanx of potentially intelligent, reasoning men and women.

After Robert Owen there were men such as Lord John Russell of the 1832 Reform Bill, Fielden, Ashley Cooper (later Earl of Shaftesbury), Michael Sadler, among many others, all working for improvement. At the other end of the scale many ordinary men were banding in trade unions, mutual improvement societies, mechanics institutes. The stories of some of these are recorded in books such as *Memoirs of James Lackington* ' Who began Business with five pounds ', and Alexander Somerville's *Autobiography of a Working Man*, ' by one who has whistled at the Plough ', of 1848. Scottish education had forged far ahead of English education. In such as Somerville, schooled in a Scottish village until twelve or thirteen, we may perceive the growth towards that majority of articulate, reasoning men Robert Owen foresaw.

But conditions improved desperately slowly. In the year 1848, when Europe had a year of political revolutions, Britain came perilously near a revolt of her workers. Yet Chartism failed. Did it fail because of the astonishing, humiliating patience of the poor? Or because of the weakness within strength of self-educated minds when confronted by clemency from trained minds ? Or was the compromise that resulted some form of reasonableness between two sets of men whose interests, though opposing, had yet much in common ?

Whatever the reason, there was the traditional British compromise. The speed of reform quickened. Industrial conditions did grow easier. Not without opposition the Education Act of 1870 made provision for all children between five and fourteen to go to school, to learn to read and glean a little knowledge. Soon franchise for men, though not yet for women, would be achieved. Women would wait until the following century—1918—for the right to vote in Britain.

Novelists

Unless we call to mind something of all this, we may miss much in the novels of the period. Novelists, like dramatists and poets, are people with an awareness of their environment often disturbing to themselves as well as to others. They are not teachers or preachers. They portray; but their art, unlike reform, refuses to indoctrinate. They symbolize. Their reflection of events and conditions does not seek to coerce.

Maria Edgeworth, the daughter of an Irish educationist, wrote *Castle Rackrent* in 1800; this tale of a still almost feudal Ireland of loyal retainers and witty, bibulous Protestant-Ascendancy land-owners, is said to have given the poet Walter Scott the idea which stirred his genius, turning from poetry, to produce some twenty novels between 1814 and 1832. In the Waverley novels Scott recreated Scotland's, and after *Ivanhoe*, England's, past: that adventurous past with, in Scotland, a background of heather-clad mountain and cotton-bog, with both countries as strongholds of ever-admired individuality and reckless independence.

Jane Austen was born in 1775, when the solid eighteenth century was beginning to change into a new age. Between 1790 and her death in 1817 she wrote ten short novels. After her youthfully spirited *Love and Friendship* and *Sense and Sensibility* (1811), *Pride and Prejudice* (1813) is considered now by most as her masterpiece. Her delicate, never quite malicious humour saw through many false values and pretensions, though she was not much in advance of the limited outlook of her time. Ignoring contemporary war and industrial cruelty, she was content to display wittily the worth or triviality of men's and women's characters. She used the lightest irony within a frame of restraint, modesty and self-control.

The daughter of an Anglican clergyman-scholar, her mother was also a clergyman's daughter with relatives in the aristocracy. The six brothers of this closely knit family prospered in the navy, the Church, banking or land. From her youth Jane's wit had been the entertainment of the clan. Of her personality we may glean most from her novels—*Sense and Sensibility*, *Pride and Prejudice*, *Mansfield Park* (1814), *Emma* (1815), *Northanger Abbey* and *Persuasion* (posthumously, 1818). She remained a spinster, and that cannot have been easy in those days. But she was, we know, a loved visitor to her affluent brothers' homes and among their children. She refused marriage at her widowed mother's behest. Since her death at forty-two her adult ironies have grown steadily more appreciated.

Though the nineteenth century is sometimes called the *laissez-faire* century, the 1840s saw a ferment of social reform. In the long run industrialism and machines can be neither blamed nor praised. But since the Napoleonic Wars discontent in Britain had remained rife. Benevolent despots such as Thomas Carlyle were still to write. But Thomas Paine's *Rights of Man* had seen education as a right. No longer could it be conferred merely by the kindly or the condescending. Young men's clubs, mechanics' institutes, mutual improvement societies, benefit societies, flourished after the days of Paine, Owen and Cobbett. The age of improvement was also an age of novels. There is certainly some connection in those two attributes of the age.

Charles Dickens believed himself to be facing head-on the misery of Britain's poor, of which much of the population was in ignorance. He created a small world of characters, in his *Pickwick Papers* (1837), *Nicholas Nickleby* (1839), *The Old Curiosity Shop* (1840), *A Christmas Carol* (1843), *Dombey and Son* (1848), *David Copperfield* (1849-50), *Bleak House* (1852), *Hard Times* (1854), to the finest of them all, *Great Expectations*, of 1861. Then the flow of great novels ceased.

With *Oliver Twist* (1838) Dickens became the first novelist to make a child the central character. His characters belong to the steaming, crowded, struggling, suffering, evil, ugly, comic, compassionate, pathetic, men, women and children whom Dickens knew as a boy and a youth in the cities of Portsmouth and London. He wrote of them in big house and slum, in debtors' prison, bad home and, later, in workhouse, factory and school. It has been said that he exaggerates the grizzly evil, as in Mr Squeers of Dotheboys Hall in *Nicholas Nickleby*, and the frailly good, as in Little Nell of *The Old Curiosity Shop*. But there is also the tough, eight-year-old marchioness in that book, and Jo the crossing-sweeper in *Bleak House*.

Dickens's method with inventing character is usually to take dominant traits, ways of speaking, and build human beings round them. He is accused of using unfairly his evidence of bad conditions. He is accused of being melodramatic. It is said that he portrayed evil conditions when these were already being improved. All this may be valid criticism. But ignorance and slums are still with us; and we are surely richer for Dickens's stories. What is surprising in them is not that so many children grew up only a century ago under adult cruelty and appalling oppression to become liars, criminals and depraved; that there were employers to work their people twelve or more hours a day; that parents—drunken, starving or of abnormal mentality—might sell children to near-slavery; what surprises is that in the world of Dickens's characters the seeds of human nobleness were so strangely steady.

Three sisters, Charlotte, Emily and Anne Brontë, from the isolation of their Irish father's Yorkshire parsonage, assuaged their gifted loneliness by writing novels before all three died of tuberculosis. As children they peopled make-believe countries—Gondal and Angria—about which they wrote stories and poems. Later, Charlotte's *Jane Eyre* (1847), *Shirley* (1849) and *Villette* (1853) sold well as soon as they were published. *Jane Eyre* tells of an unwanted orphan's struggles to happiness through her devoted love for an older man married to a maniac wife. The sensational story derives its illusion of reality from something entirely new in English novel-writing—a frank portrayal of emotion. *Jane Eyre* is the first English novel to reveal those subconscious reaches of the mind, the longings, frustrations, desires and fears, in every one of us concealed or spoken of only in changed guise, that Sigmund Freud, towards the end of this century, was to outline in his psychology.

Emily Brontë's one novel, *Wuthering Heights*, perhaps too strongly refused that well-regulated discipline of conventional values: this may have caused it to be less quickly or readily accepted by readers. With its background of foggy, rainy, northern moorland, from which spring the turbulent figures of Emily Brontë's stern imagination, *Wuthering Heights* took a long time before being recognized as the powerful novel it is.

Emily's childhood Gondal country is the ' Invisible ', the ' Unseen ' world of her inner life and lonely imagination. She wrote poems which her sister Charlotte saw as ' not at all like the poetry women generally write ', but ' vigorous and genuine '. The poems of the three sisters, published in the 1840s under the names of ' Currer ', ' Ellis ' and ' Acton Bell ', fell flat. Charlotte later published Emily's and so we have them today.

Mary Ann Evans, ' George Eliot ', was a woman of intellect and great moral courage. Her novels include *Adam Bede* (1859), *The Mill on the Floss* (1860)—its early chapters drawn from her childhood as the daughter of a farming family in Warwickshire—*Silas Marner* (1861), *Romola* (a tale of the great preacher Savonarola in fifteenth-century Florence), *Middlemarch* (1871-2), said to be her finest work, and *Daniel Deronda* (1874-6). *Silas Marner* is the story of an infant left on a miser's doorstep; how his care and later love for the child altered his life and outlook. It is a short, finely constructed novel. Silas and Effie grow and change as consistently yet surprisingly as most people do, without knowing it, through their reactions to life's experience. *Middlemarch*, far longer than *Silas Marner*, keener, sadder, less hopefully generous, older perhaps, is a penetrating study of failure in the basic human relationship of marriage. Virginia Woolf wrote of *Middlemarch* that it was one of the very few English novels for adults.

After her first book, Mary Ann Evans wrote under the masculine name, George Eliot. As did the Brontës, she wanted to be sure of a fair hearing in a society where women were the retiring half of the community. After George Eliot, no woman writer needed to hide behind a man's name in Britain.

Charles Reade trained as a lawyer and wrote a number of unmemorable dramas, or melodramas, before he turned to writing novels of didactic tone: *It is Never too Late to Mend* (1853), *The Cloister and the Hearth* (1861) and *Hard Cash* (1863) are among the best known. Reade combined an immense fertility with wide documentary knowledge. In *It is Never too Late to Mend* prison inhumanities, which the author had witnessed in Durham, Oxford and Reading, are revealed with indignation and, it is said, without exaggeration. The search for gold in Australia, in the same novel, becomes an absorbing narrative. Reade does not have the Dickensian brand of character-humour which sometimes, paradoxically, almost reconciles us to human beastliness. He is as remorselessly pragmatic and fervent as Defoe. As W. T. Young writes in *The Cambridge History of Literature*, the age is 'rich indeed which can afford to consider the author of *The Cloister and the Hearth* a minor novelist'.

Elizabeth Gaskell also wrote novels of insight and social sympathy: *Mary Barton* (1848), useful to historians, is about the early Manchester cotton-mill workers. It was criticized as being against employers but was popular. *Ruth* (1853) is a story of a girl who gave her life to nurse the father of her child who had left her to bear ignominy alone. A sentimental plot, it has been said. However, considering the age when the book was written, such a plot had some justification. A hundred years later we still penalize, in rather a primitive way, not only unmarried mothers but their offspring who are obviously ' innocent '. Mrs Gaskell's *Cranford* (1851-3) is a humorous description of ingrown, small-town life among the comfortably off; her *North and South* was published in 1855; *Sylvia's Lovers* in 1863-4; and her *Life of Charlotte Brontë* of 1857 caused complaint and some statements were withdrawn.

Anthony Trollope wrote a series of slow-moving, mildly ironic novels about the clergy of the town of ' Barchester '. Wilkie Collins, with *The Woman in White*, continued the fashion Horace Walpole began of macabre tales of mystery. Collins's *No Name*, less well known than *The Woman in White*, shows its author's capacity to make enthralling unlikeable characters whose deceptions of each other supply a compellingly commonplace ' plot '.

William Makepeace Thackeray dealt in mild social ironies in *Vanity Fair* (1848), and in semi-historical fiction in *Henry Esmond* (1852), *The Newcomes* (1853-5), and *The Virginians* (1857-9). Thackeray interposes his author-self and thus frequently breaks the fictional spell.

Charles Kingsley was an energetic clergyman whom children remember for songs of seafaring Devon such as ' Caller Herrin ', for his renderings of classical stories, *The Heroes* (1856) and *Androm- eda* (1859), and for stories of our past such as *Westward Ho!* (1855) and *Hereward the Wake* (1866). *The Water Babies*, also for children, incorporates love of nature with social compassion. Kingsley's novels *Yeast* (published in *Fraser's Magazine* in 1848 and separately in 1850), *Alton Locke* (1850) and *Hypatia* (1853) are also strongly didactic.

Benjamin Disraeli, son of a Jewish writer estimable in his day, became the Earl of Beaconsfield and Queen Victoria's trusted Prime Minister. Disraeli's many novels include *Coningsby* (1844), *Sybil* (1845), *Tancred* (1847), *Lothair* (1870). *Sybil* gives a detailed, often vivid, account of what Disraeli saw as Britain's ' two nations ', the rich and the poor. Nineteenth-century prototypes of ' teddy- boys ', ' layabouts ' and smartly dressed factory girls are described in its pages. Disraeli's remedy for the hostility between the ' two nations ' was the tried, traditional benevolence of rulers, Church and landowners. The new captains of industry, Disraeli thought, would care for decent, docile toilers.

Idealists

Scotsmen, Welsh, Irish and English had been since 1801, politically at least, one nation. In senses other than political and economic each could henceforth keep their respect for each other and at the same time retain their individuality.

There was one writer whose voice echoed over the mid-century: Thomas Carlyle, who was of Scottish parentage. From the time of his early education in a village school in Scotland, Carlyle spent his youth in a quest for learning. In his maturity he turned from sympathy for the oppressed, who grew unruly, to fear of mobs and a didactic upholding of puritan moralism. He was inspired to some extent by German philosophers. After much affliction of spirit, Carlyle found his beliefs. A ' disease ' of materialism could only be cured by purifying of souls, he thought. There must be far greater justice towards the suffering of still growing numbers of the poor. The great and the strong, the ' heroes ' of industry, must ameliorate life's radical unfairness. Carlyle's *Sartor Resartus* (published in *Fraser's Magazine* 1833-4; first English edition in volume form, 1838), a disguised autobiography of the soul's development, his *On Heroes, Hero-Worship, and the Heroic in History* (1841) and, most of all, *The French Revolution* (1837), made him, after his move from Scotland to London, one of the celebrated writers of rhetoric in an age that his authoritarian, anti-Semitic self saw as degenerate. In *Past and Present* (1843) he discussed the old, troublesome question of manhood:

A heroic people chooses heroes, and is happy; A valet or flunky [*sic*] people chooses sham-heroes, and is not happy. The grand summary of a man's spiritual condition, what brings out all his herohood and insight, or all his flunkyhood and horny-eyed dimness, is this question put to him, What man dost thou honour ? Which is thy ideal of a man ?

John Ruskin had the ardent Celtic, Anglo-Saxon awareness of natural beauty. More than Carlyle, he insisted on the preciousness of individuals whilst calling for strong leaders and service to them, and for cleansing of ugliness from urban life. He said he wrote *Modern Painters* (1843-51), *Stones of Venice* (1851-3) and *The Crown of Wild Olive* (1866) in ' black anger ' against the ignorant insensitiveness to beauty among the owners of chimney-stacks, pits, docks and wharves of Britain. The cultivation of the arts and of social beauty was his instinctual basis for moral force in industrial, political and individual life. Ruskin was laughed at by many as an impractical dreamer. But the influence of the man with the harrowed features and moving eloquence is incalculable. Twentieth-century education in the arts owes much to Ruskin.

William Morris wrote of himself as ' an idle singer ' and ' a dreamer of dreams ' born out of his time. Yet Morris, practical and of immense energy, ran the firm of Morris and Company, artistic decorators; he lectured on liberal socialism, as well as writing a great deal of readable verse based on Icelandic and European medieval legends. His rhythmic faculty was such that he wrote verse far more easily than prose. Morris's *News from Nowhere* is a utopian dream: filth and smoke and ugliness have been swept away; buying and selling for profit, prisons and war are all obsolete. Morris saw the breach, the deep ' divide ', between poetry and art for all, and poetry and art for a few, as begun only in the eighteenth century. In his essay, ' The Beauty of Life ', he summed up society's needs as: ' Art made by the people and for the people, a joy to the maker and the user.'[8] As G. D. H. Cole points out, there are more than economics and politics in the human condition, as Ruskin and Morris often said.

Critics have lately said that Morris lived a contradiction—preaching socialism whilst profiteering from a firm making tapestries, carpets and wallpaper such as none but the rich could buy. But which of us lives no contradiction ? Morris must be seen in the context of his age.

John Stuart Mill, in his essay ' On Liberty ' (1859), voiced yet once more the need for freedom of speech and action. Aware of the growing complexity of society, Mill deemed freedom to speak and freedom to act more necessary than ever. Neither freedom should be used with frivolousness or licence. To be educated was to know, without having to be reminded by authority, how to use personal liberty responsibly. Such responsible, personal liberty was the only

[8] William Morris, *Selected Writings*, ed. G. D. H. Cole (Nonesuch Press, 1948), p. 564.

attribute which could make men and women strong; and none but strong, adult human beings could be the stuff of a civilized nation at peace:

> . . . The worth of a State, in the long run, is the worth of the individuals composing it; . . . a State which dwarfs its men, in order that they may be more docile instruments in its hands even for beneficial purposes—will find that with small men no great thing can really be accomplished; and that the perfection of machinery to which it has sacrificed everything will in the end avail it nothing, for want of the vital power which, in order that the machine might work more smoothly, it has preferred to banish.

All four of these writers—Carlyle, Ruskin, Morris and Mill—betrayed fear of those whom they called the ' mob '. The mob held philistines and barbarians, rich or poor. All four are now inspired and inspiring voices of a never-dead past. In their day all spoke their minds despite severe opposition or scornful disregard. They prodded complacency. They revitalized a heavy materialism threatening to close in on Victorian riches and dominance and success. They gave fresh life to the concept that is as old as humanity but never far from submergence in the ocean of misconceptions, that of the unity of beauty and decency.

Philosophy and Biology

Social improvement and reform went hand in hand with increase of knowledge. Charles Darwin, grandson of the biologist, physician and versifying author of *The Loves of the Plants* (1789), Erasmus Darwin, published *The Origin of Species* in 1859. Charles Darwin is a key figure and his book a key work of the nineteenth century. It is an exposition of the principle, already known to Alfred Russel Wallace and other biologists, of natural selection. In prose almost entirely free of scientific jargon, Darwin's book praises life's infinite variety, but it piles proof on exhaustive proof for the theory of evolution against the long-held idea of six-day created, fixed species. It does not demonstrate a Divine purpose as inconsistent with the

climb of the primate apes' first cousin from among them. It shows
earth far older than 4004 B.C., which James Ussher, seventeenth-
century Archbishop of Armagh, had given for God's Creation, and
to which date the Christian Church adhered. Earth's creatures, in
Darwin's, Wallace's and others' views, had not been specially
designed for God's image, man, and man's sometimes arrogant use.
The *Origin of Species* roused a storm of controversy. It was felt by
some to endanger faith. But its effect, and the effect of Darwin's
Descent of Man (1870), have been far-reaching.

Poetry

Muted because of growing complexities—social, religious and
philosophic—mid-Victorian poets' voices echoed, each in his or her
own way, a loss of surety, a sometimes profoundly questioning
distress. Alfred Tennyson followed Wordsworth as Poet Laureate
in 1850. After the publication of *Poems*, in 1830 and 1833, the first
volume of which was unfavourably reviewed, and after two further
volumes in 1842, with *The Princess* in 1847 Tennyson's success was
assured. *The Princess* is an amused survey, in no way before its time,
of Victorian girls at last to be educated alongside their brothers.
In Memoriam came in 1850. This is a long elegy written round the
death, in 1833, of Tennyson's friend Arthur Hallam. Subsequently
Tennyson published *Maud* (1855), four *Idylls of the King* (1859),
Locksley Hall sixty years after (1886), *Poems* (1889), and *The Death of
Oenone and other poems* (1892).

Tennyson may be said to have dedicated his life to the perfection
of a lyrical gift that is occasionally exquisite. If, as A. E. Housman
has contended, ' poetry is not the thing said but a way of saying
it ',[9] then some of the lyrics from *Maud* and *The Princess* are near-
perfect.

But poetry is the thing said as well as a way of saying it. Tennyson, whose phonetic harmony is so expert, is said to have been
happily free of the questioning doubts of his day. *In Memoriam* shows
that in his younger days deliberately he sought to surmount,
cleverly to conceal, the fear a divided heart can give:

[9] *The Name and Nature of Poetry* (Cambridge Univ. Press, 1933), p. 37.

> I stretch lame hands of faith, and grope,
>   And gather Dust and Chaff, and call
>   To what I feel is Lord of all,
> And faintly trust the larger hope.

As he grew older, he found, as he himself told, the peace he sought. In 1832 he had published *Morte d'Arthur*. In *Idylls of the King* he retold medieval legends of King Arthur and the Round Table. He expressed the optimism of a dynamic age. In *Locksley Hall* he saw a future, when

> the war-drum throbb'd no longer, and the battle-flags were
>   furl'd
> In the Parliament of man, the Federation of the world.

> There the common sense of most shall hold a fretful realm in awe,
> And the kindly earth shall slumber, lapt in universal law.

'Knowledge comes, but wisdom lingers', he wrote, and then echoed Malthus's fear. By the time of *Locksley Hall sixty years after*, achievement and perfection were at least questioned:

> All diseases quench'd by Science, no man halt, or deaf or blind ?
> Stronger ever born of weaker, lustier body, larger mind ?

> Earth at last a warless world, a single race, a single tongue—
> I have seen her far away—for is not Earth as yet so young ? . . .

> Warless ? war will die out then. Will it ever ? late or soon ?
> Can it, till this outworn earth be dead as yon dead world the
>   moon ?

Doubt was here straight-spoken; lyricism, if appropriating symbols facile to today's ears, at last betrayed awareness that 'progress' diminished few problems.

> Ay, if dynamite and revolver leave you courage to be wise:
> When was age so cramm'd with menace ? madness ? written,
>   spoken lies ? . . .

> Chaos, Cosmos ! Cosmos, Chaos ! once again the sickening
>   game;
> Freedom, free to slay herself, and dying while they shout her
>   name.

Scepticism and Religion

Other poets who felt the mental disturbance into which enlightenment relentlessly thrust them were, first and foremost, Matthew
Arnold, his friend at Rugby and Oxford, Arthur Hugh Clough,
James Thomson, Algernon Charles Swinburne and Gerard Manley
Hopkins. Matthew Arnold was the eldest son of Thomas Arnold,
one of the most famous of the headmasters of Rugby School.
Matthew Arnold the poet became an inspector of schools and a
writer on education, religion and society, in *Culture and Anarchy*
(1869) and *Literature and Dogma* (1873). He strove to see and write
with detachment and a ' disinterested intellect '. His longer poems
and even his lyrics have this far-off, echoing quality. Following
Wordsworth he sought strength and serenity in Nature. But Nature
had for Arnold none of the joy it could give to Wordsworth; it had
none of that happiness it could strangely confer, in the worst ill-
fortune, on John Clare. Arnold's plea from ' Dover Beach ' reaches
direct from his mid-century to today's, when self-doubt and distrust
of others seem at a new nadir:

> Ah, love, let us be true
> To one another ! for the world, which seems
> To lie before us like a land of dreams,
> So various, so beautiful, so new,
> Hath really neither joy, nor love, nor light,
> Nor certitude, nor peace, nor help for pain;
> And we are here as on a darkling plain
> Swept with confused alarms of struggle and flight,
> Where ignorant armies clash by night.

Arthur Hugh Clough, whom Arnold celebrated in ' Thyrsis '
and Swinburne thought no poet at all, was a tireless, honest, ethical
questioner to the end of his life. Clough is remembered for satiric
verse, for the humorous hexameters of his long poem *The Bothie of
Tober-na-Vuolich* (1848), and for his lyric ' Say not the struggle
naught availeth '.

In 1854-6 Coventry Patmore published his domestic but not
wholly trivial *The Angel in the House*. Lord Macaulay's stirring,
imperial-minded *Lays of Ancient Rome* (1842), were immensely

popular. But most mid-nineteenth-century poets' voices echo between the gain and the loss of wisdom in the tipping scales of experience. James Thomson, the second poet of this name, was born in Glasgow and brought up in one of the poor-houses of the day. He sought refuge when he reached years of discretion in the movement of Free Thought which, even before Darwin, rejected any explanation of life beyond material phenomena. He was self-taught, as many of the aspiring were in those days, and in his early lyrics expressed the joy for which a poor boy from a workhouse yearned.

But, with poor hereditary health aggravated by poverty, with dipsomania and the recurrent guilt it induced, Thomson was soon pouring out the most hopeless poem in the language—*The City of Dreadful Night*. His desperate need for belief held with rigorous courage to reasoned non-belief:

> Speak not of comfort where no comfort is,
>   Speak not at all: can words make foul things fair ?
> Our life's a cheat, our death a black abyss:
>   Hush and be mute envisaging despair.

Swinburne may have been saved from such a city by a kindlier fate. A friend, Theodore Watts Dunton, cared for him for many years during his alcoholism. The pain of facing what he saw as truth was perhaps alleviated in Swinburne by a stronger, more innate lyricism. He was condemned in his own day for atheism. In our own century Ezra Pound saw in Swinburne's assonances, alliterations, half-rhymes and mid-line rhymes a ' tired prettiness ' overtaking nineteenth-century poetry. Edith Sitwell, in her Introduction to her selection of Swinburne, thought differently: the British nineteenth-century poetry reading public must, she wrote, have been so ' greatly bewildered ' by the ' horrible heart-rending cacophonies ' of Robert Burns, that they should have heard in Swinburne the piteously frustrated religious poet he at heart was. Swinburne has been indicted for sensual writing as for atheism and homosexuality. T. S. Eliot thought his language suggestive of weakness.

Perhaps ' romantic ' hope *was* tired. Most movements play themselves out. ' Hertha ' from *Songs Before Sunrise* (1871), ' Before a Crucifix' and 'The Garden of Proserpine' are examples of Swinburne's realization of the senses' importance and are also rejections of his century's growing emphasis on mechanical science. He was one of the first to recognize William Blake's poetry as vital. He voices his own religious view, which owed something to Blake's and Shelley's, perhaps most clearly in 'Hertha': he perceives good and evil as opposites yet one; without evil one cannot know good; without dark one cannot understand what light is. Swinburne's verbal splendour is comparable with Blake's 'energy'.

The poetry of Gerard Manley Hopkins belongs to the mid-nineteenth century. But it was not published until 1918. Robert Bridges, the friend to whom Hopkins sent it, put the bulk of it in print long after Hopkins's death. Poets such as Robert Graves, Geoffrey Grigson and Charles Williams knew at once that Hopkins, in his search for the authentic indigenous cadence, was important. The structure and technique of Hopkins's poetry make him one of the most original of British poets. He wrote in what he termed ' sprung rhythm ', or else in ' common rhythm counterpointed '. Sprung rhythm relied on the spoken or natural stresses, tone, or pitch of words, rather than on the syllables the eighteenth century had declared should be counted and used under the most careful laws derived from the syllabic length and weight of Greek and Latin words in classical poetry.

Hopkins's poems are strong but not simple. For him, as in ' Pied Beauty ', ' The Windhover ' and ' Margaret ', God, ' whose beauty is past change ', ' fathers forth ' all beauty here below. Though a devoted priest, Hopkins did not shirk the anguish of widening, inescapable knowledge, following *The Origin of Species*:

> No worst, there is none. Pitched past pitch of grief,
> More pangs will, schooled at forepangs, wilder wring.
> Comforter, where, where is your comforting?
> Mary, mother of us, where is your relief? . . .
> O the mind, mind has mountains; cliffs of fall
> Frightful, sheer, no-man-fathomed. Hold them cheap
> May who ne'er hung there. Nor does long our small
> Durance deal with that steep or deep. Here! Creep,
> Wretch, under a comfort serves in a whirlwind: all
> Life death does end and each day dies with sleep.

One or two poets of this period escaped doubt if not rigour: Charles Kingsley, Henry Kingsley, William Barnes, Dante Gabriel Rossetti, his sister Christina Rossetti, Elizabeth Barrett Browning, Robert Browning and Coventry Patmore.

William Barnes was a scholar and a curate-schoolmaster. Few, his friend Thomas Hardy the novelist wrote, were simpler or more direct. Barnes was determined to write poems in the dialect he heard all around him in Dorsetshire. He thought it a tragically vanishing speech. Perhaps inwardly he knew that, no more than Wordsworth, was he putting down words ordinary countrymen used; his attempt to reproduce the Dorsetshire Sturminster dialect he had heard in boyhood, in dialect spelling, neither improves nor spoils the content or the sound of his poems. Barnes's exploration of rural life is second only to Clare's in its rich understanding.

Dante Gabriel Rossetti, half-English, half-Italian, poet as well as painter and brought up in orthodox Christian belief, sought to render heavenly beauty direct in terms of earthly, sensuous delight. His best-known poem is perhaps ' The Blessed Damozel '. With William Morris he belonged to the Pre-Raphaelite group of painters.

Rossetti's sister Christina's fine, small talent is characterized by a quiet, often renunciatory, economy of feeling.

Elizabeth Barrett became known, in 1841, for her poem of social protest, ' The Cry of the Children '. This played its part in directing attention to outrage against English children in factory, mine and mill. In 1846 she eloped with Robert Browning from her father's house in London to Italy. She wrote of their love in *Sonnets from the Portuguese* (1850). Her long, leisured novel in blank verse, *Aurora Leigh* (1857), with its high-minded characters, was popular enough to draw attention to the independence of women; that problem, like girls' education, was beginning to claim wider thought.

Robert Browning faced his age's changes with the most boisterous, high, genial yet stoic intelligence. He saw art (poetry) as ' the one way possible of speaking truth '. No doubt his optimism in the face of what he saw as life's staggering limitlessness must be correlated with robust physical health and freedom from money worries. It was not, in Browning's case, linked with early public recognition and easy success as a poet. When Elizabeth Browning became popular with *Aurora Leigh*, her husband declared himself the most unpopular poet there ever was. He tried plays, but drama was almost non-existent at the time and his plays failed.

He published *Paracelsus* in 1835, *Sordello* in 1840. Literary magazines damned both as obscure, discordant, uncouth. Browning, his head seething with knowledge and his interest fascinated by what, with Tennyson, he called the development of the human soul, produced *Mr. Sludge the Medium*. *Paracelsus* is a story of a sixteenth-century alchemist of Basle, Theophrastus Bombastus, from whose wordy addresses the word ' bombast ' is derived. Browning saw in Bombastus a man of dynamism whose power of convincing showed the need of the many to be convinced. Browning was intrigued by natural cunning and the urge in some to make others believe in them.

Sordello is a difficult story of a Visconti prince whose Hamlet-like character allowed much ill to befall many people. *Mr. Sludge the Medium* is a brilliantly jocular exposure of the fraudulent in spiritualism. Browning disliked Elizabeth Barrett's belief and interest in the American spiritualist, D. D. Home.

When Elizabeth Browning died, Browning returned to England. At last, in 1868, his Roman crime story in verse, *The Ring and the Book*, met with approval from critics and with interest from provincial readers in Britain who clamoured for more and more books. *The Ring and the Book*, in twelve parts, recounts, with prologue and epilogue, a murder from the viewpoints of eleven people involved. There is also a conclusion giving representative public opinion, as also the lawyers' and judge's views of the case. Browning's sympathy with each character shows the bewildering complexity of how no two people see the simplest happening in the same light. After *The Ring and the Book* Browning was acknowledged as a great poet.

He alienated readers once more with *Fifine at the Fair* (1872) and *Red Cotton Night-cap Country* (1873), both of which were considered to be shocking stories of illicit love. In *Parleyings* and *Asolando* (1889) Browning returns to his earlier theme of love that can temper but may never govern reason and intellect.

Children know Robert Browning by finely told action-poems: ' How They brought the Good News from Ghent to Aix ' and ' The Pied Piper of Hamelin ', and by lyrics such as ' Home-thoughts, from Abroad '.

In the same year as the publication of Darwin's *Origin of Species*, a translation of a poem was issued that has been among the most often read and well loved of English poems between then and now. Yet the poem is English in neither theme nor background: Edward FitzGerald's translation of the eleventh-century Persian poet Omar Khayyám is a free rendering of some 110 four-line verses, or *Rubáiyát*. It is variously said to be a devotional poem of the Sunni doctrine of Islam; a poem celebrating ' eat, drink, and be merry, for tomorrow we may die '; and an agnostic, devout rendering of the beauty, pain and delight of being alive. Khayyám's poem's subtlety lies partly in the fact that, as in most early Middle East poetry, it is on at least these three levels. A certain accuracy may be contained in the statement that the *Rubáiyát* are on as many levels as they have readers; each reader receives what he brings to them plus that articulate insight never quite definable which the poet offers. A new translation in 1967 by Ali-Shah and Robert Graves, whilst it makes some meanings clearer, does not alter the essential beauty, worth and content of FitzGerald's version.

In the Oxford movement of the advancing nineteenth century, high churchmen and broad churchmen travailed again over allegiance to Rome. John Henry Newman inspired the Anglican movement of revival during the mid-century. Then he found himself impelled to return to Roman Catholicism. Newman's *Apologia pro vita sua* (1864) is a patient and detailed explanation of his reasons for what some thought of as desertion. It is an answer to Charles Kingsley's accusation of Newman's beliefs as ' unconscious hypocrisy '. Newman defends the lie in certain circumstances. Not always fairly, he saw Kingsley's liberalism as opening the door to many evils. His meticulous ' circular ' reasoning on theological subjects that for some will always be important is akin to seventeenth-century reasoning such as Samuel Clarke's in *The Being and Attributes of God*. Such way of thought is totally different, different in essence, different in premises, from what men such as Hume, Darwin or T. H. Huxley called reasoning, and hence truth. Newman's hymn ' Lead, Kindly Light ' was written whilst the orange-boat in which he voyaged back from Rome to England lay becalmed between Palermo and Marseilles.

Writers of the Century's End

The final quarter of the nineteenth century saw Britain briefly at peace, imperial, self-satisfied. Much reform had been carried through for helping the growing multitudes of her people. Ease produced a generation of writers on personal subjects, each writer ready to be concerned with private interests. George Borrow was one of these many self-taught Victorian scholars. He acquired a knowledge of some thirty languages. He wrote of his travels as a chapman (or, as he more euphoniously named it, a ' colporteur ') of the Bible in *The Bible in Spain* (1843). He completed a dictionary of the language of those roving, independent cosmopolitans, gipsies; this was followed by *Lavengro* (1851) and *The Romany Rye* (1857). Finally, his *Wild Wales* (1862) illustrates the remote beauty of much of that slow-changing, mountainous land. David Livingstone's *Last Journals*, of 1874, tell of his exploring, and of converting men and women in East Africa to Christianity. Livingstone engendered trust between Black and White, in contrast to the hatred and fear provoked by an equally intrepid explorer, Henry Morton Stanley.

Richard Jefferies, a victim of ill-health, returned, in *Wood Magic* (1881), *Bevis* (1882) and *The Story of my Heart* (1883), to the sustaining power, known to Anglo-Saxon and Celtic poets and people, through a millennium and a half, of nature in temperate, northern lands.

The naturalist W. H. Hudson, born of American parents, came to live in England and published, among many books, *Birds in London* (1898), *Birds and Man* (1901), *Green Mansions* (1904), *Afoot in England* (1909), *Far Away and Long Ago* (1918), *A Traveller in Little Things* (1921) and *A Hind in Richmond Park* (1922).

Kenneth Grahame's *Dream Days* (1898) and *The Wind in The Willows* (1908) have become classics which both children and adults still enjoy.

Edward Lear published in 1846 a *Book of Nonsense*. This was followed by *More Nonsense Rhymes* in 1871, and *Laughable Lyrics* in 1876. Lafcadio Hearn brought back from the Far East contemplative lore which fascinated if it could not temper British imperialist activism. Charles Dodgson (Lewis Carroll), writer of hymns and treatises on mathematics, also wrote *Alice's Adventures in Wonderland* (1865) and *Through the Looking-glass* (1872).

J. M. Barrie, a Scottish novelist and dramatist, came to make his literary fortune in London. Barrie wrote sketches such as *A Window in Thrums* (1889), and his plays include *The Little Minister* (1891; produced in 1897), *Quality Street* (1901), *The Admirable Crichton* (1902) and one that has joined the Christmas pantomime tradition —*Peter Pan* (1904).

Some poets of the Victorian nineties have been called decadent and effete, scions of a cultural and religious decay in an overripe civilization. But the many poets in the 1890s were very different from each other. The term ' decadent ' by no means fits, even if it *seems* to fit those who died young, such as Oscar Wilde, Lionel Johnson and Ernest Dowson. Alfred Austin is of this age, and also Rudyard Kipling, W. E. Henley, Francis Thompson, Arthur Symons, A. E. Housman and John Davidson. Oscar Wilde's witty social comedies were *Lady Windermere's Fan* (produced in 1892), *A Woman of No Importance* (1893), *The Importance of Being Earnest* (1895) and *An Ideal Husband* (1899). His novel *The Picture of Dorian Gray* (1891) is concerned with moral disintegration in a fashionable socialite. His *Ballad of Reading Gaol* (1898) and *De Profundis* (1905), written whilst serving a prison sentence for homosexual offences, reveal his talents in a very different, serious strain. Alfred Austin followed Tennyson as Poet Laureate. Arthur Symons was a critic as well as a poet.

Ernest Dowson was the only son of a not very prosperous London merchant. He and his father travelled in Europe, not staying long enough in one place to allow the boy consistent education. Oxford gave him a love of poetry but no degree. He squandered his frail health for some years at the Rhymers' Club in London, and after his father's death he made a meagre living in Paris by efficient translations. The French poets, Verlaine, Valéry, Rimbaud, Baudelaire and Laforgue were influencing English poetry. In *Marius the Epicurean* (1885) Walter Pater revived ornamental prose, and in 1889, in *Appreciations*, gave his theory of Art for Art's sake; Art, not as part of living but separate and distinct from it.

Dowson's books, *Verses* and *Decorations in Verse and Prose*, careful and metrical, contain echoes from Keats and Swinburne. Dowson's and his group's revolt was against the rigid self-righteousness of the majority of the older generation. In Dowson hopelessness became a clinging to childhood's innocence, remorse for his own squandered health, and a strong death-wish.

Francis Thompson's devout mysticism led him into poverty and hardship from which he was rescued by Alice and Francis Meynell. In an age of doubt Thompson's strength was his Catholic faith. His poem ' The Hound of Heaven ' has a solemnity and a traditional harmony rather than a late-nineteenth-century sense of a past in any way relinquished.

W. E. Henley and Rudyard Kipling made a heroic ideal of the British Empire, then being consolidated for its brief heyday. Their ethos is one of strong leadership of less technically advanced peoples; of bravery in out-of-the-way places by the ' advanced '. A cripple and invalid, Henley chanted passionately and elevatedly of the will, the endurance, self-mastery and patriotism that have to do with worldly glory and ' greatness '. His best-known poem is perhaps ' Invictus '.

Both Henley and Kipling rejected subtlety of thought and feeling. Kipling chose to use both his considerable fictional and his varied lyrical talents to become the confident, occasionally strident, public voice of what may now sound like an outdated and obsolete imperialism. His ' Ballad of East and West ', rather than *The Jungle Book* or *Puck of Pook's Hill*, states the first essential, the admiration of traditional, manly bravery, for such an outlook:

Oh East is East, and West is West, and never the twain shall
meet,
Till Earth and Sky stand presently at God's great Judgment
Seat;
But there is neither East nor West, Border nor Breed, nor Birth,
When two strong men stand face to face, though they come from
the ends of the earth !

The scholar A. E. Housman published *A Shropshire Lad* in 1896. His *Last Poems* (1922) and *More Poems* (1936) link him with the twentieth century. Together, these two volumes of ballad-lyrics disclose Housman's resolute resignation to his ' hidden grief '.

John Davidson was born of fairly poor Scottish parents of great piety. He came to London to live a life of what he called poetry's ' storm-clad strength '. Soon he was in revolt, not only against needless poverty but against what he saw as the smugness of some Victorian Christianity. He wrote *Fleet Street Eclogues* (1893), *The Testament of a Man Forbid* (1901), *Mammon and his Message* (1908) and other books. But making a living by poetry was no easier than it had ever been. Davidson's mind brooded in loneliness until it became bitter and clouded. He could be flayingly contemptuous of the ' human hod-me-dods ', the Londoners of his poem ' The Crystal Palace ':

> They can't tell why they come; they only know
> They must shove through the holiday somehow.

But his ' Thirty Bob a Week ' of 1894 was something new in the poetic language of the day. It was as different from what had gone before in Victorian verbal melody as Wordsworth's speech of the common man was from Pope's poetic diction.

Besides his conversational tone of ' Thirty Bob a Week ', his contemptuous tone, Davidson could summon the courage of ' while I live the victory is mine ' and could fall into the near-despair of ' The world has cast me out '. He received little notice, no acclaim. In 1908 George Bernard Shaw gave him £250 to ' cast aside all commercial considerations ' and write a poem on Lucretian Materialism. Instead, Davidson wrote (according to Shaw) ' a popular commercial drama '. He ' had thrown away his big chance '. But Davidson had written ' The Last Journey ', in a rhythm that re-enacts the swing of a long walk:

> I felt the world a-spinning on its nave,
>> I felt it sheering blindly round the sun;
> I felt the time had come to find a grave:
>> I knew it in my heart my days were done . . .
> Deeds all done and songs all sung
>> While others chant in sun and rain,
> 'Heel and toe from dawn to dusk,
>> Round the world and home again.'

Before he drowned himself he recorded:

> I come a hundred years before the time—that time foreseen by Wordsworth—when what is now called science, familiarized to men, shall be ready to put on a form of flesh and blood.[10]

Some may think Davidson's outlook presumptuous and his poetry morbid. Others see his life as one man's regirding of his loins after the Darwinian crisis, in the midst of so-called poetic decadence. His poetry's rhythms sounded a strong note for twentieth-century verse.

The New Literacy

Like poetry, prose changed profoundly towards the close of the nineteenth century. After fourteenth-century ballads the rift had grown wider between the people's poetry and literary poetry. Following Shakespeare, British drama had become the recreation of the aspiring rather than of all or many Londoners. Throughout the nineteenth century, cheap reading matter, in weekly magazines, had been accumulating. Commercial prose or 'journalese' came in.

The deepest wedge grew between the novel read by all and the intellectual novel for a few. Circulating libraries, begun in the eighteenth century, multiplied. Fifteen or twenty years after the 1870 Education Act a literate generation had grown up. In 1869 Matthew Arnold took for granted that 'culture' would prevail. By 1889, the year after his death, in *Questions at Issue* those opinions were revised: state education, he declared, would produce a revolt by the 'mob' against literary masters and against authority. Chaos in standards could result.

As soon as the majority were literate they wanted freedom of selection. Hitherto they had had little to choose from. Many books in the future would be for relaxation. What the eighteenth century called 'taste' had been ordained. When publishers and authors

---

[10] *John Davidson: A Selection of His Poems*, ed. Maurice Lindsay (Hutchinson, 1961), p. 50.

realized that people had freedom of choice, they prepared to offer at least some of what would sell most profitably.

In 1891/2 Arthur Conan Doyle began detective fiction or crime stories with *The Adventures of Sherlock Holmes*. *The Mighty Atom* (1896), by Marie Corelli, was among the first best-selling novels. This is the story of a child's reaction to scientific threat. But overwriting and sentimentality plunge the book in emotional slush.

A growing readership brought a much heavier responsibility to writers. The public was aware, on many different levels, of the questioning in established eschatology and of the new revelations about the hitherto unsuspected subtleties and depths of its own mental and emotional make-up. Both the naïve and the highly intelligent writer might distort or vulgarize in many different ways.

Novelists of the Turn of the Century

There was a strong group of novelists at work in the last decades of the nineteenth century. R. L. Stevenson wrote historical adventure tales, as well as essays and poems: *Treasure Island, Kidnapped, The Master of Ballantrae, Travels with a Donkey*, and *Virginibus Puerisque*. In *Robert Elsmere* Mrs Humphry Ward wrote of the conflict between faith and doubt though rather confusing conscience with convention. Arnold Bennett, a native of the industrial English Midlands, the Potteries, began his regional novels. John Galsworthy, with his series *The Forsyte Saga*, showed money-loving, treasure-collecting Britons in a rosy light. Joseph Conrad, a Pole from the Ukraine, after several years at sea came to Britain and became naturalized in 1884.

Conrad's chief books include *Tales of Unrest* (1898), *Lord Jim* (1900), *Youth* (stories, 1902), *Heart of Darkness* (stories, 1902), *Nostromo* (1904), *The Secret Agent* (1907), and *Chance* (1914). Usually they deal with human flotsam in the earth's four corners—characters who often introduce ' modern civilization'—and their impact on the local inhabitants. *Heart of Darkness* is the most subtly ironic exposure yet written of the madness which could be the jungle's gift to pitiless, ' superior ' exploiters in the past century.

George Meredith, Samuel Butler, George Gissing and Thomas Hardy are linked in that they would have none of the blinkered idealism of their age. Meredith, who wrote more than a dozen novels as well as a long sonnet-series, *Modern Love*, and much other poetry, deliberately wrote in a dense and heavily charged prose that yet delicately outlines his characters. In what is perhaps his best-known book, *The Ordeal of Richard Feverel* (1859), Meredith exposes the folly of trying to bring up a boy within the rules of a philosophical system. Samuel Butler was a religious critic and the author of two ironic utopias, *Erewhon* (1872) and *Erewhon Revisited* (1901). His bitter, autobiographical novel, *The Way of All Flesh* (published posthumously, 1903), tells of a boy's growing up in the care of parents completely convinced of their own righteousness. George Gissing, whom Raymond Williams has called a lesser Dickens, is remembered for grim novels of poverty-stricken London, and of starving writers—*Demos* (1886), *New Grub Street* (1891), and for *The Private Papers of Henry Ryecroft* (1903).

Thomas Hardy's Wessex Novels are deeply English. *Under the Greenwood Tree* (1872) and *Far from the Madding Crowd* (1874), to *Tess of the D'Urbervilles* (1891) and *Jude the Obscure* (1896), are all stories that depict human lives swayed by dark, unknown forces much greater than themselves: Tess, an innocent girl, is yet a bewildered victim of powerful, ruthless, ironic circumstances; Jude and Sue are utterly unable to alter their fate, for all their sincerity.

Jude the Obscure outraged the Britain of the 1890s; Hardy turned to poetry. His *Wessex Poems* of 1898 influenced English poetry through the succeeding century. His mystic verse-tapestry of the three parts of *The Dynasts* (1904-8) showed the ' littleness ' of the human movers in Napoleon's European war, under the Immanent Will, the Spirit of the Years, the Pities, the Shades, all those invisible shapers of the universe which remind us of Shelley's in *Prometheus Unbound*.

None of these writers compromised in what they felt they had to say. None was popular in his day.

The socialist H. G. Wells became a best-seller towards the turn of the century. His books include *The Time Machine* (1895), *The Island of Dr. Moreau* (1896), *The Invisible Man* (1897), *The War of the Worlds* (1898), *The First Men in the Moon* (1901), *The Way the World Is Going* (1928) and *The Shape of Things to Come* (1933). More than any previous writer Wells made readers aware of the adventures and the perils of the future. His rather coarse prose concentrates on the ingenuity of original, daring, technical action. It does not attempt to convey subtlety or sensitivity of character. It is competent, confident, scientific and, in novels such as *Ann Veronica* (1909) and *The History of Mr. Polly* (1910), socially analytic yet humorous.

He also believed in the efficient popularizing of knowledge. *An Outline of History* (1920) and *A Short History of the World* (1922), which he helped to write, are readable if only for their conception and growth of a cosmic way of seeing our earth, as world communications become quicker. This marks a further attempt at approach to the wholeness of knowledge Francis Bacon, in the early seventeenth century, Hobbes a little later, and Herbert Spencer in the nineteenth century wished to see.

Drama

Nineteenth-century British literature began with a Scottish enrichment—by Beattie, Ramsay, Burns and Walter Scott. It ended with enrichment from Irish culture, the Gaelic Renaissance. This came in both poetry and drama. Set on foot when terror and fighting continued between Ireland and England, when hate and oppression were unresolved between the two disparate race-stocks and the Catholic and Protestant religions, the Irish revival echoes the great early period of Gaelic-Irish prose and poetry before and after the sixth century. Beginnings of revival may be discerned in mid-nineteenth-century Irish poets and journalists of the 1842 *Nation*—Thomas Davis, James Clarence Mangan and Samuel Ferguson.

George Bernard Shaw, William Butler Yeats, John Millington Synge, Sean O'Casey, Lady Gregory, Katharine Tynan, James Stephens, Padraic Colum, George Russell, better known as A.E., and George Moore—all these were inspired by the Irish Renaissance. The theatre in England had been dead enough during the nineteenth century. There were a few social comedies, of Pinero, Henry Arthur Jones and others. Farquhar, Sheridan and Goldsmith, the well-known playwrights in London of the seventeenth and eighteenth centuries, were Irish.

Like James Joyce later, Shaw deliberately turned from Gaelic influence. He admitted he owed much to the irony of Samuel Butler in *The Way of All Flesh* and *Erewhon*. He was further in debt to the early, practical socialism of Robert Owen, to the Christian socialism of Charles Kingsley during the sufferings of British workers and children in the earlier part of the century, as well as to Croce's idea of a Life Force, to Nietzsche and Karl Marx's *Das Kapital.* This last Shaw read in the French edition of 1884 and became a socialist. *Das Kapital*—full of *saeva indignatio* that sounds like hate, but should be studied, if only for its many undeniable facts—did not reach English and England until 1887. Technically Shaw owed much to the Norwegian dramatist Ibsen. Under Ibsen's inspiration he revived British drama, first in Dublin, then in London. A brilliant imitator and mimic himself, with a sparring, flashing intellect, his plays, and the prefaces he invariably gave them, have that audacious humour we associate with the richly voluble, unquenchable Irish mind. His works include *Mrs. Warren's Profession, Arms and the Man* and *Candida*—all in *Plays Pleasant and Unpleasant* (1898)—*Man and Superman* (1903), *Pygmalion* (1912), *Back to Methusalah* (1921), *St. Joan* (1924) and *The Applecart* (1929). Rarely whole truths, Shaw's astringent overstatements contain lively germs of the elusive element. His belief in a Life Force inclined him to admire dictators and the power they could command. His characters are more often mouthpieces or intellectual puppets rather than men and women.

Synge's plays, such as *The Shadow of the Glen* (performed 1903), *The Playboy of the Western World* (1907) and *Deirdre of the Sorrows* (1910), turned back to Gaelic, still-living speech rhythms: what Synge called the ' realities ' of the Gaelic background or rural West Ireland. The myths of *The Playboy* and of *Deirdre* have their roots in a far Celtic-Gaelic past. The rhythms and cadences of the Irish-English which Synge's characters use continue to enrich the language, as do those of Welsh and Scottish, often in unconscious, certainly in unexpected, ways. Synge died tragically young.

Sean O'Casey, too, used his early Dublin slum background, Irish idiom and childlike, drinking, bouncing Irish characters, in his early plays such as *Juno and the Paycock* (1925). Those of his characters who mock at faith offended his Catholic countrymen, and *The Silver Tassie* (1928) was refused by Yeats for the Dublin stage. O'Casey lived most of his life in England. His later plays include *Red Roses for Me* (1942), *Oak Leaves and Lavender* (1946), *Cock-a-Doodle Dandy* (1949) and *The Bishop's Bonfire* (1955). All his plays have a love of life voiced by a variety of characters, none of whom is evil and all of whom have an engaging Gaelic volubility.

Historians, Critics, Philosophers

By the end of the nineteenth and the beginning of the twentieth century English literature had a rich past and a complex, diffuse and by no means wholly English present. Historians of the nineteenth century include J. A. Froude, Thomas Macaulay, John Richard Green, William Stubbs, and S. R. Gardiner. Literature, freed from direct political dissensions, was the voice for most other dissensions. Besides journalists, there were writers of essays and belles-lettres, and experts on the various sciences.

At the turn of the century well-known critics included Edmund Gosse, Leslie Stephen, Arthur Quiller-Couch, George Saintsbury and Stopford Brooke. Not all critics were practitioners in the novel, poetry, or plays they undertook to criticize.

G. K. Chesterton and the French-born Hilaire Belloc were writers of light verse, epigrams, religious controversy and journalism. Their verse belongs with that of Rudyard Kipling in that it has a flamboyant, tongue-in-cheek, Little Englandism. Both chose to be influenced by the coming of commercial journalism. Both were believers in ancient wisdoms and orthodoxy; both rather despised the new. But their quipping optimism and clever paradox prevent many readers feeling they have any underlying seriousness.

G. E. Moore published *Principia Ethica* in 1903. Bertrand Russell's *Principles of Mathematics* appeared the same year. The three volumes of *Principia Mathematica*, by Bertrand Russell and A. N. Whitehead, were published in 1910. Russell's *Human Knowledge, Its Scope and Limits*, with the same kind of inclusiveness as Wells's *Short History of the World* (1922), came out in 1948. Russell is the most widely known of modern British philosophers, but it will need the distance of time to assess fully his importance as a twentieth-century thinker.

Russell, Bernard Shaw, Thomas Hardy, W. B. Yeats, Joseph Conrad, Galsworthy, Arnold Bennett and H. G. Wells link the crowded nineteenth century of wealth and exploration, empire and reform with the testing century to follow.

G

VII

The Twentieth Century

1914 to the Present Day

Time took on modernity. The twentieth century has become the Scientific Age. Men have learnt to make science so precise, so strictly accurate, by disciplining, curbing, sometimes wholly rejecting, the wayward, ' blind ' imagination. The outward triumph of this process is apparent today.

Under more and more rapid growth of education for the many the century also came to be called ' the age of the man-in-the-street '; under staggering scientific advance it has become the ' Technological Age '. As problems have multiplied, it has been variously labelled the ' Space Age ', ' Atomic Age ', ' Megaton Age ', ' Electronic Age ', ' Computer Age ', as well as the ' Age of Anxiety ', ' Age of Unrest ', ' Age of Self-consciousness ', ' Age of Distrust '. Change itself has grown more rapid. This rapidity can be delusive if scanned only from urban areas of development.

About the turn of the nineteenth century Sigmund Freud, a Viennese, Jewish doctor, disclosed his hypothesis of the self, emotional and impulsive, below man's conscious, intelligent self. Freud claimed that more basic (though not necessarily more important) than human reason are inborn urges, many of which we share with our animal ancestral relatives. Thinking, and morally self-conscious emotion, constitute progress beyond the ape in us. But reason, therefore, cannot be in sole, or even totally secure, command. Based in feeling and the senses, reason Freud saw as incapable of ' pure disinterest '. Rationalists from the eighteenth century onwards have supposed reason man's infallible guide. It is, of course, still his guide; but rationalism, Freudian thought held, if unaware of its emotive basis, could be incognizant of when it departed from reason.

After such a ferment of enlightenment about the human make-up, disagreed with by many of course, novelists were eager to experiment in form and content. Freud's doctrines, popularized, sometimes misrepresented, made people more than ever curious about what one of the great twentieth-century novelists was to call the nine-tenths of the human iceberg submerged beneath consciousness.

New Techniques in the Novel

Freud's, Jung's, Adler's and other psychologists' work showed that the deep, unconscious mind has memories of racially inherited, archetypal or myth assumptions. Behind or below the conscious, the subconscious is inchoate but not formless. Both the conscious and the unconscious relate to individual memory and personality. Disclosures such as these influenced Dorothy Richardson in her novels. She began what critics have since called the ' stream-of-consciousness ' novel: *Pointed Roofs* (1915), *Dawn's Left Hand* (1931) and *Clear Horizon* (1935), with five in between, are the best known of her eight collected under the title *Pilgrimage* in 1938. All show events happening in the mind rather than in outside action.

In 1915 Virginia Woolf published *The Voyage Out*. Not until *Mrs Dalloway* (1925) and *To the Lighthouse* (1927) did this dedicated writer seek, with what Leonard Woolf has called ' quicksilver ' intensity, to express what she saw as the ' butterfly wing ' of inward experience. *To the Lighthouse* does away with ' plot ' as Scott, Wilkie Collins, Dickens and Hardy understood it, highly complicated happenings often more full of coincidence than life is. *To the Lighthouse* is largely Mrs Dalloway's private reactions to a house-group of people, including her husband and eight children, during an evening disappointing to the youngest boy because the father has decided a promised visit to the lighthouse cannot take place on the morrow. Virginia Woolf has a fine sense of human frailty. Her later novels, *The Waves* (1931) and *The Years* (1937), where she uses what has come to be called the ' flash-back ' method with place and time in a story, have had considerable influence on twentieth-century novel technique. Her experience of people was dominated by her own consciousness, but within her own limits she is highly original.

D. H. Lawrence's first novel, *The White Peacock*, was published in 1911, and this was followed by *The Trespasser* (1912) and *Sons and Lovers* (1913). Rejected on account of tuberculosis for the 1914-18 war Lawrence wrote *The Rainbow* (1915). This was banned in Britain. Then came *Women in Love* (1920), first published in the United States, where it was seized by the Society for the Suppression of Vice but afterwards released. Restless but not daunted Lawrence travelled and wrote *Aaron's Rod* (1922) and *Kangaroo* (1923) from Australia, *The Plumed Serpent* (1926) from Taos in Mexico, shorts stories, *England, My England* (1922) and *The Woman Who Rode Away* (1928). His studies *Psychoanalysis and the Unconscious* (1921) and *Fantasia of the Unconscious* (1922), vivid and fascinating, contain profound sense and some nonsense. His critical *Studies in Classic American Literature* came in 1923; his travel books *Sea and Sardinia* and *Mornings in Mexico* were published in 1921 and 1927 respectively; and in 1928 came *Lady Chatterley's Lover*.

Lady Chatterley's Lover was banned in Britain until the right to issue it in paperback was fought in a 1960 court: Penguin Books won; Regina, State and Crown lost. The book and the case raised much public discussion as to whether the book was obscene and in what obscenity or pornography lies. Books have been burnt and banned since the days of papyrus. In *Areopagitica* Milton wrote against censorship, of which, three hundred years later, the puritan Lawrence became a victim. *The Rainbow* and *Women in Love* show the emotional turmoil and happiness that accompany the fulfilment of desire and sexual love between a man and a woman. They are also about the running battle and guerrilla warfare between men and women before they accept each other's ' otherness '. Both novels are intricately intuitive and richly detailed. Lawrence cared nothing for standardized, intellectual labels—what he called ' skin and grief form '. *Lady Chatterley's Lover* is a novel with blemishes beyond, as F. R. Leavis has said, its didacticism and class-animus. Some readers find it ' fine '; some ' beautiful '; others find it ' revolting '; still others wonder what ' all the fuss is about '. The hero Mellors's hearty over-use of the male Anglo-Saxon verb for ' to love ' or ' to make love ' produces different reactions in different readers. The novel is a poet's cry against the deadness and mechanicalness he thought were steadily seeping into every vein of life in the twentieth-century machine age.

Lawrence's sincerity, however passionate, could not and did not always ensure artistry of content. Novels such as Jane Austen's *Pride and Prejudice*, George Eliot's *Middlemarch*, Dickens's *Great Expectations*, Conrad's *Lord Jim*, are all firmly based in a well-tried, moral and intellectual body of law. Lawrence believed in a ' dark blood-conscious ', primitive intuition wiser than intellect and beyond law. But there is no way back to such primitiveness as this belief entailed. Although he affirmed an ancient, lost truth, exemplified in the tangled myths of Tristan and Yseult, Lancelot and Guinevere and other legends, his rebellion against his age continued even when restraints and hypocrisies had receded after the end of the First World War. *Lady Chatterley's Lover* is a courageous failure by a dying genius who detested libertinism but whose subconscious mind could not play the part the subconscious mind does play in successful writing. Lawrence reveals a profitable seam for the serious novel of the future to explore. A vital quality in his portraits, and what his champion, the critic F. R. Leavis, has labelled Lawrence's ' terrifying honesty ', are unsurpassed.

Lawrence put out *Love Poems* in 1913, and—already marked for death—wrote poems and novels until his *Collected Poems* came out in 1928 and 1932. Beginning with rhymed verse, later he followed the century's change sufficiently to use a snarling near-prose in *Nettles* and uneven, unrhymed, ' prose-cadences ' in the second volume of his *Collected Poems*. The sequence from ' Coldness in Love ' to ' The Virgin Mother ' and the second sequence ' Look ! We Have Come Through ' of between 1912 and 1917, may be read alongside *The Rainbow*, *Women in Love* and *Lady Chatterley's Lover* as Lawrence's commentaries on the strife, mystery and fulfilment of sexual and family love. After that Lawrence wrote a poem-sequence on flowers, fruits, birds and animals. Writing—prose or poetry—for him was so much a part of being alive that his poems have a startling, deliberately uncontrolled directness. Lawrence's power, which he called his ' demon ', rarely fails to the last to quicken, to bring into bright, temporary being, the kindred life in snake, bat, mosquito, Sicilian cyclamen, in almost everything his pen touched, as his novels bring man, woman and child to a kind of pulsing aliveness rather than to any imperceptible but sure growth.

Katherine Mansfield (Kathleen Beauchamp), born four years after Lawrence, but in New Zealand, was naturalized in Britain as the wife of the critic and utopian socialist, John Middleton Murry.

She wrote short stories and poems; her *Journal* and *Letters* were published after her death. These last reveal a self-awareness and an awareness of others akin to D. H. Lawrence's, Virginia Woolf's and Dorothy Richardson's in this self-conscious age. They belong totally with the already chafed sensibilities of the new century. They could not have been written in any previous age.

They also reveal their author's attitude to her own life and writing harried by the disease which killed Keats, Dowson and Lawrence. Secretly dissatisfied with her inability to be ' simple ' and honest enough, at thirty-three Katherine Mansfield retired to a retreat at Fontainbleau. Her death there, three months later, now seems, with the advance of treatment, tragically needless.

Her volumes of short stories were *In a German Pension* (1911), *Bliss* (1920), *The Garden Party* (1922) and *The Dove's Nest* (1923). Her originality is that she lets her characters reveal, betray themselves, not only by actions, but by the tiniest, physical attributes, movements of features and bodies; everything they say betrays, even to slips of the tongue. What they do not say betrays too. This is a brilliant realization. She knows as much as Jane Austen about the artistic, impressionistic use of the withheld or the unsaid. Only to the acutest observers do we betray ourselves, in what we say, in the subjects we talk of, the subjects we avoid, what our tongues say unintentionally or when we are off-guard. In no sense a literary or intellectual writer, Katherine Mansfield had little sentimentality. She has been accused of cruelty as in the short ' Poison ' and in many other admirable stories. Clear-sighted with a childlike inwardness is one way of describing her method. She owed something to Chekhov. But her tone or flavour, and her legacy in short-story writing, are essentially her own.

Ronald Firbank wrote short novels of social irony: *Vainglory* (1915), *Inclinations* (1916), *Caprice* (1917), *Valmouth* (1919), *The Flower Beneath the Foot* (1923) and *Sorrow in Sunlight* (1925; U.S. edn titled *Prancing Nigger*, 1924). His delineation of the effete culture of some of the English *nouveaux riches* immediately prior to 1914 is achieved by a use of materialistic preoccupations to highlight inanities in almost incessant small-talk of a society utterly out of touch with any reality beyond its own closed circle.

Of this group of early twentieth-century innovators in form and content is the Irishman James Joyce. Joyce was born in Dublin in

1882. Teaching on the Continent and then settling in Paris, he was part of the Gaelic revival whilst being beyond and outside it. He published *Chamber Music* (poems) in 1907, *Dubliners* (stories) in 1914, *A Portrait of the Artist as a Young Man* (serially) in 1914-15 and *Ulysses* in 1922; *Anna Livia Plurabelle* and *Haveth Childers Everywhere* were fragments from *Work in Progress* which, in 1939, became *Finnegans Wake*. There are many studies and at least two glosses of *Finnegans Wake*. It is a kind of surrealist, symbolic, Gaelic-Anglo-Saxon ' Jabberwocky ', highly inventive in its word juggling associations, echoes and relationships.

With *Ulysses* Joyce became an innovator both in artistic form and in language. Literary and intellectual as it is, nevertheless it is much more readable and easy to enjoy than *Finnegans Wake*. It is an immensely long series of scenes in twenty-four hours in the intersecting lives of three contrasted yet related characters: the young Stephen Dedalus, the middle-aged, Jewish, Leopold Bloom, and Bloom's wife Marion. Its background is the vast, static, well-defended citadel of Roman Catholicism, in Dublin's underworld, in the fortresses of the characters' minds. Against the overpowering Catholic guard Stephen is rebelling. The bedroom soliloquy of Bloom's wife, Marion, which closes the book, is brilliantly arid. There are finer scenes. Much of *Ulysses* belongs to the ' stream-of-consciousness ', ' thought-pattern ' method of earlier twentieth-century writing. To read in *Ulysses* for the first time in one's life Stephen Dedalus's ' soliloquy ' as he walked by Dublin harbour shore is to become aware, with the shock adolescent discovery of self-consciousness gives, what our minds are up to during all their waking hours when we are apparently unobservant.

In *Pilgrimage* Dorothy Richardson shows us minds more restricted in range, aware of tiny importances all round; but amid the hurry of material living these importances are often ignored, slurred over. Joyce shows us mind gyrating beyond external ' good ' and ' evil ', perilously free of both. He reveals how mind repeats itself; how it works in associations seemingly random, beyond consciousness, but tied to that memory the workings of which we still know so little about. He shows minds, male and female, meandering through individual, private labyrinths, lurching into the unforeseeable future.

Novelists after the First World War

1914 darkened windows in Europe and Britain. Powers, conventional restraints, previous structures and self-confidence crumbled. After 1918 perfectionism, with many other illusions, died.

The novelists Hugh Walpole and Compton Mackenzie, whom Henry James thought better novelists than D. H. Lawrence, spanned the war years. Wells, Bennett, Galsworthy and Conrad, were still writing. E. M. Forster built his reputation on five novels— *Where Angels Fear to Tread* (1905), *The Longest Journey* (1907), *A Room with a View* (1908), *Howard's End* (1910) and *A Passage to India* (1924). In each novel Forster explores the lives of people whose fumbling desires to believe others are complicated by an almost equally instinctive urge to distrust. Self-aware, mutual trust between people Forster saw as hampered by differences in cultures and environments. These differences, often imaginary or self-invented, created monstrous misunderstandings. People, Forster seemed to be saying, are often so much better than they seem; human friendship is the important thing, human beings are much more alike than different; human warmth is more important than culture. In *A Passage to India* the real—or fancied—difference between potential friends, an Indian and an Englishman, fights with personal, instinctive trust and cannot avert tragedy. On the friends cultural differences force final estrangement. Forster presents a strong plea, first and foremost, for tolerance above cultural and racial differences.

Norman Douglas's travel books *Old Calabria* (1915) and *Alone* (1921), and novels *South Wind* (1917) and *In the Beginning* (1927), illustrate the influence Roman and Italian cultures have had on Britons.

Aldous Huxley sought a way through, or from, the burden of increasing knowledge and self-consciousness in the fascinations, first of ' pure ' detached intellect, then of extrasensory perception. Instead of concerning himself with describing ' middle-class interiors ' Huxley at first tried to make ' ideas bombinate ' in his novels, as he put it. *Crome Yellow* (1921), *Antic Hay* (1923), *Those Barren Leaves* (1925), and *Point Counter Point* (1928) show some of the sophisticated relishing the post-war, physical and mental relief after the strain of the 1920s. Later he ventured into further illusions of detachment under the drug mescalin. His interest in science produced in 1932 the satiric ' Utopia ' of the future, *Brave New World*. An émigré Russian, Yevgeny Zamyatin,[1] in his novel *We* (1922) originated this theme. Whether Huxley read *We* in its French edition is not certain. *Brave New World* depicts a test-tube produced community. Almost completely non-human, nobody within the society realized how ' dead ' they were until a ' noble savage ' spoke in defence of feeling: emotions mean constant fear of constant threat; they mean remorse, guilt, tragedy, despair. More than ever, as this century progresses, do we seek to subordinate them to science and reason. Yet they, united with intellect, are what help us to remain humanly compassionate. The ' noble savage ' was a romantic eighteenth-century conception that sprang up in the twentieth century because of a new Western realization of an ethical simplicity in black people sometimes thought to have been corroded by white civilization. Huxley's later novels include *Eyeless in Gaza* (1936), *After Many a Summer* (1939) and *Island* (1962). His other works include the essay collections *Grey Eminence: A Study in Religion and Politics* (1941), *Ape and Essence* (1948), *The Devils of Loudoun* (1952) and *Heaven and Hell* (1956).

George Orwell, educated at Eton, trained in the Indian Imperial Police, died tragically early. Orwell hated cant in high places and shallow thinking anywhere. He published *Down and Out in Paris and London* in 1933, *The Road to Wigan Pier* in 1937, *Homage to Catalonia* in 1938. *Animal Farm* (1945) and *Nineteen Eighty-Four* (1949), minatory and ironic, became very popular. They are prophecies concerning our possible future, more joyless than *Brave New World*, forecasting a Balance of Terror between two great world powers in which all personal liberty is jeopardized. Orwell's parables are part of this new age of man's acceptance, late and reluctant, of his own responsibility; and, as John Wain has said, Orwell's essays and fables are as relevant today as they were when he wrote them.

Threat to man's future and the challenge of that threat were beginning to dominate the novel. A preceding bleakness, seen by some as realism or naturalism, had been a persistent note in Ivy Compton-Burnett's novels; and these range from the time when

---

[1] Yevgeny Zamyatin (1884-1937), a naval engineer, spent some time in England between 1914 and 1918 and wrote two scathing tales about English life, ' The Islanders ' and ' The Manhunter '. See Janko Lavrin, *An Introduction to the Russian Novel* (Methuen, 1942), pp. 169-70.

Lawrence, Virginia Woolf, Dorothy Richardson, and Ronald Firbank began to write. Ivy Compton-Burnett's books include: *Dolores* (1911), *Pastors and Masters* (1925), *Brothers and Sisters* (1929), *Men and Wives* (1931), *More Women than Men* (1933), *A House and Its Head* (1935), *Daughters and Sons* (1937), *A Family and a Fortune* (1939), *Parents and Children* (1941), *Elders and Betters* (1944); and other novels up to *The Mighty and Their Fall* (1961). She creates a small family world of the period between 1890 and 1900. In each novel she peoples this with related grown-ups, Victorian servants and children, who all seem shut up in country houses surrounded by a kind of claustrophobic, blank, outer dark. Their ingrown lusts and greeds, their plots and stone-hearted jealousies are shown almost entirely through highly stylized dialogue. Children speak in this way as well as grown-ups. No retribution, no kindly justice, seem ever to intervene in, quell or alleviate savage hates and family passions; yet from the point of view of craftsmanship, all is superbly carried out.

Mr Weston's Good Wine (1927) is perhaps the best known of the many fables by T. F. Powys, member of a Welsh family and brother of Littleton Powys, Llewelyn Powys and J. C. Powys. *Mr Weston's Good Wine* is a rural parable or mystic story celebrating the country people whom industrialism is causing to disappear.

Charles Williams wrote seven novels, *War in Heaven* (1930), *Many Dimensions* (1931), *The Place of the Lion* (1931), *The Greater Trumps* (1932), *Shadows of Ecstasy* (1933), *Descent into Hell* (1937) and *All Hallows Eve* (1944). All have philosophical depth as well as the suspense of a thriller; all explore a supernatural reality. Ethical, occult, this reality is the spirit life beyond death and its effect upon life on earth. Besides these and his verse play *Thomas Cranmer of Canterbury* (1936) Charles Williams wrote theological studies, including *The Descent of the Dove* (1939), *The Foregiveness of Sins* (1942), both collections of essays, and *The Figure of Beatrice: A Study in Dante* (1943).

Ford Madox Ford, founder in 1908 of *The English Review*, included in his large output of novels the Tietjens sequence, *Some Do Not* (1925), *No More Parades* (1925), *A Man Could Stand Up* (1926) and *Last Post* (1928). His work *The March of Literature from Confucius' Day to Our Own* (1938-9), like H. M. and K. Chadwick's *The Growth of Literature*, sees as necessary a wider, intercultural view of prose and poetry.

Malcolm Lowry completed four of a planned seven novels to be called 'The Voyage Never Ends': *Ultramarine* was published in 1933. Then came *In Ballast to the White Sea*, completed in 1936. *Lunar Caustic* (not printed until it appeared in the *Paris Review* of 1963) recounts an alcoholic's useless stay in a New York mental hospital. *Under the Volcano* (1947; repr. 1967) is a subtle analysis, written in lyrically beautiful prose, of a man, physically and mentally tormented and self-tormented by alcoholism, in his slow descent to death and Avernus. It is a powerful, original novel with autobiographical undertones.

L. H. Myers's *The Root and the Flower* (1935) and *The Pool of Vishnu* (1940) explore the India of the last Mogul. Myers's lofty, deeply serious, style aptly illustrates how slowly, after all—for all this century's real change and illusions of change—time and institutions alter basic human nature. The guru, believer in natural goodness, is Myers's most admirable of men; gurus are not interested in public power or external disciples. Authority imposed in terms of original sin or human folly by a godhead, rather than through humanly godlike possibilities, has no lasting usefulness, Myers might have said. As E. M. Forster's emphasis on friendship is relevant for life and novels of all time, so is this statement of L. H. Myers.

Through the 1930s and the 1940s, with slow, detailed insights, R. C. Hutchinson explored further the difficulties of seeing, or even approaching, in an age of wide communications and needed understanding, each other's point of view. *The Unforgotten Prisoner* (1933), *One Light Burning* (1935), *Shining Scabbard* (1936) and *Elephant and Castle* (1949) have European as well as English backgrounds and have been much translated. As Forster, Myers and Hutchinson have done, so Joyce Cary explored difficulties of understanding between people of a developed culture of less developed civilizations. His *Mister Johnson* (1939) was one of the few novels by a white man in which the portrayal of Africans was acceptable to the latter. But since *Uhuru* this acceptance has changed to rejection. The subject explored in *A Passage to India*, *Mister Johnson* and by a younger novelist, P. H. Newby, in his *A Guest and His Going* (1959), is fertile ground for present-day novelists, white and black.

Joyce Cary also published *To Be a Pilgrim* (1942), *The Horse's Mouth* (1944) and *A Fearful Joy* (1949). His trilogy *Prisoner of Grace* (1952), *Except the Lord* (1953) and *Not Honour More* (1955) is concerned with politics, while *The Captive and the Free* (1959) has a religious theme. Cary's *A House of Children* (1941) is autobiographical.

Storm Jameson has also written novels on the question of reciprocal sympathies within various cultures. In this she may be linked with E. M. Forster, R. C. Hutchinson, Joyce Cary and P. H. Newby. Her books published between the two wars include *That Was Yesterday* (1932), *A Richer Dust* (Pt 3 of trilogy, 1933), *None Turn Back* (1936), *Cousin Honoré* (1940), *Europe to Let* (1940), *The Fort* (1941), *Then We Shall Hear Singing* (1942) and *The Road from the Monument* (1962). Rosamond Lehmann in *Dusty Answer* (1927), *The Weather in the Streets* (1936) and *The Ballad and the Source* (1945) used a delicate perception to tell stories that fascinated by their sense of youth's beauty and vitality. Phyllis Bentley has written regional novels of Yorkshire. Winifred Holtby's *South Riding* (1936) was memorable.

Elizabeth Bowen in *The Death of the Heart* (1938), *The Heat of the Day* (1949) and other novels has a similar intuition, often concerning the young. There is, or there was up to the 1950s, a masculine and a feminine way of writing novels. Even an intellectual such as George Eliot has a depth of personal intuition very different from a man's broader, far more comprehensive, perceptions. Rosamund Lehmann and Elizabeth Bowen are both very ' feminine ' novelists. Rose Macaulay, with *Dangerous Ages* (1921), *I Would Be Private* (1937), other novels and travel books, belongs to this group.

Vera Brittain's *Testament of Youth* (1933) showed how the flower of a generation was crushed between 1914 and 1918. Rebecca West's examinations of notorious criminal trials enthral many: her *Black Lamb and Grey Falcon* (1968), on Yugoslavia, reveals a writer who makes no compromise with slick journalism. Another great journalist was H. J. Massingham. Another, who was also a writer with perceptivity, was H. M. Tomlinson. His well-known book about the First World War is titled *All Our Yesterdays* (1930). Countrymen such as George Sturt in *The Wheelwright's Shop* (1923) have recorded the way of rural life and crafts vanishing under the century's technology.

V. S. Pritchett, critic and novelist, is also a highly gifted short-story writer. He endows all his characters with a flesh-and-blood vitality, and often their comic liveliness seems, miraculously, to be self-generated. His autobiography, *A Cab at the Door* (1968), may

be one of the significant life stories of the century. So may Bertrand
Russell's. And so may Leonard Woolf's, concluding with *The
Journey Not the Arrival Matters*, which appeared in 1969, the year of
his death.

Osbert Sitwell, poet, essayist and novelist, is well known for his
five-volume autobiographical work, *Left Hand, Right Hand!*
(1945-50), broadly a family saga of wit, erudition and literary
elegance. George Orwell, in a review of the first three volumes—
Left Hand, Right Hand! (1945), *The Scarlet Tree* (1946), *Great Morning!* (1947)—wrote: ' It is to Sir Osbert Sitwell's credit that he has
never pretended to be other than he is: a member of the upper
classes, with an amused and leisurely attitude which comes out in the
manner of his writing. . . . How easy it would have been to write of
Eton or the Grenadier Guards in a spirit of sneering superiority. . . .
Or how easy, on the other hand, to stand on the defensive and try
to argue the injustice and inequality of the world in which he grew
up. He has done neither, with the result that these three volumes,
although the range they cover is narrow, must be among the best
autobiographies of our time.'[2] In the concluding volume, *Noble
Essences* (1950), Osbert Sitwell gives vivid pen-portraits of a number
of artists and writers, including Arnold Bennett, Firbank, Gosse,
Ada Leverson, Wilfred Owen and W. H. Davies—poet and author
of *The Autobiography of a Super-Tramp* (1908), a book much admired
by Bernard Shaw.

Evelyn Waugh wrote biting, detached satires. Among his best-
known novels are *Decline and Fall* (1928), *Vile Bodies* (1930), *Scoop*
(1938), *Put Out More Flags* (1942), *Brideshead Revisited* (1945), *The
Loved One* (1948) and his trilogy *Men at Arms* (1952), *Officers and
Gentlemen* (1955) and *Unconditional Surrender* (1961). All convey a
certain contempt for ordinary, sophisticated man. Most became
best-sellers. They reflect some of the self-distrust and self-disgust
which grew in Britain in the inter-war years. But because a writer
cannot hide what he is, a sense of Waugh's own divided heart comes
disturbingly through his writing, assuaging the harsh satire.

Somerset Maugham's first novel *Liza of Lambeth* (1897) began a
long career for its author as a best-selling novelist, playwright and
short-story writer. Maugham was a diligent craftsman. His values,
admittedly ' realistic ', are tied to much that is now both past and
of past interest. His best-known novels are *Of Human Bondage* (1915)

[2] *The Adelphi* (July-Sept. 1948), p. 250.

and *Cakes and Ale* (1930), his best-known plays, perhaps, *The Land of Promise* and *The Constant Wife* (1927).

J. C. Powys's novels, of which the best known is *A Glastonbury Romance* (1933), are Celtic and enriching in the sense that their passionate prose is inseparable from, and used in praise of, an ancient, mystic, earthy love.

J. B. Priestley's *The Good Companions* (1929) is a rollicking, Pickwickian entertainment; and Priestley has also written successful plays—*Dangerous Corner* (1932), *Time and the Conways* (1937). He is a man of the people, seeing for them, speaking for them, even in *Literature and Western Man* (1960).

Many people have read, and critics have praised, L. P. Hartley's trilogy, *The Shrimp and the Anemone* (1944), *Eustace and Hilda* (1947) and *The Go-Between* (1953). L. P. Hartley's values, and his characters Eustace and the elder sister Hilda, are Victorian and worldly. The author's understanding, as in *The Go-Between* where seeing two people make love seems to precipitate a nervous breakdown in the boy, dips occasionally towards melodrama.

Charles Morgan's idealistic novels, *Portrait in a Mirror* (1929), *The Fountain* (1932), *Sparkenbroke* (1936) and *The Judge's Story* (1947) have a precise style and a background of Platonism that appeal to the French: Morgan is more admired in his French translations and in France than by his own countrymen.

Henry Williamson's long sequence, *The Flax of Dream*, written from the 1914 war onwards, may perhaps be less important than his more original, intimately observed nature stories, *Tarka the Otter* (1927) and *Salar the Salmon* (1935).

Richard Hughes's *A High Wind in Jamaica* (originally published as *The Innocent Voyage*, 1929), a discerning story of children's reaction to a murder at sea, was much praised. Richard Hughes has written other sea stories, such as *In Hazard* (1938). *The Fox in the Attic* (1961) is the first volume of a long work in progress, *The Human Predicament*.

C. S. Lewis, scholar and critic, wrote, among many other books, *The Problem of Pain* (1940) and *The Screwtape Letters* (1942). He also devised allegories of Good and Evil, a new Devil, a new Eve. Such is the trilogy *Out of the Silent Planet* (1938), *Perelandra* (1943) and *That Hideous Strength* (1945). A leaning to sensationalism cheapens the frequent beauty in these. Their threat of doom approaches the blunt, gloating horror found in some science fiction.

Arthur Koestler, Hungarian by birth, has lived in England and written in English since 1940. His novels include *Darkness at Noon* (1940), *Thieves in the Night* (1946) and *The Age of Longing* (1951). His best-known collection of essays is perhaps *The Yogi and the Commissar* (1945).

Nigel Balchin, as an industrial psychologist, is an informed, easy, competent novelist. *The Small Back Room* (1943) and *Mine Own Executioner* (1945) are psychological whodunits—economical, confident, and finished.

Henry Green (pseud. of Henry Vincent Yorke) is a novelist of whom W. H. Auden has spoken as ' the best English novelist alive '. C. P. Snow has seen in Henry Green's work ' all the signs we have come to associate with artistic diffidence and decay '. Green's novels include *Living* (1929), *Caught* (1943), *Loving* (1945), *Back* (1946), *Nothing* (1950) and *Doting* (1952). They are all shapely novels; they use talk, as Ronald Firbank, Katherine Mansfield and Ivy Compton-Burnett have all used it, brilliantly to portray and betray personality.

C. P. Snow, a scientist and a civil servant, has written the novel series *Strangers and Brothers*. With an economical, flat, emotionless prose, Snow's novels lay bare the jealousies and intrigues in university, business and political life. His characters are representative of men who will influence our immediate future.

Some critics and readers find novels such as *The Corridors of Power* (1964) ' authentic ', ' realist ', ' healthy '; they see characters observed with clarity yet with due admiration, Snow's values as real and salutary. Others find his values materialistic, his politics tendentious and his human outlook confined to neon-lit, political and career men, committee men, administration men, eating-and-drinking men. Perhaps the fact is that *Corridors of Power* and Snow's other novels are a needed diagnosis of the unlessening conflict between self-interest and professional integrity. *The Sleep of Reason* (1969) returns to the theme that reason can achieve the fullest analysis of that blind and subtle struggle towards what is still called liberty.

Grahame Greene established his reputation with *The Power and the Glory* in 1940. His novels are often set in foreign lands. His characters are usually seedy, shoddy, Catholics, sinning, repenting, lonely. His style is terse. Often he uses a film-shot technique; frequently one or two brilliantly selected details spotlight a close-up. The drunken old priest of *The Power and the Glory* goes on fornicating until the eleventh hour but is ' saved ' by martyrdom. Scobie of *The Heart of the Matter* (1948), hopelessly without God, is also ' saved ' by suicide, we are to suppose, at the last minute. In most of Greene's internationally read books the query is: ' damned ' or ' not damned '; shabby, wilful sinner, or futile, besmeared, but saved.

Anthony Powell has observed, through the eyes of his narrator-character Nicholas Jenkins, the social turnabout of the 1950s and 1960s in the series *The Music of Time*. These novels, written in dry, witty prose, such as *A Question of Upbringing* (1951) and *The Military Philosophers* (1968), show the violent, sinister, absurd, often cruel, changes in two decades. They are in the social-realist pattern of the English novel.

Lawrence Durrell, in *Alexandria Quartet* weaves a Middle East exoticism around Europeans living in the Mediterranean or in Egypt. G. S. Fraser has called Durrell's prose and poetry ' flashy '. Certainly in the novels Durrell's people do not reach down to any plane of everyday reality. The language in which they are described and the background and subjects of their talk glitter and shimmer with sensuous fantasy that delights many in Europe and Britain. The same verbal richness pervades Durrell's poems.

Rex Warner in *The Professor* (1938) shows up a perennial human dilemma: an intellectual liberal goes down with inept unawareness before the ruthless physical and mental strength of the power-seeker. The conflict between different strengths is still relevant for twentieth-century, sophisticated man seeking to rid himself of war and its holocaust.

Mid-Century Novelists

Three novelists, P. H. Newby, Angus Wilson and William Golding, have broken new ground whilst rejecting experimentation in form. P. H. Newby began with *A Journey to the Interior* (1945). That interior was both the actual desert and wilderness of the mind. Since then Newby has written, among other novels and stories, *The Snow Pasture* (1949), *A Step to Silence* (1952), *The Retreat* (1953), *The Picnic at Sakkara* (1955), *A Guest and His Going* (1959) and *Something to Answer For* (1968). *The Picnic at Sakkara* and *A Guest and His Going* compare favourably with E. M. Forster's *A Passage to India*, except that African culture replaces Indian culture and unexpectedly different problems of mutual understanding arise between an Egyptian student, Muawiya, and his English tutor and friend, Perry. In both books Muawiya's spontaneous behaviour is contrasted with the poker-face coolness of the Englishman Perry. Unpretentiousness is of prime importance in P. H. Newby's novels.

Angus Wilson at first wrote satirical short stories—*The Wrong Set* (1949) and *Such Darling Dodos* (1950). His first novel was the compact *Hemlock and After* (1952). The story here is of the problems of Bernard Sands, a married man with grown children, who discovers in himself a moralism that results in a rigid need to expose a friend; the other man, also suffering from homosexual impulses, is driven to suicide. The realization in Sands of the hell of dishonesty that is his fear, causes, rather melodramatically, his own death. What interests Angus Wilson in this and his later novels is the illusion sentimental liberals may harbour about their own breadth and integrity of mind.

In this author's more recent and perhaps his most celebrated novel, *The Old Men at the Zoo* (1961), the old men crack into monsters when the country collapses under war. *The Middle Age of Mrs Eliot* (1958) and *No Laughing Matter* (1967) are subtly woven and never sensational; they show English middle-class people seeking to know themselves better in this century of introspective groping.

William Golding is best known for his novels *Lord of the Flies* (1954), *The Inheritors* (1955), *Pincher Martin* (1956), *Free Fall* (1959) and *The Spire* (1964). *Lord of the Flies* is a story with a Crusoe-Coral-Island theme—about a score of boys marooned from a plane-wreck in wartime on an island and how quickly the quarrel for leadership among them turns to war, treachery and murder. Children are no longer thought to be 'innocent'. They have potentiality for most grown-up guilts, powers and frailties. *Lord of the Flies* suggests the thesis of original sin. Golding has written that 'man produces evil as a bee produces honey'.

The Inheritors, the least talked about of Golding's novels, is perhaps the most profound. A family group of early people (presumably Neanderthalers or Boscops) retreat before *Homo Sapiens*. The easy-going earlier people are unorganized, with no understanding of, and no interest in, fighting. Familial, kindly, they talk a sort of image-language. The intruders are quick, shrewd, hard, more abstract in speech, greedier; they are aware, as the others are not, that survival is precarious. The earlier people will go down before them. This may or may not be something of what happened in the pre-history of man. Our ancestors survived not only by virtue of a grimly ruthless intelligence, but through a loyalty, a mutualism and a self-sacrificing care for their pedomorph young. By ' purist ' canons of artistic criticism, canons which hold that art should be ' disinterested ', distanced, rather than an integral part of life and living, the truth or non-truth of Golding's fable could be said not to matter. It is allegorical: a fable's truth is important only symbolically. Yet the truth or non-truth in Golding's story matters in the way the meaning of W. H. Auden's much-discussed line matters: ' We must love one another or die.'

Golding's *Pincher Martin* concerns a man overboard who clings to a bare rock. The artistry lies in the suspense from the story's beginning until almost its end. One reads on to find whether Pincher Martin, for whom all sympathy is aroused because of his endurance under the overwhelming odds against him, will die. Almost on the final page the author discloses that the drowning man was never on the rock at all. He drowned in a matter of seconds; the rock was an aching tooth; his efforts to live—epitome of all human endeavour that so wrought our sympathy—were his obstinate, lifelong refusal to submit to God's will. This shift from one reality to another is so abrupt that the willing suspension of disbelief is surely needless. Without that final turn-around *Pincher Martin* would retain power as a picture of human helplessness and courage; of man's persevering obstinacy that is at the same time one of his strengths.

In 1950 William Cooper gave to the novel an eighteenth-century twist by reintroducing the non-serious ' hero '. The whole tone of *Scenes from Provincial Life* is tough, light facetiousness. This has been called ' naturalism ' and the term is applicable if we skim off a top layer of existence and call that the ' natural ' one. A young man is bent on American-imitated sexual promiscuity rather than on getting caught falling in love. Wanting to ' get on ' he is aggressively unsure of himself in a ruefully comic way.

Kingsley Amis also introduced a non-serious hero in his best-selling first novel *Lucky Jim* (1954). This was followed by, among others, *That Uncertain Feeling* (1955), *I Like It Here* (1958), *Take a Girl Like You* (1960), *One Fat Englishman* (1963), *The Anti-Death League* (stories, 1966), *I Want It Now* (1968) and *The Green Man* (1969). Like *Lucky Jim* the later novels are all rampageously comic, set in a go-getting culture. Their decent-at-heart young men are great sexual warriors. Some critics see profundity lurking behind the competent, slapdash, comic rictus of this novelist.

John Braine, who has acknowledged William Cooper's influence, published *Room at the Top*, a best-seller, in 1957. It is written in cliché-ridden prose. The new ' natural ' hero-un-hero, tongue-tied in all beyond materialist values, is the old, old male Cinderella. Determined to ' get on ', like Ronnie Appleyard of *I Want It Now*, Braine's non-hero tests his sexual prowess in the traditional way by marrying a girl ' above ' him socially. John Braine makes use of sentimental ' thriller ' horror: a car accident, in which the married woman with whom the married ' hero ' is having an affair dies, punishes the ' guilty ' one.

John Wain, poet, critic and novelist, believes in the novel artform as one of Western man's means of learning about himself. He has published *Hurry On Down* (1953), *Living in the Present* (1955), *The Young Visitors* (1956) and *The Smaller Sky* (1967). In John Wain's novels the wit and seriousness reinforce each other. Wain is an able literary critic.

Alan Sillitoe, a sombre writer, involves his novels and stories in the often brutal, intractable war between intelligent members of the industrious classes and in the more fortunate ' them '. Sillitoe's *Saturday Night and Sunday Morning* was published in 1958. His long short story, ' The Loneliness of the Long-Distance Runner ' (1959) conveys the thought of a boy running a cross-country five miles for a Blue Ribbon inter-Borstal Cup. The response of this ' menace to decent lads ', to what he sees as the hypocritically inept ' do-gooding ' of the governor and the preaching of the militarized staff, is: ' You don't kid me, you bastards ! ' His lonely and bewildered defiance is convincingly portrayed as he forces himself not to win the race, not to give ' honour ' to his prison. The empathy with which Sillitoe works out the boy's outlook and the interconnections between it and his social surroundings is profound in the way William Golding's skill and sympathy are in working out the suspense of Pincher Martin's obstinate holding fast to a rock. Alan Sillitoe's other novels are *The General* (1960) and *Key to the Door* (1961). He has also written *The Rats and Other Poems* (1960).

Iris Murdoch's first novel, *Under the Net* (1954), has a non-hero similar to those of William Cooper, John Braine and Kingsley Amis. But, as John Wain does, so Iris Murdoch relates the non-hero to a philosophical reality. Comic happenings imperil the self-confidence of the young man of *Under the Net*. Other novels of this prolific writer include *The Flight from the Enchanter* (1956), *The Sandcastle* (1957), *The Bell* (1958), *A Severed Head* (1961), *An Un-official Rose* (1962), *The Nice and the Good* (1968), *Bruno's Drema* (1969) and *A Fairly Honourable Defeat* (1970). She endows her characters with psychological traits rather than flesh and blood. These ' composed ' people act in a sometimes wildly coincidental manner which is rarely inevitable. Their rapidly changing sexual attractions are rooted in private fantasies such as many of us harbour, but they are not always given credibility.

Some of Anthony Burgess's novels of the sixties, such as *enderby outside*, also contain a richly individual, comic vein. Muriel Spark has given us *Memento Mori* (1959), *The Bachelors* (1960), *The Prime of Miss Jean Brodie* (1961) and *The Mandelbaum Gate* (1965). She has an international reputation as an entertainer, is sparkling, witty to the verge of insensitiveness and enormously competent.

Doris Lessing's contribution to the modern novel in her two most recent books is her attempt to avoid what she sees as the novel's ' deformed form '. *The Golden Notebook* (1962) and *The Four-Gated City* (1969) are her most significant work. *The Golden Notebook* tries to set down experience and characters as the first is being lived anp the second unfolding. Life-form, ' nailing Anna to the page ', is what Doris Lessing seems to aim at. *The Golden Notebook* is rather like an exhaustive record of ' group therapy ' sessions. It is loaded with sensitive insights; it is long and turgid, but no more formless than—say—*Dr Zhivago*. It is important because it repudiates the fantasy currently so relied on. It explores fictional-actual, intract-ably hostile areas of human relationships that are often clumsily handled in popular fiction.

The Four-Gated City is a long *bildungsroman* examining the modern world under its threat of collapse from nuclear war with intelligent insight and refusal of defeatism.

Experimentalists

Among younger novelists, Christine Brooke-Rose, B. S. Johnson and Robert Nye are experimenting with technique, as well as with substance and tone or atmosphere. The novel of plot reached a first peak of excellence, not only in Britain but in Russia, France and Germany, in the nineteenth century. Dorothy Richardson, Virginia Woolf, James Joyce—and, of course, the Anglo-American Henry James—narrowed but deepened the English novel's landscape to inscape early in the twentieth century. The future of this youngest of written art-forms (begun in Britain by Deloney, Sidney, Lyly, Nashe and Greene in the sixteenth century) is currently thought by a few to be uncertain.

Samuel Beckett's prose, in both his novels and drama, is vital to discussion of the novel's future. Beckett is sometimes thought of, as Shaw, Joyce and even Yeats have been, as an English writer. These four, Beckett, Shaw, Joyce and Yeats belong to the important and distinctive Gaelic-Irish branch of English letters. Not only since 1922, when Yeats gained recognition for it, but through many centuries, often in the mixture of prose and poetry Gaelic writers know as *crosánacht*, has this second-oldest literature of Europe influenced both overtly and hiddenly prose and poetry in English.

Born in Dublin in 1906 Beckett has lived in Paris since the Second World War and has written novels as well as plays, both in French and English. His *Murphy* (Eng. 1938) and trilogy—*Molloy* (1951; Eng. trans. 1955), *Malone Dies* (1951; Eng. trans. 1956), *The Unnameable* (1953; Eng. trans. 1959)—continue the novel of thought-pattern of the inner, non-rational soliloquy which reason would prefer not to recognize. Molloy, Malone, Moran and the Unnameable of the third story inhabit a dark, near-empty landscape in which a few obscure figures lurk now and then. In all Molloy, the Unnameable and the rest say or think, there is a pitiable doubt or uncertainty, a brilliantly conveyed sense of isolation, and of the way they see themselves, which is different from the way all others see them. Hobbling, bare-boned, ragged, filthy, alone, they let loose a paragraphless, echoing prose. Towards the close of *The Unnameable* his words grow more and more strangled and stopless:

. . . you must say words, as long as there are any, until they find me, until they say me, strange pain, strange sin, you must go on, perhaps it's done already, perhaps they have said me already, perhaps they have carried me to the threshold of my story, before the door that opens on my story, that would surprise me, if it opens, it will be I, it will be the silence, where I am, I don't know, I'll never know, I'll never know, in the silence you don't know, you must go on, I can't go on, I'll go on.

If Molloy were an imbecile, one might say that in Beckett's portrayal there is a compassionate exploration of a neuro-psychotic mind. But Beckett intends that Molloy should be seen as normal. Molloy, Murphy in Beckett's earlier story, Moran, Malone and the Unnameable, all have essential humanity, within a despairing refusal of despair. Such despair man feels he has never known. Yet he has always known it. Perpetually he faces it afresh. These characters are shut in and alone. Yet they are today's everyman. They register an occasional, passionate awareness of earth's beauty. They are all the time only just not overcome by other people, by life, by things. They are obsessed by time running out. Their speech soliloquies echo and so convey the disjointedness of the mind. But an added incapacity is also conveyed. This is almost a dislexia, that physical-mental disorganization which attacks when the mind must confront overwhelming new knowledge, as today it must.

Molloy, Murphy, Malone and the Unnameable are Beckett's symbols of twentieth-century human distress, loneliness, valour. Characters and stories identify the ' real ' and the imaginative— as perhaps these two aspects of human beings are, after all, identified. The Unnameable finally says: ' I'll go on ' after weeks of feeling that he couldn't ' go on '. Beckett's seeming negations evoke in us a sense of life's perpetual conquest of despair. His language makes words chafed by time speak freshly in the immediate context of today.

Frank Kermode, after quoting James Hutton's ' No Vestige of a Beginning—No Prospect of an End ' of 1790, wrote: ' . . . it is obviously relevant that the novel developed as the time of the world expanded, and that the facts are related '.[3]

Christine Brooke-Rose forsook poetry to write *A Grammar of Metaphor* (1958) and novels, *Out* (1964) and *Such* (1966). *Such* joins

[3] *The Sense of an Ending* (New York: Oxford Univ. Press, 1967), p. 167.

a dehydrated, space-age poetry to symbolic prose: a man's heart stopped beating during an operation and doctors revived him. The efforts of this intellectual to recommunicate with relatives and friends on his return to life show us a back-to-the-wall future for the feeling mind through a warning fog of biological, computerized, stratospheric hazard. Perhaps only an art-form such as the serious novel can deal with not to be evaded subjects such as this.

B. S. Johnson is also a poet who seeks to link poetry more closely with prose. So far he has written three novels, *Travelling People* (1963), *Albert Angelo* (1964) and *Trawl* (1966). The last is an account of a young man who sets out to learn more about his sense of isolation and his failure in relationships. B. S. Johnson's fictional people, as the title of his play *You're Human Like the Rest of Them* (1967) indicates, are seen without sensationalism, and without fantasy: they are normal. Inner and outer description of them has a dense, conversational, outspoken rhythm. Until this century we have been instructed to be ashamed of, to restrain and deny, at least to disguise with so-called decency, the troublesome contents of that Pandora's box, our common minds. One of today's tendencies in the novel is to falsify by means of sensational overstatement.

Robert Nye, too, is a poet, novelist and critic who believes in the imaginative relationship of prose and poetry known in the Gaelic literary tradition. He has written three volumes of poems, *Juvenilia I*, *Juvenilia 2* and *Darker Ends* (1969). His novel *doubtfire* (1968) owes something to Rabelais, Sterne, James Joyce and Samuel Beckett. It is composed of inwoven, cross-referenced disclosures such as the acutely observed mind will render up. A growing boy learns to dare not to evade (as in self-defence minds do evade, fail to see, ignore and misinterpret) the experience of senses, feeling, mind, or the experience of the body. Only if he meets all these ' realities ' as the moth burns in the candle, or as the mirror reflects the eidolon, will life render up its logic and its reward; *doubtfire* does something towards restoring Coleridge's ' vital ' imagination to its place in the development of mind-heart-body. This has importance because contemporary science for at least the past three decades has rejected the complex waywardness of imagination in favour of factual precision, whilst much competent science fiction is exploring a fantastic unreality.

Drama

Older dramatists such as Shaw, O'Casey, Barrie, Galsworthy, Priestley and Somerset Maugham were writing plays up to the 1940s. But yesterday's language and themes cannot be today's. Today's pass almost overnight into tomorrow's. Most plays depend on colloquial language; and change is so unpredictable that its chameleon facts and facets perpetually demand fresh treatment and rethinking.

Drama following the First World War did not get under way until the 1930s. There was an attempt to revive poetic drama. The naturalized American from New England, T. S. Eliot, wrote verse plays between the thirties and the fifties. His first full-length play was *Murder in the Cathedral* (1935). Others were *The Family Reunion* (1939), *The Cocktail Party* (1950), *The Confidential Clerk* (1954) and *The Elder Statesman* (1959). *Murder in the Cathedral* is the story of Thomas à Becket, the poor twelfth-century boy who rose to be Chancellor of England and Archbishop of Canterbury. Thomas then rejected his King's—Henry II's—authority for that of Rome. Underneath this story lies the image of a strong spirit seeking to resist the temptation to gain martyrdom's sainthood through pride and ambition.

Since 1922, when his long poem *The Waste Land* was published, Eliot had become the literary mouthpiece of a generation which had temporarily lost its way. In days of severe unemployment in Britain, in *The Rock* (1934), Eliot stated causes:

Men have left God . . . this has never happened before . . . what
                                                    have we to do
But stand with empty hands and palms turned upwards
In an age which advances progressively backwards ?

All Eliot's plays are, at their centres, religious, didactic. In *The Family Reunion* Harry, Lord Monchensey, arrives home haunted by the suspicion that he has pushed his wife overboard on the voyage. He is pursued by ' Furies '. That his father had loved his mother's sister and wished to murder Harry's mother before the child's birth emerges. Harry's mother wishes him to take responsibility for the estate. But the play ends with Harry's setting out on affluent travels again. Why a father's unacted-on wish should have power to cause a son to imagine he himself *had* done murder is difficult to see. Whether Harry had murdered his wife is not made clear.

In *The Cocktail Party* a nagging wife and her faithless husband await guests. The guests include a strange, priestlike psychiatrist and Celia, the husband's mistress. With the psychiatrist's help the husband and wife at the play's end settle down to:

> . . . casual talk by the fire:
> Two people who know they will never understand each other,
> Breeding children whom they do not understand
> And who will never understand them. . . .

To atone, Celia becomes a missionary. She is murdered by ' savages '—an eighteenth-century touch, very similar to the conclusion of Joyce Cary's novel *Aissa Saved* (1932), though in Cary's novel the incident is ethnically plausible. Questions such as the usefulness of Celia's ' atonement ' pursue one after reading Eliot's plays. When we see the plays acted their dialogue covers weaknesses of theme. The verse, which Eliot ' diluted ' (his own word) towards prose, haunts. Even at its flattest and most Drydenesque, the words of this poet, crystal-hard, emphasize Eliot's central point: compassion has little to do with the romantic sentimentality he decried.

Between 1918 and 1940 W. B. Yeats's verse plays became known chiefly to the scholar. Among Christopher Fry's plays, which deal with themes of goodness in a scabrous world, are *A Phoenix Too Frequent* (1946) and *The Lady's Not for Burning* (1949). Fry's verse glitters and scintillates with ornamental words. It reminds us of the *Euphues* of John Lyly or of Shakespeare's euphuistic early comedies.

Auden's and Isherwood's *The Ascent of F6* (1936) is a youthful, Freud-inspired play about the corroding need of a son to live up to parental ambition for him. Spender's and MacNeice's plays are socialist and political. Norman Nicholson's are *The Old Man of the Mountains* (1946), *Prophesy to the Wind* (1950), *A Match for the Devil* (1955) and *Birth by Drowning* (1960).

The attempt to revive verse drama lapsed. After Shaw and Synge died, Sean O'Casey, the most considerable Western communist dramatist, with his ' uncondemning imagination ', continued to write prose drama.

New Voices in Prose Drama

Samuel Beckett's was the first of newer voices in drama. He may be called the last dramatist in the Gaelic dramatic revival of the last century's close and the first one in the present century. His best-known plays are *Waiting for Godot* (1952; Eng. trans. 1956), *All That Fall* (1957), *Endgame* (1957; Eng. trans. 1958) and *Krapp's Last Tape* (1959). In *Godot*, two tramps, Didi and Gogo, mutually incapable of leaving each other, wait at some undefined roadside for an Unknown who has promised to come. Pozzo enters, a cruel master, pulling his slave, Lucky, on a rope. They, too, are tied to each other by more than rope: on their next entry, Pozzo though still a tyrant has become blind. Little else happens—except that a small boy comes to tell Didi and Gogo that Godot is not coming. The play leaves Didi and Gogo at the end, still waiting.

But waiting for whom ? Waiting for what ? What does this play mean ? One can only say what the play signifies for oneself. Beckett does not like to be asked to interpret his plays. A sense of twentieth-century man, bound, fettered, irrationally and still primitively cruel ? Towards his fellows ignorantly quarrelsome ? His speech incapable of communicating ? Is he lost because he no longer feels sure about any end, purpose, for himself here ? For what they once had faith in, have men now substituted their own too finite end ? A scientific affluence of which they are only now beginning to perceive the savagery ? Through threats of their own making, they grow aware of their dissatisfactions ? Some take *Waiting for Godot*, as all Beckett's plays, to contain a sense of the hilariously comic: but to some the play's statement, ' Nothing is funnier than un-happiness ', is of an unutterable, ' hopeless hope '.

This mingling of comedy and tragedy is Beckett's way of meeting the challenge of the age's new science, violence, confusion, self-alienation, and sense of time as non-perfecting. The mind reels before all this almost in neurosis. Yet comedy and tragedy, as Samuel Johnson was one of the first to remind us, have always been equally part of daily life; and life has never lacked joy and fun and threat and agony. All these Beckett has interwoven in *Waiting for Godot*. The dialogue is clipped, staccato, threadbare, repetitive—poetry, yet everyday, charged prose. This sparser and sparser rubric of lost certainties is Beckett's contribution to the

British theatre as well as to the novel, to his century's abandonment of previous ages' concept of steady ' progress '. As Beckett's novels hold inspiration for younger novelists, so his plays have inspired younger dramatists.

John Osborne's *Look Back in Anger* was first performed in 1956, at the Royal Court Theatre, Chelsea—once Shaw's and Granville-Barker's theatre. Quickly this play produced a critic's label for Osborne's generation—' Angry Young Men '—to include novelists such as Kingsley Amis and Alan Sillitoe. ' Angry Young Men ' were speaking for a post-atom-bomb youth's resentment against the world their parents had not managed to avoid passing on to them. The hero, or non-hero, of *Look Back in Anger*, Jimmy Porter, is a child of the new age. His father—like so many others of this generation—died in war. Jimmy feels himself condemned to mediocrity. Justly or unjustly he feels himself better than but help-less under conditions he sees thrust at him in rat-race-conscious press and radio. He is nihilistically critical of self-righteous religion, of bland, non-comprehending moralism; and he sees all these all round him. He talks—but he remains inert. He cannot direct his relationship with his very young wife: Alison has come, as Joe Lampton's wife had in *Room at the Top*, from the liberal better-off whom his frustration makes him see as sententious and false. He is, as Lawrence prophesied for the next generation, no Mellors power-fully potent in a love-making which (we are to suppose) can unify two lives. Unfaithful, he drives his wife to an abortion. On her return, ill and abjectly submissive, they are left playing with toys like the children we must suppose they still are. The ending of this powerful play leaves a queasiness no doubt intended. The whole is a brilliant analysis of post-war generations. More affluence, wider education, but no less crude industrial work, which means mental slavery for the millions, do not offer satisfying life. At once threatened and materially indulged, the impulse of the young towards what is too complacently called maturity is delayed. The play's problem revives in modern form that ancient crux visible in literature since days of chivalry—how to achieve true human maturity.

Osborne's *Luther* (1961) is said to owe much to the great German dramatist, Bertolt Brecht, and his *Galileo* (1943; Eng. trans. 1952). Both plays are reassessments of past great men's characters. History changes, and often distorts these: as in the case of Richard III of England. Brecht shows Galileo selfish, hypocritical, smarmy, to those whom he thought could harm him; at the end of his life he becomes a lonely glutton. We would like to imagine Galileo as a brave thinker who defended his discovery, that the earth went round the sun, against the angry power of the Church. Which is more important, the historical picture or a great man's personal character? Whichever is, it is rarely without contradictory elements. Osborne's *The Entertainer* (1957) and *The World of Paul Slickey* (1959) contain slashing attacks on British social and political life.

Harold Pinter's best-known play is *The Caretaker* (1960). It cannot but remind us of *Waiting for Godot* in that so little happens in it. There are three characters: Mick, who shares a junk-room with his brother Aston, who has received treatment in a mental hospital; Aston is ' cured ' but reduced as a human being; and Davies, a tramp. Davies see his chance of a roof over his head when Mick offers him the job of caretaker of the room and looking after Aston. The dialogue, their conversation, has a quality of the great Russian dramatist Chekhov; speakers do not answer each other so much as pursue their own track of thought. But Pinter's dialogue has a lost, ' cracked ', ' not all there ' quality similar to the dialogue in *Waiting for Godot*. It echoes, even relays, human conversation, and not only among tramps and the mentally injured.

Arnold Wesker's three most important plays to date are two from his trilogy, *Chicken Soup with Barley* (1959), *Roots* (1959) and *Chips with Everything* (1962). Wesker is socialist, intellectual, full of drive. *Roots* is a movingly sympathetic, and in a sense poetic play about the intense, naïve, but often hidden, desire in most working families to acquire more knowledge, more culture, more being. One might think that this enthusiasm, to have more of the happiness and inner confidence of knowledge, died with Dickens or with the 1870 Compulsory Education Act. From Wesker's play, and from books as convincing as Richard Hoggart's *The Uses of Literacy* (1957), peasant ambition and vitality are seen to be much as they evidently were in Caedmon the poetic swineherd's day.

John Arden is also fiercely committed, strongly critical of post-1945, post-Empire Britain. A socialist and an intellectual, his plays —*The Waters of Babylon* (1957), *Live Like Pigs* (1958), *Serjeant Musgrave's Dance* (1959) and *The Happy Haven* (1960)—have all been produced at the experimental Royal Court Theatre, Chelsea. The theme of *Serjeant Musgrave's Dance* is the intolerable one of Force versus Survival, pacificism as a weapon to overcome violence, blood-lust, cruelty, cant.

Live Like Pigs is a near-the-bone yet hilarious study of how law-abiding council-house dwellers attack and drive from their midst a ne'er-do-well ' family ' moved by the Council from a caravan to their neighbourhood. No suspicion against immigrant neighbours could be more intolerant. *The Happy Haven* is about a home for old people where the doctor in charge is inventing, secretly, an elixir to make them young again. But of course they do not want, they would not know how, to be young again. They discover what he is up to, administer his own elixir, and reduce him to a foolish child. John Arden intended *The Happy Haven* to be played in masks, on an ' open stage '. He wants to open out the modern dramatic conventions: presumably to allow, as in Shakespeare's theatre, an audience to take more part. Masks, this dramatist believes, may have much use in the theatre. They bring to mind medieval Morality and Miracle plays. They also suggest present-day, African masked plays where the audience participates in the performance.

John Whiting's *A Penny for a Song* and *Saint's Day*, both produced in 1951, and his plays *Marching Song* (1954) and *The Devils* (1961)—based on Aldous Huxley's book, *The Devils of Loudoun*—all aroused controversy. Whiting's common theme is the inescapable bondage which attends any human ideals of greatness, the evil which at the same time is the good.

In the 1960s Shelagh Delaney's *A Taste of Honey* was among the first searchlights on the often carefully hidden discrimination of older people in Britain against those who do not belong to an ' in-group '. John Bowen's *Little Boxes* are plays about the desperate courage in isolated ' out-groups ' of our day. Other contemporary dramatists of note are Robert Bolt, Peter Shaffer and N. F. Simpson.

Before this present century, the stage, like the earliest preserved poetry, was concerned with the lives of the princely, the rich, the warrior-great. All this held social decorum and intellectual fastidiousness. It is no more relevant to label any of the plays of the 1960s ' kitchen-sink ' drama than it is to suppose that a royal and aristocratic tradition behind theatre gives it validity as art. Shaw and Eliot did not attempt to broaden theatre audiences as O'Casey and Synge did. Since the 1950s dramatists have sought to bring theatre-going closer to what it was in Shakespeare's day. They have not yet succeeded; but there are theatres such as the Hampstead (Experimental) Theatre, the Stratford Theatre Royal of East London, the Century Theatre and the Round House; and there are dedicated youth theatres and theatre groups in many provincial cities, many of which are working towards communication with wider audiences.

Poetry

Just before the 1914-18 war Robert Bridges succeeded Alfred Austin as Poet Laureate. Bridges was a classical scholar, a believer in ' pure ' poetry: poetry, he thought, should be unlinked with the gross imperfections of day to day. He was not widely known until he published, in 1929, *The Testament of Beauty*. This is a far-ranging poem about providence, goodness, civilization's progress: a progress now doubted. Bridges's 1,450 ' hexameters ' are not stressed but classical in long or short syllables. Couched in half-Miltonic spelling, they seem now a little pedantic. Both their versification and their optimistic surety go against the very way English poetry is flowing and has been since 1918. Yet, for a short period in the 1920s people of all ages did think that the ' Great War ' might really end all wars. Ease and confidence had not then been overlaid.

Between 1912 and 1922 Edward Marsh published five volumes of *Georgian Poetry*. Some of the poets who from those volumes received the label of ' Georgian ' were Alfred Noyes, Laurence Binyon, Laurence Housman, Lascelles Abercrombie, John Drinkwater, John Masefield (Laureate until 1968), Wilfrid Gibson, James Elroy Flecker, W. H. Davies, Ralph Hodgson, Edwin Muir, Richard Church.

But as early as 1910 a few vigorously critical scholars were beginning to say that English poetry, grown tired, vague, faded, trivial, needed new vitality. F. S. Flint wrote[4] that non-rhymed cadences were used by the earliest autochthonous poets such as Cynewulf. In fact, both rhyme and metre as well as non-rhyme all go much further back than Cynewulf in the evolution of European

---

[4] In the Preface to his collection of poems, *Other-world, Cadences* (London Poetry Bookshop, 1920).

and Asian poetry and therefore of ours. T. E. Hulme in *Speculations* (published in 1924, though Hulme was killed in the war in 1917)[5] already saw a new age in poetry dawning. A poem, Hulme wrote, should be definite, accurate, non-rhymed description. Words should be ' dry ', ' hard ', free of romantically ' damp ' sentiment. Richard Aldington in *Images, 1910-1915* (1915) and *Images of War* (1919) claimed that precision, unblurred by the emotion nineteenth-century poets from Keats to Dowson had exploited, was what twentieth-century poetry should aim at. Metre, stanza, particularly rhyme, Flint, Hulme and Aldington claimed, over-ornamented and so debased the meaning of a poem. Through emotionalized rhyme, meaning slid too easily and became vague. These freer cadences, conversational or breath rhythms, with uneven line-lengths, resembled free verse. French poets had adapted *vers libre* out of their traditional alexandrines; this free verse was what British innovators recommended. Any one of the five poems of Hulme's poetic output in *Speculations* makes the new aim clear:

> A touch of cold in the Autumn night—
> I walked abroad,
> And saw the ruddy moon lean over a hedge
> Like a red-faced farmer.
> I did not stop to speak, but nodded,
> And round about were the wistful stars
> With white faces like town children.

T. S. Eliot, educated at Harvard and the Sorbonne, and reaching England in 1915, published *Prufrock and Other Observations* in 1917, *Poems* in 1919 and *The Waste Land* in 1922. He became a naturalized British citizen in 1927.

The Waste Land's five parts employ the unrhymed prose cadences Flint and Hulme advocated. These, Ezra Pound, Eliot's fellow-expatriate to whom he owed much, believed in and used. Among Eliot's cadences the occasional rhymed couplets and adroitly varied iambic lines shine in *The Waste Land* like gems.

The poem's theme is the one of a dead land and fevered, sterile people such as Morris, Ruskin and Carlyle had cried out against in the nineteenth century. Eliot's central theme was that the barren

---

[5] *The Complete Poetical Works of Hulme*, appended to Ezra Pound, *Ripostes* (1912), reprinted in *Speculations*, ed. Herbert Read (1924; repr. 1960).

land could live again only by sacrifice and submission; by the fear
in the lustful, evil hearts of its people towards God: ' I will show
you fear in a handful of dust.'

That theme Langland impressed on listeners to *Piers Plowman* in
the fourteenth century. In Eliot's poem the myth of the sacrificed
king of ancient fertility rites is linked to Christ's sacrifice; and in
seemingly unrelated pictures, episodes of drab, brutalized modern
sex-encounters follow each other. These express the break-up, as
Eliot and others saw the more open, often sadder but little wiser,
sexual *mores* after gross war. Most of Eliot's enactments of sexuality
are renderings of human misery and ignorance heard frag-
mentarily in pubs. Nobody would guess from them that making
love was any deep joy at all; much less that it held beauty or
fulfilment. Eliot wrote *The Waste Land* under a breakdown of nervous health and in circumstances of great personal tragedy. The
brilliant, ' sick ', disillusioned poem touches those raw wounds
none of us wholly escapes:

> I can't help it, she said, pulling a long face,
> It's them pills I took, to bring it off, she said.
> (She's had five already, and nearly died of young George.)
> The chemist said it would be all right, but I've never been the same.
> You *are* a proper fool, I said.
> Well, if Albert won't leave you alone, there it is, I said,
> What you get married for if you don't want children ?
> HURRY UP PLEASE IT'S TIME. . . .

He pictures the Thames in grey London winter dawn and noon:

> Sweet Thames, run softly, for I speak not loud or long.
> But at my back in a cold blast I hear
> The rattle of the bones, and chuckle spreads from ear to ear.
> A rat crept softly through the vegetation
> Dragging its slimy belly on the bank. . . .

Nothing is carefree, nothing clean, not even half an hour by the
sea beach:

> On Margate sands
> I can connect
> Nothing with nothing.
> The broken fingernails of dirty hands. . . .

These conversations and vignettes Eliot mingles with quotations from Spenser, Webster, Shakespeare, Swinburne, from writers in other tongues, from Dante and Provençal poets. Though his poem is designedly ' caviare to the general ', he draws it towards a close with a quotation from the old play from which Shakespeare took the plot of his Hamlet story, followed by a phrase attributed to Buddha: ' Why then Ile fit you. Hieronymo's mad againe./Datta. Dayadhvam. Damyata.'

The last line of *The Waste Land* is the Sanscrit Peace Chant from the final Upanishad of the Hindu Scriptures: ' Peace ! Peace ! Peace !/Shantih Shantih Shantih.'

G. S. Fraser, the poet-critic, has written in *The Modern Writer and His World* (1953; rev. 1964) that *The Waste Land* ' does not quite stand up on its own '[6] as a poem. This, the critic thinks, is partly because of Eliot's use of Christian, Pagan and Eastern myth mingling with his puritan association of sexual love with sin; it is also because Eliot felt impelled to give notes on his obscurer references. He was raising the expressly simple imagist verse of Flint and Hulme to the intellectually impressive level of seventeenth- and eighteenth-century English poetry he admired; and he owed much to nineteenth-century French poets such as Laforgue and Baudelaire. In the 1930s Michael Roberts wrote against ' esoteric ' poetry— poetry with learned or private allusions needing notes for its understanding. But Eliot's poem became the doxology of at least two generations.

Before he published his poem, Eliot, advancing step by step as critic as well as poet, paid ' homage to John Dryden ' the creator of ' poetic diction '; Eliot wrote that poetry ' must be difficult '— the poet must even ' dislocate ' his language to different levels of meaning. Coleridge held that ' poetry gives most pleasure when not perfectly understood '; and it is true that *The Waste Land* haunts and impresses alike those who agree with and those who cannot assent to Eliot's theology, and those who do not understand all his meanings.

' The Hollow Men ', in which Eliot is indebted to Conrad's *Heart of Darkness* for his general theme, was published in 1925. Yet the poem dipped deeper into disillusion, and a terrible despair under a heaven ' lonely of a God ' becomes audible:

[6] Penguin edn, p. 270.

H

For Thine is the Kingdom

For Thine is
Life is
For Thine is the

> *This is the way the world ends*
> *This is the way the world ends*
> *This is the way the world ends*
> *Not with a bang but a whimper.*

In both *The Waste Land* and ' The Hollow Men ', anxiety, almost gibbering disgust and loss of direction, powerfully and impersonally set out, exactly mirrored the drained and bitter hopelessness, the misery and the phoniness that were Britain's awakening after the short-lived, hysterical relief following that ' war to end war '.

Eliot's next poem, *Ash-Wednesday* (1930), reveals submission following from disillusion and sexual despair, to the solace offered by Anglo-Catholicism. He became Anglo-Catholic in 1927. In his *Essays* he has upheld orthodox dogma, conservatism, authoritative standards and culture for the ablest few. He has spoken of the influence on him of Victorian poets, James Thomson of ' The City of Dreadful Night ', that poet of echoes from Shelley and Swinburne, and ' laureate of pessimism '; of the influence on him, too, of Ernest Dowson and John Davidson at the turn of the century. Eliot jettisoned the rich rhyme, the lush, Victorian rhythms seen in such poems as Thomson's ' The Doom of a City ' and in some of Dowson's lyrics. Yet the dipsomaniac Thomson could be toweringly strong, as in the final section of that poem. Eliot imbibed this desolate strength that reaches back to Byron's ' I learn'd to love despair ' and through Arnold and Clough. It speaks, almost more than Victorian optimism from the last century, going beyond Eliot to today's tough hopelessness. ' From these men,' Eliot has written, ' I got the idea that one could write poetry in an English such as one would speak oneself. A colloquial idiom.'[7]

' Burnt Norton ', ' East Coker ', ' The Dry Salvages ' and ' Little Gidding ' make up the *Four Quartets* Eliot published between 1940 and 1942. The *Four Quartets* are in iambic verse, which is not blank verse, and were influenced by Dante. They are reflections on the poet's own life, on war, on ' unredeemable ' time; exquisitely perceptive and devoid of self-pity:

[7] Quoted from *John Davidson: A Selection of His Poems*, ed. Maurice Lindsay, p. 9.

. . . the rending pain of re-enactment
Of all that you have done, and been; the shame
Of motives late revealed, and the awareness
Of things ill done and done to others' harm
Which once you took for exercise of virtue.

William Butler Yeats published *Responsibilities* in 1914. Almost
fifty years old, Yeats then embarked, in troubled Ireland, upon a
steadier devotion to ' the fascination of what's difficult ' in poetry.
Yeats was one of those who did not turn aside from a deeply rooted
lyric strength at the imagist call to modernism. He did not understand either Eliot or Ezra Pound, or they him. With the wide
horizons of a great poet and so a little outside the Gaelic heart of
Ireland, he yet wished his roots to spring out of the ' bare hills and
stunted trees ' of Sligo. In ' Under Ben Bulben ', written in the last
year of his life, he applauded ' indomitable Irishry '. Critical of the
new Irish Free State which he had watched emerge, he wished
Ireland, a land which had escaped industrialism, to retain her
peasant-aristocratic tradition. He praised the rich continuity, in one
respect democratic, of Gaelic ballad-poetry and prose from her
long past. He identified himself with ancient Gaelic heroes—
Cuchulain, Oisin. He saw a (not wholly improbable) link, historically, between Gaelic Ireland and ancient Greece.

Ireland's 1916 Sinn Fein ' troubles ', the bitter, hate-and-fear
induced bloodshed of 1922 and after, turned Yeats into being, in
his maturity, in some respects a reactionary. Searching for that
vanishing, or at least protean, ideal of manhood—a search which
runs through all English poetry—he commended violence:

Know that when all words are said
And a man is fighting mad,
Something drops from eyes long blind,
He completes his partial mind,
For an instant stands at ease,
Laughs aloud, his heart at peace.

Yeats believed in authoritarianism, not knowing, or else not caring,
how inhumane and backward-looking that can sometimes be. He
confessed that poets ' had no gift to put a statesman right '; but he
recalled the almost sacred position of the *filé* or poet in ancient
Ireland. He spoke of himself as one of the ' last romantics '. By that

much abused word 'romantic' he did not mean one who cannot or will not face up to actuality. He meant one who, without being deluded any more than he can help, refuses to lose a positive, vigorous idealism. The contradictions in himself and the external anomalies he saw he accepted as part of the 'real'. He enjoined himself: 'seek out the actual'.

By the 1930s idealism was in Britain almost totally unfashionable. Being a Gael Yeats tried to keep idealism and 'lust', self and soul, soul and body, united. He found them almost impossibly irreconcilable. 'Never,' he wrote towards the close of his life, 'after bidding good-bye to physical vigour, 'had I more excited, passionate, fastastical Imagination.' Deeply religious but not in any usual or puritanical way, he believed in the 'cyclic' return of the great religions, in the supernatural and in a world of death here around the living. In *The Use of Poetry and The Use of Criticism* (1933) Eliot said of him: 'He was much fascinated by self-induced trances, calculated symbolisms, mediums, theosophy, crystal-gazing, folklore and hobgoblins.'

A poet of great lyrical variety, Yeats wrote—besides occult expoundings—folk drama in verse: *The Shadowy Waters* (1900), *Cathleen ni Houlihan* (1902), *The Hour-Glass* (1903), *The King's Threshold* (1904), *Deirdre* (1907); many volumes of poems, such as *The Stolen Child*, *The Happy Townland*; ballads like 'The Fiddler of Dooney'; complexly mature lyrics such as 'Sailing to Byzantium', 'Byzantium', 'The Wild Swans at Coole'; and familial lyrics like 'A Prayer for My Daughter'. The lyric impulse, more usually dead in poets after their 'thirtieth year to heaven', produced in him late songs 'in a marrow bone '—'John Kinsella's Lament', 'The Wild Old Wicked Man', 'Why Should Not Old Men Be Mad?' 'The Three Bushes', the 'Crazy Jane' poems, the expert *terza rima* of 'Cuchlain Comforted' and 'The Black Tower'. W. H. Auden has seen some of these late poems as insufficiently 'anonymous', too full of rage and lust. Other critics have seen Yeats young and old as out of touch with his age, or as lacking a profound mind. All these criticisms must be accepted with his 'wild', reckless nonchalance, and his beliefs inspired by Blake and Shelley. His final 'heavenly voices', his 'high invisible ones', helped him not so much to submit to what most others saw as the 'real', as to see the 'filthy modern tide'. His 'embittered

heart ' ' worn out with dreams '—set down the unresolvable
antinomy: From ' The Circus Animals' Desertion ':

> Those masterful images because complete
> Grew in pure mind, but out of what began ? . . .
>   . . . Now that my ladder's gone,
> I must lie down where all the ladders start,
> In the foul rag-and-bone shop of the heart.

The question is an open one: whether the American-reared
Eliot or the Irish Yeats steeped in the ideas and rhythms of one of
the oldest cultures in Europe, will, in the long run, have the stronger
influence on English poetry, with its Gaelic undercurrent which
Yeats helped to revive.

After *Songs of Childhood* (1902) and *The Listeners* (1912) Walter de
la Mare was thought by some to have shut himself in a fairy-tale
world of nursery magic:

> ' Is there anybody there ? ' said the Traveller,
> Knocking on the moonlit door; . . .

> ' Tell them I came, and no one answered,
> That I kept my word,' he said. . . .

' Peacock Pie ', ' The Song of Finis ', ' Old Shellover ' or ' Hi !
Handsome Hunting Man ', undoubtedly enthral children. ' Look
thy last on all things lovely ' has its own sufficiency of warning.
' In the Dock ' might sting in an area of needed enlightenment:

> Pallid, misshapen he stands. The world's grimed thumb,
> Now hooked securely in his matted hair,
> Has haled him struggling from his poisonous slum
> And flung him, mute as fish, close-netted there.

De la Mare did not understand or else deliberately rejected what
Yeats called, and the more worldly Eliot knew, the ' safety in
derision '. He is never satiric, coarse, hard. Lascelles Abercrombie
has set down how poetry is a repeating pattern of words in which
monotony is avoided by imposing a counter pattern.[8] A sense of
such verbal and musical rhythm is inherent in almost all of us from

[8] *The Principles of English Prosody* (Secker, 1923), pp. 41-3.

birth. Most often it is not brought out. It remains stifled. Tirelessly de la Mare explored rhythmic variations and stanza patterns and produced many innovations. Yet perhaps he has not thought ' long and deeply ' as Wordsworth said a poet should have. To say, however, that de la Mare retreated into a world of magic or of childhood is to disregard his last long poem, *Winged Chariot*. He explores dark, evil, deserted houses, the hidden, the unknown, the hard to see and hear. Like Eliot he regrets irreparable time's echoes. But constantly and courageously he refuses to seek answers, has no report to make on the mystery of our being here. The strength of such philosophic acceptance of not-knowing is part of the twentieth-century outlook.

> Darkness had fallen. I opened the door:
> And lo, a stranger in the empty room—
> A marvel of moonlight upon wall and floor . . .
> The quiet of mercy ? Or the hush of doom ?

Edmund Blunden spent three years or more in what he called an area of ' destroyed lives '—the Flanders trenches between 1914 and 1918. That stay, which began when the poet was a youth just turned eighteen, ' branded ' him, made him old before his day, ' Dead as the men I loved ', gave him, as it gave many when they came back, sleep with ' strange agonies racked '. Edmund Blunden's prose reminiscences of the long ' fight with the lapping slime ' is titled *Undertones of War*. Not published until 1928, this uncondemning record belongs among the books of English prose that will not be forgotten whilst wars are with us. Edmund Blunden has also written on other poets: Christopher Smart, Shelley, Leigh Hunt, Lamb, Kirke White and John Clare.

What Edmund Blunden speaks of as his ' brighter morning ' was spent in the Kentish countryside. He admits ' the power of country life ' for him. After war, and Oxford, and spells of being an emissary for British prose and poetry in Tokyo University and Hong Kong University, he returned to woods and pathways thousands of years old. The modernists accused the Georgian poets, to which Edmund Blunden may be said to belong, of covering, with a soft and faded prettiness, the week-enders' countryside. But what Shakespeare, Spenser, Traherne, Collins, Smart, Cowper, Thomson, Burns, Clare, Emily Brontë, Hardy, William Barnes, Francis Thompson, Gerard Manley Hopkins, Edward Thomas, Geoffrey Grigson,

Ted Hughes, Seamus Heaney, and a fine green line of English lyric poets have in common, has little to do with sentimentalizing British poetry or nature or land. The Indian writer Nirad Chaudhuri has said that this love of earth in the English people was a revelation to his countrymen.

Edmund Blunden's poetry eschews cynicism or disillusion. Its balance does nothing to exacerbate this century's self-pitying sense of guilt, wrong, ill. Among poems of his are ' The Midnight Skaters ', ' Resignation ', ' Values ', ' The Sunlit Vale ', ' Return ', ' Chances of Remembrance ', ' The Kiss ', ' Report on Experience '. These lines are taken from the last named:

> I have seen a green country, useful to the race,
> Knocked silly with guns and mines, its villages vanished,
> Even the last rat and last kestrel banished—
> God bless us all, this was peculiar grace. . . .
>
> Say what you will, our God sees how they run.
> These disillusions are His curious proving
> That He loves humanity and will go on loving;
> Over there are faith, life, virtue in the sun.

Robert Graves, also in the 1914-18 war like Edmund Blunden, has acknowledged a debt to Thomas Hardy. Graves's war autobiography, *Good-bye to All That*, was first published in 1929. He has written historical novels, *I, Claudius* (1934) and *Claudius the God* (1934), and historical-cultural interpretations such as *The White Goddess* (1948; repr. 1952, 1961). He was probably the first to recognize the greatness of the poetry of Gerard Manley Hopkins,[9] a greatness Eliot questioned.

In poetry Graves has held to the Anglo-Irish tradition in which he was born. He has published four columns of collected poems— in 1926, 1938, 1947 and 1959. The balladry of his early poems changed to serious exploring of experience; and this in turn matured to a rueful readiness to leave ' the rest unsaid '—' Rising in air as on a gander's wing/At a careless comma '.

Graves's poems all have this hit-or-miss quality. One of the last poems in his 1959 volume, ' The Twin of Sleep ', has the Irish, quipping acceptance of his mental-physical self which ' Down,

---

[9] In *A Survey of Modernist Poetry* (with Laura Riding) (Heinemann, 1927).

wanton, down ', a poem of his early maturity, has. Here is ' The Twin of Sleep ':

> Death is the twin of Sleep, they say:
>   For I shall rise renewed,
> Free from the cramps of yesterday,
>   Clear-eyed and supple-thewed.
>
> But though this bland analogy
>   Helps other folk to face
> Decrepitude, senility,
>   Madness, disease, disgrace,
>
> I do not like Death's greedy looks:
>   Give me his twin instead—
> Sleep never auction off my books,
>   My boots, my shirts, my bed.

Herbert Read, poet, social critic and art critic, also went early into the First World War. His war poems were, he says, ' as imagist poems should be, coldly objective '. But in his autobiography, *Annals of Innocence and Experience* (1940) he discloses how, in the ' earthly paradise ' of his father's farm in the Yorkshire dales, he discovered poetry before war's impact drove him to the painful realism of ' The Happy Warrior '. Later Herbert Read came to believe that the intellect and the imagination were not disparate: They were united ' organically '. Reason and feeling should not be separated as seventeenth- and eighteenth-century philosophers, following Aristotle, have separated them, as they are still being thought separate. Herbert Read speaks of an ' intelligence of the heart ' and the ' natural imagination '. Yet more and more during his life he disciplined his powerful romantic imagination under his intellect; until, by the 1960s, as G. S. Fraser wrote, he was the only imagist poet we had.

But as an art critic and educational writer Herbert Read did equally important work. He was the writer most responsible for the revolution British schools have undergone since 1920 in the teaching of drawing and art. For forty years he crusaded against the neglect he saw Plato as being the first to discern in the necessary education of all children's artistic faculties. Without the arts we cannot be fully human, he says. In books such as *Art and Industry* (1934) and

Education through Art (1943) this intellectual poet-critic has done immeasurable service to his age.

Poets lost in the First World War were Edward Thomas, Francis Ledwidge, Rupert Brooke, Wilfred Owen, Charles Sorley, Isaac Rosenberg. Rosenberg—and David Jones, who survived the war and is best known for his book *In Parenthesis* (1937)—wrote almost wholly in prose cadences.

For years Edward Thomas struggled to earn a living by literary criticism and biographies, of which he wrote many. It was Thomas's friend Robert Frost, the American poet, who just prior to the war recognized and encouraged Thomas's poetic gift. In *As It Was* (1926) and *World Without End* (1931)—published in one volume in 1956—Helen Thomas has told of his struggle with the melancholy in his Celtic temperament. Edward Thomas's quiet, conversational poems have the phonics of traditional English verse. Their subjects —such as ' Fifty Faggots ', ' The Path ', ' The Chalk-Pit ', ' Roads '—point to Thomas's direct, unaffected way of observing, often within an original rhythm, as is apparent in this poem:

> Out in the dark over the snow
> The fallow fawns invisible go
> With the fallow doe;
> And the winds blow
> Fast as the stars are slow.
>
> Stealthily the dark haunts round
> And, when a lamp goes, without sound,
> At a swifter bound
> Than the swiftest hound,
> Arrives, and all else is drowned;
>
> And I and star and wind and deer,
> Are in the dark together,—near,
> Yet far,—and fear
> Drums on my ear
> In that sage company drear.
>
> How weak and little is the light,
> All the universe of sight,
> Love and delight,
> Before the might,
> If you love it not, of night.

Thomas was killed in 1917 at the age of thirty-nine.

In the last year of his short life, 1917, Francis Ledwidge turned to his own Gaelic tradition and its verse style. Ever since the displacement of the language in the eighteenth century, after which Irish poets have written in English, the rhythms persist. The following is taken from Ledwidge's last poem, ' Fate ':

> These things I know in my dreams,
> The crying sword of Lugh,
> And Balor's ancient eye
> Searching me through,
> Withering up my songs
> And my pipe yet new.

Before 1914 Rupert Brooke lived the secure, comfortable life of a well-to-do young man of the day and in his early poems he expressed an almost breathless excitement at being young and alive in England. After Rugby he went up to Cambridge, where he seems to have experienced some kind of awakening. In a letter to F. H. Keeling, written in September 1910, Brooke reveals something of his outlook after joining the Fabians:

> . . . Why do you say you are becoming a pessimist ? What does it mean ? . . . that the Universe is bad as a whole, or that it's bad just now, or that, more locally and importantly, things aren't going to get any better in our time and our country, no matter how we preach Socialism and clean hearts at them. . . .
>
> Are you telling me that the world is, after all, bad, and, what's more horrible, without enough seeds of good in it ? . . .
>
> The remedy is Mysticism, or Life, I'm not sure which. Do not leap or turn pale at the word Mysticism, I do not mean any religious thing, or any form of belief. . . .
>
> It consists in just looking at people and things as themselves—neither useful nor moral nor ugly nor anything else; but just as being. . . . I suddenly feel the extraordinary value and importance of everybody I meet, and of everything I see. . . .[10]

Brooke had one book of verse to his name and five ' war sonnets ' when he died of blood-poisoning in the Aegean in 1915, while on

[10] *The Collected Poems of Rupert Brooke, with a Memoir* (Sidgwick & Jackson, 1925), pp. ii-iii.

his way to Gallipoli. In the public mind he had come to personify the spirit of patriotic youth, an heroic ideal amidst the squalor and bestiality of war. He was twenty-seven. His sonnets were quoted to help divert public attention from the carnage of the 1914-1918 war. Like so many young officers fresh from school or university Brooke saw war in terms of honour, pride, patriotism, nobleness: ' the laughing heart's long peace there '. To lay down one's life was sacrifice, even desirable: ' the worst friend and enemy is but death '. Some have said that Brooke did not come to grips with war or with life, or with poetry. His youthful, musical verse has suffered criticism on each of these counts. The tribal complacency of that ' richer dust ', those ' men with Splendid Hearts ', the implications of ' their skins are white ' and ' we are earth's best ', belong to an imperial past from which needed rigour has torn us. Yet Brooke's

> Hasten, hand in human hand . . .
> And in the water's soft caress
> Wash the mind of foolishness

still speaks to some as the words of the last optimist.

Wilfred Owen had not Brooke's background of confidence, ease, wealth. In Owen's war poetry, written during a gruelling period in front-line trenches, his diffidence is overcome by his rejection of inflated thought. In a fragment of preface to his war poems Owen explained:

This book is not about heroes. English poetry is not yet fit to speak of them.
Nor is it about deeds, or lands, nor anything about glory, honour, might, majesty, dominion, or power, except War.
Above all I am not concerned with Poetry.
My subject is War, and the pity of War.
The Poetry is in the pity.
. . . All a poet can do today is warn. That is why the true Poets must be truthful.

Yeats could not understand Owen's ' passivity ' in suffering. It has also been said by later critics that the pity in Owen's poems occasionally overcomes the poetry. He did not always follow the poetic law of using adjectives with strict economy. But with poems such as ' Anthem for Doomed Youth ' and ' Strange Meeting ' his influence was considerable.

Siegfried Sassoon became Owen's friend when he was in an Edinburgh hospital with him. Sassoon had had an upbringing like Brooke's. His time in France as an infantry officer convinced him of the obscenity of that front-line war of attrition when men in thousands were turned into ' gun-fodder '. In hospital Sassoon became a conscientious objector. The army medical staff treated him as shell-shocked.

Where Owen's poetry deals with the pity of war's human waste, Sassoon's is seering satire of those, often elders, who watch and plan wars but do not fight them. After ' They ', ' The General ', ' Base Details ', Sassoon came to feel that neither his stand against war nor his war poetry had done much or any good:

Have you forgotten yet ? . . .
For the world's events have rumbled on since those gagged days . . .
But the past is just the same,—and War's a bloody game . . .
Have you forgotten yet ? . . .

New Voices in the Thirties

The movements of surrealism and Dadaism arose out of disillusion in post-war France and Germany, though they had roots in the rebel symbolism of Mallarmé and Rimbaud. Surrealism reached Britain after the financial crisis of 1931 and war's aftermath of two million unemployed. Surrealism refuses the use of conscious intellect in the arts. It rejects the carefully wrought poem for an ' organic ' association of images which may spring spontaneously from the subconscious mind. There must be no mental wrestling and no polishing. Apparently random associations, connected with individual response to experience, rise through racial and private memories. Surrealism may be seen as a non-rational means of preserving sanity in desperate dilemma.

James Joyce showed the method in the prose soliloquies of *Ulysses*. Subconscious linking of word and idea can make poetry private and hence often difficult. Among the most powerful poets who subscribed to surrealism's usages in poetry were Dylan Thomas with *18 Poems* in 1934, David Gascoyne, George Barker and Edith Sitwell. Reading Edith Sitwell's poetry is like trying to see, through stained glass windows, what lies beyond. All four sought to use the ancient incantatory power of words as well as a neo-surrealist symbolism. All four have written verse beyond the private and the esoteric.

In 1931 the Statute of Westminster changed an already obsolete British Empire into a precarious Commonwealth of Free Nations. Quicker communications made the world seem smaller. Communism—or at least communalism—was vocal. Poets in Britain were strongly anti-fascist. A few were communist, though briefly. They bypassed honour, freedom, nightingales, dawns. Thought, and hence language, was made to fit ' collective ' man and his communications in a growing technology. Poets wrote of dynamos, pylons, electric drills, magnetos, on ' power that corrupts ', on Freudian realizations such as the presence of hatred within love, on ' international wrong ' and on new ' patterns of frustration '.

Poets of the 1930s include W. H. Auden, Cecil Day Lewis (who succeeded John Masefield as Poet Laureate in 1968), Stephen Spender, Louis MacNeice, Henry Reed, Rex Warner, William Empson, Bernard Spencer, Geoffrey Grigson and A. S. J. Tessimond. Day Lewis is also a critic, a translator of Virgil's *Georgics*, and of the *Aeneid* and, under the pseudonym Nicholas Blake, a writer of detective fiction. Stephen Spender, journalist as well as poet, was also joint editor of the magazine *Encounter*. Louis MacNeice, Anglo-Irish as is Day Lewis, advanced from abstraction to realism, as typified in *Autumn Journal* (1939) and later in *The Burning Perch* (1963). He also wrote radio dramas and translated Aeschylus' *Agamemnon* and Goethe's *Faust*.

Geoffrey Grigson founded and edited *New Verse* (1933-9), an important outlet for poetry. He judged poetry, he has written, by its taking ' notice of the universe of objects and events '. His own poetry is full of coloured evocations of the rural present and of man's rich past in shapely, exact verse.

But by the early thirties a second war loomed. Progressively Hitler's boast of ' intuition ' helped to discredit feeling's place beside reason. Helplessness to avert catastrophe grew more and more overwhelming. The gigantic problem that one-third of the world population already had too much food and two-thirds still too little had to be faced. W. H. Auden, the leading poetic voice, wrote of poetry as ' a serious game '.

> . . . no one exists alone
> Hunger allows no choice
> To the citizen or the police;
> We must love one another or die.

The meaning or the use of the word ' love ' is less ambiguous if the term is not restricted to its sexual connotation.

Auden's *City without Gates* (1969) contains, John Gross has commented, unflagging energy and ' undiminished verbal cunning '. The Auden of 1969 remains a ' conjurer in words ' both in light verse and poetry.

In 1939 a group of young poets published a manifesto. They called it *The New Apocalypse*. Points in its four statements included:

1.   That Man was in need of greater freedom, economic no less than aesthetic, from machines and mechanistic thinking.
2.   That no existent political system, Left or Right, no artistic ideology, Surrealism or the political school of Auden, was able to provide this freedom.
4.   That Myth, as a personal means of reintegrating the personality, had been neglected and despised.

Poets concerned with the New Apocalypse were Henry Treece, J. F. Hendry, Nicholas Moore, Vernon Watkins, Tom Scott, Norman MacCaig and the poet and interpreter of other men's poetry, G. S. Fraser. These sought to tap the inner logic of archetypal imagery from which human myths, intercultural as these are, spring. They published *The New Apocalypse* (1939) and *The White Horseman* (1941); and they founded the International Workshop— the first, surely, of an important international activity in modern poetry. These poets set feeling—human brotherhood—both symbolized in myth, before the sociotechnical, cerebral reason which Day Lewis and Auden seemed to advocate.

But six more years of war fell upon Europe and other parts of the world again. In 1945, the Americans, with the practical help of Britain, dropped the first atom bomb on Hiroshima, killing and maiming some hundred thousand people. Nothing on earth could be the same again. The Second World War did not so much cease as lapse into a Cold War of Megaton threat, Balance of Terror, secret biological and germ war research, air spies, a political distrust stronger than before. Committed to a higher and higher standard of living, labouring vainly in the wake of a United States richer from two wars fought chiefly in Europe, Britain, though said to be bankrupt, continued in prosperity for many of her citizens. In Africa, Asia and South America new nations achieved independence. These were unindustrialized. They faced problems such as Britain faced three centuries ago. Their greatness lies still in the future. The Computer Age came in.

Literary and Popular Poetry after the Second World War

After this second devastation the revival of poetry in Britain took time. By the late 1940s and 1950s, when poets were again vocal, those led by Auden were much less politically committed than before. William Empson and Ronald Bottrall, both intellectuals, have not been prolific; but Empson has a continuing influence.

Anne Ridler is a religious and personal poet in *The Golden Bird* (1951) and *A Matter of Life and Death* (1959). She has also written verse drama. Her *The Trial of Thomas Cranmer* (1956) is comparable with Charles Williams's *Cranmer*, even with *Murder in the Cathedral*.

Kathleen Raine has an intellectual vision of a neo-Platonic language for poetry. She presents her poems from a sense of inorganic to organic life, as if from pre-Cambrian rocks of over 4,000 million years old up to an inexhaustible present. This inorganic time she sets within a human time contemporary with each freshly created minute. To this non-everyday but true and vital way of seeing life whole she is totally committed.

W. H. Auden and his contemporaries mellowed into middle age's greater reliance on tradition and orthodoxy. John Betjeman's cheery, insular lightness slowly grew popular; his *Summoned by Bells* (1960) is well known, as is his nostalgia for the Victorian age.

New coteries of young poets followed the Apocalypse. To the 1950s and 1960s belong the Movement, the Mavericks and the Group.

By 1955 and *The Less Deceived* Philip Larkin's sense of quietness and quietness's limits proclaimed an original new voice. Philip Larkin's third volume, *The Whitsun Weddings* (1964), emphasizes his acquiescence in what is left to live for rather than in causes to die for. This acceptance of what—however crudely—IS, yet holds glimpses of almost invisibly far horizons.

> It becomes still more difficult to find
> Words at once true and kind,
> Or not untrue and not unkind.

In ' Reference Back ':

> Truly, though our element is time,
> We are not suited to the long perspectives
> Open at each instant of our lives.

There are many poets of the 1950s and 1960s, other than those mentioned, whose work it is not possible to mention or discuss within the limits of this volume. These, to name comparatively few, include: Thomas Blackburn, Charles Causley, Robert Conquest, Hilary Corke, Iain Crichton-Smith, Patric Dickinson, D. J. Enright, W. S. Graham, Michael Hamburger, Ian Hamilton, John Heath-Stubbs, Geoffrey Hill, Elizabeth Jennings, Laurie Lee, George MacBeth, Christopher Middleton, F. T. Prince, Jon Silkin, Robin Skelton, Stevie Smith, Jon Stallworthy, Terence Tiller, Rosemary Tonks, Sydney Tremayne and David Wright.

Poets of varied tone, W. R. Rodgers and Patrick Kavanagh have been major voices in Irish poetry of this century. Rodgers's ' Easter Sequence ' in his *Europa and the Bull* (1952) compares with T. S. Eliot's ' The Coming of the Magi '. Hugh MacDiarmid is the most important Scottish poet. Of Welsh poets, R. S. Thomas is probably the best known. P. J. Kavanagh, Seamus Heaney, Thomas Kinsella, John Montague and Brenden Kennelly are all Irish poets. Basil Bunting, a very interesting poet, seeks to bridge the gap between the generations by extending understanding to the young and receiving it from them.

Roy Fuller has been called ' the most Freudian of English poets ', and, until recently, ' our most undervalued poet '. Between the 1930s and the late 1960s he has written seven or eight volumes of poems besides several novels. His poems have a technical and cerebral excellence that latterly is more and more often matched against feeling deliberately renounced for ' emotions not your own '. He was elected Professor of English Poetry at Oxford in 1969.

Thom Gunn is a poet whom we may read two or three or more times before the meaning behind his compassionate, unpitying observer's mind becomes clear. He is perhaps the most intellectual of today's poets: he is intent on the thing said as well as on a way of saying it. Calling himself ' a presence without full being ', with authentic twentieth-century courage he explores the mysteries of touch, movement, isolation.

Donald Davie seems sometimes to despair, not only of the contemporary scene and people in Britain, but of the English language. James Reeves and Martin Seymour-Smith, critics as well as poets, have recently put out a *New Canon in English Poetry*. Michael Hamburger is a translator of distinction—from German—as well as a poet. With Ted Hughes and others he works towards that extremely difficult goal set by the Apocalypse poets—to foster poetry from different cultures by translations into English from works by writers such as Voznesensky, Yevtushenko, Zbigniew Herbert, Günter Grass, Miroslav Holub, Jorge Luis Borges, Pablo Neruda.

The 1960s saw a popular upsurge of poetry. This manifested itself in scores of poetry groups whose members read and wrote verse. These groups were urgent with a need to speak against the threats under which a younger generation felt itself to have been born—against biological and germ warfare, against intellectual hypocrisy, against the injustice of privilege, against all the discords of present reality. The voices of this popular movement in poetry were—and are—not always anti-rational or unreasonable. They are, and only occasionally violently, eager to expose the expedience sometimes to be found masquerading as reason among elders.

Standard English, like ' classes ', has come to be of less importance in the last decade. Dialects and provincial accents are in speech deliberately retained. Verse may have what amounts, sometimes, to a cliché-ridden exploration of the commonplace. It imitates American words, phrases, outlook. Much of it has echoes of Eliot, Dylan Thomas, D. H. Lawrence. Some of it postures, discarding verbs and capital letters, running words together. Most of it eschews any demand for more than Bondo drum-beat rhythm. Its themes may be repetitive, narrowly personal, or of fringe importance:

Questions such as whether human aggression can be overcome by ' love ' (whatever is meant by that ill-used word), or whether physical force can be subdued by Eastern mysticism, are not wholly sterile and the initiated young may not always think thoughts down to the roots in the way George Orwell recommended, yet their writing adds some perspective.

> Ignorant of any tenderness we hide in each other's lives
> A clue to our loneliness.
> Boredom shares our beds,
> It turns whats living dead in us—
> Yet among the drifting populations mock love suits us fine,
> We wear our personalities well !
> Twenty. Already inside us
> Something has fallen asleep.[11]

The strong popular revival of ballads, songs and verse owes much to the virility of fourteenth- and fifteenth-century Scottish and English ballads and to Irish ballads of the nineteenth century. Groups of the young meet often in pubs, and ballad or song is usually accompanied by the guitar or by the jazz of African *sitar* music, Negro lament and Bondo microtonic drum-beat in a world movement made possible by technologically rapid communications. This popular poetry movement indicates a youthful vitality and courage which belie an outward attitude of sophisticated cynicism.

Criticism

Modern critics include the veterans I. A. Richards, F. R. Leavis, V. S. Pritchett, and also Frank Kermode, Raymond Williams, A. Alvarez, Richard Hoggart, Edward Blishen, G. S. Fraser, Bernard Bergonzi and Cyril Connolly. Connolly founded and edited the important literary magazine *Horizon* (1939-50), and his journal, *The Unquiet Grave* (1944), by ' Palinarus ', has become a contemporary classic.

Recently A. Alvarez asked whether British and European poets

---

[11] Brian Patten, *Little Johnny's Confession* (Allen & Unwin, 1967), p. 49.

could help to create 'a politics of sanity and survival'. English poets must refuse complaisance about a threatened future out of which assurance had dropped. But are we, A. Alvarez asked, still 'too cushioned against violence'? We recall Beckett's characters in his prose and drama, Edmund Blunden's and W. H. Auden's poems, Christine Brooke-Rose's *Such*, Robert Nye's *doubtfire*, poems by Ian Hamilton. The antithesis between violence and the reasonableness that is A. N. Whitehead's 'persuasion' against force in his *Adventures of Ideas* (1933) treads close on the heels of all technical triumphs. More acutely than ever, age-old questions in new guise plague, through literature, our conscious minds and our inherited, subconscious memories. Modern civilization is potentially more, not less, ferocious than primitive men. Are we approaching an alienation from ourselves akin to brutalism through our addiction to and excessive faith in science? Talk of human trust may be naïve. Yet mental and 'spiritual' strength is no past dream but incident to human as opposed to animal nature. Either the sympathetic imagination can unite with brute intelligence or, equally likely, both have always been one. Yet civilization is still caught between whatever Chaucer meant by 'Gentilesse' and the pitiless cruelty Shakespeare's contemporaries, Webster and Tourneur, obsessively warned against.

Writers are never more than voices. Yet they are significant, inextinguishable voices. Their influence cannot be measured. They are concerned with the links between honesty and the lie, between affluence and hunger of all kinds, between cosy hypocrisy and all new forms of violence. Knowing at last that there is no ease of sure answers, rejecting consoling, mystogogic explanations, we face a future of uncertainty, but equally of possibly limitless horizons.

Donald Davie contends that there is more than doom, pain and stress for poetry to explore. Of course there is. In contemporary poetry, symbolist and post-symbolist, there is certainly an absence of enthusiasm or joy. Today's floriation of verse, its double line of poetry, intellectual as well as popular, is often a far cry from Wordsworth's, Shelley's, Keats's, and Clare's of only a century ago:

> At dusky eve or sober silent morn
> For such delights 'twere happy Man was born.

But as Keith Douglas insisted, absence of expectation is not the same as apathy. Some present British poetry may have an air of the peripheral, or deliberately keeping to the past, or the promiscuous minute, or the personal, accepting what is neurotic, or flat, conventional, trivial. A vogue for ' concrete ' poetry suggests either an attempt at verbal and pictorial confluence, or that some writers of verse cannot find a ' true voice of feeling ' in this mathematical, nuclear, computer age. But then again, there is ' immense resilience ' in the human make-up.

English literature has come a long way in prose and poetry: from timeless tale in prose-rhyme to Irish *filé* of the sixteenth century; from Celtic bard or Anglo-Saxon *scôp* reciting lines of praise or punishment from memory before royal audiences at drinking feasts; from popular minstrel chanting to ordinary people at births, puberty rites, marriages, deaths, or ritual gatherings on May Day, at Midsummer or New Year; from the Christian beginner of written prose, the Venerable Bede, and the verse-contestant, the swineherd Caedmon; from the early four cycles of Irish saga, the Celtic *Gododdin*, and the Anglo-Saxon ancestral poem *Beowulf* with its myth of Evil in the shape of the fiend Grendel; from Celtic and English ballads courtly and popular; from Mystery and Miracle and Morality plays, to Langland, Chaucer, Skelton, Spenser, Sidney, Shakespeare, the Bible translators, Ussher the Irish scholar, Milton, Dryden, Blake, Lamb, Wordsworth, Keats, Browning, Dickens, George Eliot, Carlyle, Ruskin, Mill, Tennyson, Hopkins, Hardy, Yeats, Eliot; to Robert Graves, Edmund Blunden; to Patrick Kavanagh, Hugh MacDiarmid; to W. H. Auden, Philip Larkin, Thom Gunn; to all the others at the thorny cross-tracks of poetry today.

Much, and many names, will inevitably have been omitted from this short account of the growth of English poetry and prose. There is a long way yet to travel. English literature itself is far from being any longer the literature of the British Isles only. Christopher Okigbo, the young Nigerian poet killed in the Biafran war, reading his poems in an English city in 1966, reminded his audience: ' English is the language of all those who learn it, as I learnt it, in infancy.' Prose and poetry in the malleable English tongue, for well over a century now, has been defining and sometimes uniting growing traditions in Canada, Australia, India, parts of Africa, Asia, New Zealand, the West Indies. Many and varied cultures are thus enriching each other. Already British literature is part of, and but one of, all these. W. H. Auden has remarked that poetry has little or no influence on society. In an age of computers and statistics it would be folly to underestimate growing scientific forces. But as long as the written word is read, the intangible strength of poetry, and of creative literature as a whole, will continue to extend individual consciousness.

GENERAL REFERENCES

Abercrombie, Lascelles, *The Idea of Great Poetry*, Secker, 1925.
——————————————, *Principles of English Prosody*, Secker, 1923.
Alexander, Michael (ed.), *The Earliest English Poems*, Penguin Books, 1966.
Beowulf, a metrical trans. by J. R. Clark Hall, Cambridge Univ. Press, 1914.
Beowulf, ed. A. J. Wyatt and R. W. Chambers, Cambridge Univ. Press, 1914, repr. 1920.
Beowulf, trans. Kevin Crossley-Holland, Macmillan, 1968.
Beowulf and Its Analogues, trans. G. N. Garmonsway, Jacqueline Simpson and Hilda Ellis Davidson, Dent, 1968.
Bradley, A. C., *Oxford Lectures on Poetry*, Macmillan, 1909.
Brooke, A. Stopford, *English Literature from* A.D. *670 to 1832*, Macmillan, 1917.
The Cambridge History of English Literature, Vols I-XIV, Cambridge Univ. Press, revised edn 1964.
Chadwick, H. Munro, and Kershaw (afterwards Chadwick, Norah), *The Growth of Literature*, Cambridge Univ. Press, 3 vols, 1932-40.
Chaucer, Geoffrey, *The Canterbury Tales*, trans. into modern English by Nevill Coghill, Penguin Books, revised edn 1966.
—————————— *Troilus and Criseyde*, trans. into modern English by Margaret Stanley-Wrench, Centaur Press, 1965.
Collingwood, R. G., and Myres, J. N. L., *Roman Britain and the English Settlements*, Oxford, Clarendon Press, 1936, repr. 1949.
Cook, A. S. (ed.), *A Literary Middle English Reader*, New York, Ginn & Co., 1915.
Dillon, Myles (ed.), *Irish Sagas*, Mercier paperback, 1968.
Eliot, T. S., *Selected Essays*, Faber & Faber, 1932.
The Faber Book of Modern Verse, ed. Michael Roberts, revised edn ed. Anne Ridler, Faber & Faber, 1960.
Ford, Ford Madox, *The March of Literature*, Allen & Unwin, 1939, revised edn 1947.
Fraser, G. S., *The Modern Writer and His World*, Pelican Books, 1964.

————————, *Vision and Rhetoric: Studies in Modern Poetry*, Faber & Faber, 1959.

Furnivall, F. J. (ed.), *The Babees' Boke*, Early English Text Society, Trubner, 1868.

The Gododdin—The Oldest Scottish Poem, ed. and trans. Kenneth Hurlstone Jackson, Edinburgh Univ. Press, 1969.

Grigson, Geoffrey (ed.), *The Poetry of the Present*, Phoenix House, 1949.

Hoggart, Richard, *Speaking to Each Other*: Vol. I *About Society*; Vol. II *About Literature* (originally published in one volume as *Essays on Literature*), Chatto & Windus, 2 vols, 1970.

————————, *The Uses of Literacy—Aspects of working-class life with special reference to publications and entertainments*, Chatto & Windus,1957.

Housman, A. E., *The Name and Nature of Poetry*, Cambridge Univ. Press, 1933.

Kane, George, *The Autobiographical Fallacy in Chaucer and Langland Studies*, Chambers Memorial Lecture, London, H. K. Lewis & Co., 1965.

Kermode, Frank, *The Sense of an Ending*, New York, Oxford Univ. Press, 1967.

Knott, Eleanor, *Irish Classical Poetry*, Dublin, Colm O Lochlainn, 1957.

Leavis, F. R., *Revaluation*, Chatto & Windus, 1936.

Legouis, Emile, and Cazamian, Louis, *A History of English Literature*, Dent, 1926, revised edns 1960/4.

The Mabinogion, ed. Thomas Jones and Gwyn Jones, Dent, Everyman edn, 1957.

MacDonagh, Thomas, *Literature in Ireland*, Dublin, Talbot Press, 1916.

The Oxford Companion to English Literature, ed. Paul Harvey, 4th revised edn ed. Dorothy Eagle, Oxford, Clarendon Press, 1967.

The Oxford Book of Eighteenth Century Verse, ed. D. Nichol Smith, Oxford, Clarendon Press, 1951.

The Oxford Book of English Verse, ed. A. Quiller-Couch, Oxford, Clarendon Press, 1919.

The Oxford Book of Irish Verse, chosen by Donagh MacDonagh and E. S. Lennox Robinson, Oxford, Clarendon Press, 1960.

The Oxford Book of Scottish Verse, chosen by John Macqueen and Tom Scott, Oxford, Clarendon Press, 1966.

The Oxford Book of Seventeenth Century Verse, ed. E. K. Chambers Oxford, Clarendon Press, 1934.

The Oxford Book of Victorian Verse, ed. A. Quiller-Couch, Oxford, Clarendon Press, 1922.

The Penguin Book of Contemporary Verse, ed. Kenneth Allott, Penguin Books, 1951.

Penguin Modern Poets, Vols 1-12, general editor Nikos Stangos, Penguin Books, 1962-9.

Power, Patrick C., *Anglo-Irish Poetry*, Mercier paperback, 1967.

Schofield, W. H., *English Literature from the Norman Conquest to Chaucer*, Macmillan, 1906.

Seymour-Smith, Martin, *Poets Through Their Letters*, Constable, 1969.

Sweet's Anglo-Saxon Reader, revised by Dorothy Whitelock, Oxford Univ. Press, 1967.

The Vision of Piers Plowman, trans. into modern English by Nevill Coghill, Phoenix House, 1949.

Wain, John, *The Living World of Shakespeare*, Macmillan, 1964.

Williams, Gwyn, *The Burning Tree: Poems from the First Thousand Years of Welsh Verse*, selected and trans. into modern English by G. Williams, Faber & Faber, 1956.

INDEX

Note: In general, titles of novels, plays and poems are not included, excepting anonymous works or those discussed individually in the text. Main page references are given in bold. All dates are A.D. unless otherwise indicated. Dates appended to monarchs denote years of reign. Living writers born after *c.* 1930 are listed without birth dates.